Leasehold Enfranchisement and the Right to Manage

Related titles available from Law Society Publishing:

Commonhold
Gary Cowen, James Driscoll and Laurence Target

Conveyancing Checklists
Frances Silverman and Russell Hewitson

Conveyancing Handbook
General Editor: Frances Silverman, Consultant Editors: Annette Goss, Peter Reekie, Anne Rodell, Michael Taylor, Bernadette Whitters

Environmental Law Handbook (6th edn)
Trevor Hellawell

Home Information Packs
Michael Garson

Licensing for Conveyancers
Tim Hayden and Jane Hanney

Planning and Compulsory Purchase Act 2004
Stephen Tromans, Martin Edwards, Richard Harwood, Justine Thornton

Profitable Conveyancing
Stephanie Dale

Renewal of Business Tenancies
Michael Haley

Understanding Stamp Duty Land Tax (8th edn)
Reg Nock

Understanding VAT on Property (2nd edn)
Dave Jordan

Titles from Law Society Publishing can be ordered from all good legal bookshops or direct from our distributors (Prolog, 0870 850 1422, **lawsociety@prolog.uk.com**). For further information or a catalogue, email our editorial and marketing office at **publishing@lawsociety.org.uk**.

LEASEHOLD ENFRANCHISEMENT AND THE RIGHT TO MANAGE

A Practical Guide

Christopher Sykes

The Law Society

All rights reserved. No part of this publication may be reproduced in any material form, whether by photocopying, scanning, downloading onto computer or otherwise without the written permission of the Law Society except in accordance with the provisions of the Copyright, Designs and Patents Act 1988. Applications should be addressed in the first instance, in writing, to Law Society Publishing. Any unauthorised or restricted act in relation to this publication may result in civil proceedings and/or criminal prosecution.

Whilst all reasonable care has been taken in the preparation of this publication, neither the publisher nor the author can accept any responsibility for any loss occasioned to any person acting or refraining from action as a result of relying upon its contents.

The views expressed in this publication should be taken as those of the author only unless it is specifically indicated that the Law Society has given its endorsement. The author has asserted the right under the Copyright, Designs and Patents Act 1988 to be identified as the author of this work.

© Christopher Sykes 2007

ISBN-13: 978-1-85328-999-6

Appendix A2, 'Participation Agreement', is reproduced with the kind permission of the Leasehold Advisory Service. It appears here with some minor amendments made by the author of this book. The original unamended document can be viewed at **www.lease-advice.org**

Appendices A6, A7, A16 and A17 are reproduced for illustrative purposes only by kind permission of the Solicitors Law Stationery Society Ltd. Appendices A13, A14, A15, A18 and A19 are Crown copyright. Crown copyright material is reproduced here with the permission of the Controller of HMSO.

Published in 2007 by the Law Society
113 Chancery Lane, London WC2A 1PL

Reprinted in 2007

Typeset by J&L Composition, Filey, North Yorkshire
Printed by TJ International Ltd, Padstow, Cornwall

Contents

Foreword	xiii
Preface and acknowledgements	xiv
Table of cases	xvii
Table of statutes	xviii
Table of statutory instruments	xxi
Abbreviations	xxiii

PART I   INTRODUCTION   1

1   A brief history   3

1.1	The initial stages	3
1.2	The rationale	3
1.3	Pre-1967 Act legislation	4
1.4	Post-1967 Act concerns	4
1.5	Leasehold Reform, Housing and Urban Development Act 1993	4
1.6	Impending changes to the right to collective enfranchisement	5
1.7	Right to manage	5

2   The rights   7

2.1	Overview	7
2.2	Collective rights	7
2.3	Individual rights	8
2.4	Comparison of rights: pros and cons	9

CONTENTS

PART II COLLECTIVE RIGHTS   13

3 Managing the collective process   15

3.1	General	15
3.2	Obtaining preliminary information	16
3.3	Assessing potential interest	16
3.4	Valuation	16
3.5	Assessment of the options	17
3.6	Communication and provision of information	17
3.7	Costs and contributions	18
3.8	Binding the tenants to the process	18
3.9	Nominee/RTE/RTM company	20
3.10	Professional issues for solicitors	20
3.11	Looking forward	22

4 Collective enfranchisement   24

4.1	Overview	24
4.2	Finding your way around the legislation	24
4.3	Key terminology	25
4.4	Key features	25
4.5	General comments	26
4.6	Preliminary investigations	28
4.7	The nominee purchaser	34
4.8	RTE companies	36
4.9	Initial notice	37
4.10	Timetable and procedure following service of initial notice	41
4.11	Leasebacks	50
4.12	Completion	51
4.13	Application to the court	52
4.14	Application to the LVT	53
4.15	Withdrawing from the process	53
4.16	Other issues	54
4.17	Extending the leases of participating tenants	54

5 Right to manage   56

5.1	Overview	56
5.2	Finding your way around the legislation	56
5.3	Key terminology	57
5.4	Key features of the right	57

5.5	General comments		58
5.6	Preliminary investigations		59
5.7	Qualifying criteria		61
5.8	The RTM company		66
5.9	Notice of invitation to participate		67
5.10	Acquisition date		67
5.11	Absent landlords		68
5.12	Claim notice		69
5.13	Position following service of the claim notice		71
5.14	Information notice		72
5.15	Landlord's position following service of claim notice		74
5.16	RTM company's position if the right is disputed		76
5.17	Costs		77
5.18	Management contracts		77
5.19	Withdrawal of claim notice		79
5.20	Management after the acquisition date		79
5.21	Ancillary issues for the RTM company		84
5.22	Issues for the landlord		85
5.23	RTM company: membership, voting and management		86
5.24	Cessation of right to manage		90
5.25	Miscellaneous		90

PART III INDIVIDUAL RIGHTS   93

6 Right to extend the lease of a flat   95

6.1	Overview	95
6.2	Finding your way around the legislation	95
6.3	Key terminology	96
6.4	General	96
6.5	Qualifying criteria	97
6.6	Preliminary investigations	98
6.7	Tenant's notice	101
6.8	Procedure following service of tenant's notice	103
6.9	Counter-notice	105
6.10	Timetable following service of the counter-notice	108
6.11	Conveyancing procedure	108
6.12	New lease	109
6.13	Mortgages	111
6.14	Assignment of the right	112

CONTENTS

	6.15	Collective enfranchisement	112
	6.16	Withdrawal	112
	6.17	Costs	113
	6.18	Redevelopment compensation	113
	6.19	Price	113
	6.20	Absent landlord	114
	6.21	Special categories of landlord	115
7	**Right of a tenant to acquire the freehold of their house**		**116**
	7.1	Outline of the right	116
	7.2	Finding your way around the legislation	116
	7.3	Key terminology	117
	7.4	Key features of the right	117
	7.5	Qualifying criteria	118
	7.6	Preliminary investigations by the tenant	121
	7.7	Other premises included	123
	7.8	Tenant's notice	123
	7.9	Landlord's response	125
	7.10	Procedure subsequent to landlord's reply	128
	7.11	Completion	131
	7.12	Valuation	132
	7.13	Merger	133
	7.14	Withdrawal	134
	7.15	Costs	134
	7.16	Position where more than one landlord	135
	7.17	Rentcharges	136
	7.18	Mortgages and debentures	136
	7.19	Special landlords	137
	7.20	Forum	137
	7.21	Contracting out	137
	7.22	Missing landlord	138
	7.23	Death of the tenant	138
8	**Right to a new lease of a house**		**140**
	8.1	Overview	140
	8.2	Finding your way around the legislation	140
	8.3	Key features	140

PART IV MISCELLANEOUS   143

9 The Leasehold Valuation Tribunal   145

  9.1   Overview   145
  9.2   Key points of the procedure   145
  9.3   Service   146
  9.4   Dismissal for abuse of process   146
  9.5   Pre-trial review   146
  9.6   Statements of case   146
  9.7   Inspections   147
  9.8   Hearings   147
  9.9   Use of intermediate hearings   147
  9.10 Postponement   147
  9.11 Costs   148
  9.12 Appeals to the Lands Tribunal   148
  9.13 LVT decisions   148

10 The valuer and valuation issues   149

  10.1   Introduction   149
  10.2   Key terminology   149
  10.3   How to select a valuer   150
  10.4   How to instruct a valuer   151
  10.5   Valuer's fees   152
  10.6   Key practice points   153
  10.7   Understanding the report   154
  10.8   Negotiations   155
  10.9   Leasehold Valuation Tribunals   156
  10.10 Collective enfranchisement: structuring and financial
         considerations   157
  10.11 Valuation principles   157
  10.12 Recent developments in valuation   158

11 Companies, corporate formalities and taxation   164

  11.1 Overview   164
  11.2 Collective enfranchisement structures   164
  11.3 RTE company   167
  11.4 RTM company   167
  11.5 Directors' duties   167

11.6	Voting rights	168
11.7	Tax issues	168

12 The Commonhold and Leasehold Reform Act 2002 and other relevant rights — 172

12.1	Overview	172
12.2	Commonhold and Leasehold Reform Act 2002	172
12.3	Obtaining information from the landlord	173
12.4	Right of first refusal	174
12.5	Notice of assignment of the freehold	175
12.6	Service charges	175
12.7	Administration charges	177
12.8	Insurance	178
12.9	Ground rent	178
12.10	Estate charges under Estate Management Schemes	179
12.11	Consultation on major works	179
12.12	Consultation on long-term agreements	180
12.13	Works under long-term agreements	181
12.14	Appointment of a manager	181
12.15	Variation of leases	181
12.16	Forfeiture and possession	183

APPENDICES

A Precedents — 185

Collective enfranchisement

A1	Letter of intent	188
A2	Participation agreement	190
A3	Breakdown of costs	195
A4	Specimen spreadsheet of basic information	197
A5	Specimen Articles of Association	198
A6	Initial notice	207
A7	Counter-notice	214
A8	Specimen Leasehold Valuation Tribunal application	221

Right to manage

A9	Letter of intent (right to manage)	224
A10	Breakdown of costs	226

A11	Participation agreement	228
A12	Information notice	233
A13	Claim notice	239
A14	Counter-notice	242
A15	Notice of invitation to participate	244

Lease extension

| A16 | Section 42 notice of claim | 248 |
| A17 | Section 45 counter-notice | 252 |

Acquisition of freehold or extended lease (house)

| A18 | Notice of tenant's claim to acquire the freehold or an extended lease | 258 |
| A19 | Notice in reply to a tenant's claim | 263 |

B	**Flowcharts and checklists**	**265**
B1	Collective enfranchisement timetable flowchart	267
B2	Checklist of preliminary matters on collective enfranchisement claim	268
B3	Right to manage timetable flowchart	271
B4	Checklist of preliminary matters on right to manage claim	272
B5	Right to extension of lease of a flat timetable flowchart	276
B6	Checklist of preliminary matters on service of tenant's notice to extend the lease of a flat	278
B7	Right to acquire the freehold of a house timetable flowchart	281
B8	Checklist of preliminary matters on service of tenant's notice to acquire the freehold of a house	282

C	**Useful addresses**	**285**

Index 287

Foreword

From modest beginnings, the law of leasehold enfranchisement has come to assume major importance, as an area of the law which affects many, often high value, residential properties. Some knowledge of the law of leasehold enfranchisement is essential for those who deal with residential property let on long leases, and for those who have an interest in and/or live in such property. The acquisition of such knowledge is not easy. The legislation is complex, not easily accessible, and often difficult. The procedures prescribed by the legislation for exercising rights under the legislation are themselves complicated, and contain many traps for the unwary.

In these circumstances, the publication of this book on leasehold enfranchisement is much to be welcomed. The emphasis of the book is on the practical. The book gives clear and simple guidance on the workings of the law of leasehold enfranchisement and on the exercise of the rights thereunder. The right to manage created by the Commonhold and Leasehold Reform Act 2002 is also dealt with in the same way. This is all accompanied by timetable flowcharts, checklists and guidance on procedure and valuation issues.

I am pleased to be able to welcome this book as a practical handbook and guide to a difficult and complicated area of law. It will be of use to lawyers seeking clear and simple guidance on the law. It will also be of use to valuers and other professionals involved in leasehold enfranchisement or right to manage claims. Most important of all, it will also be accessible to those landlords and tenants who wish to acquire their own knowledge of their rights and obligations in this area of law. I commend the book to all these readers.

Edwin Johnson QC
April 2007

Preface and acknowledgements

BACKGROUND AND PURPOSE

Leasehold enfranchisement can briefly be described as the right of a tenant or a group of tenants holding property under a long lease to acquire the freehold of their property or to extend their lease. It comprises a number of rights emanating from different statutes. It is an area of law which has developed rapidly over recent years. The qualifying criteria have been simplified. Tenants are increasingly aware of their rights and are seeking to use them. The Commonhold and Leasehold Reform Act 2002 ('the 2002 Act') introduced the 'right to manage', enabling tenants of flats to collectively take over the management of their block on a no-fault basis. When considering collective action, the right to manage will often need to be compared with the right of collective enfranchisement.

The law on the relative subject area is complex. It can often be difficult to navigate around the legislation. There are a number of pitfalls for the unwary. The aim of this book is to summarise the relevant law, to put it in a practical context and to guide the reader in a clear and concise way through the procedures applicable to each right. It is not intended to be a theoretical analysis of the law for which there are other texts but to focus on practice and procedure.

HOW TO USE THE BOOK

Part I contains a brief history of the development of the rights, in order to show the rights in their context. There is an outline of the rights and a comparison of them. In many cases, tenants and their advisers will need to consider which of different rights might be appropriate.

Part II deals with collective rights, primarily collective enfranchisement and the right to manage. There is an overview which deals with some of the practical and organisational issues which commonly arise.

Part III looks at the rights of individual tenants, namely the right to extend of their flat, to acquire the freehold of a house and, briefly, to extend the lease of a house.

Part IV contains useful ancillary information such as timetable flowcharts and checklists, an overview of Leasehold Valuation Tribunal (LVT) procedure, valuation principles and company law issues.

In Parts II and III are chapters dealing with each right in turn. Each right is governed by a primary Act often amended by subsequent legislation. For each right, the relevant chapter will identify the appropriate sections of the particular statute and the key statutory instruments to which reference may need to be made. The statutes are not reproduced in this book. It is assumed that most readers will have access to them from an online or other source.

There is an overview of the key features of each right and the procedure for exercising and responding to each right and consequent procedure. Key practice points and potential pitfalls are identified.

Precedents, flowcharts and checklists are contained in the Appendices and CD-ROM. The precedents are mostly limited to the primary forms for initiating and responding to a claim and to those which are less or not commonly available, rather than ones which can easily be obtained from a law stationer. The flowcharts set out the timetable of key steps for each right and the checklists are of the preliminary matters which need to be undertaken in preparation for, and including, service of the notice exercising the right in question.

ACKNOWLEDGEMENTS

As one would expect, a work of this nature could not be undertaken without the help of others. I would particularly like to express thanks to my secretary, Dorothy Dickinson, for typing and general administrative support, including the deciphering of my handwritten notes for seemingly endless revisions. Also to my colleagues at Sykes Anderson, including Amrik Tumber, Stephan Weber, Peijun Xia and Susanna Heley, for assisting me in undertaking research and providing material, particularly in respect of some of the ancillary chapters. In addition, I would like to thank Grant Gleghom of Macintyre Hudson LLP, Chartered Accountants, for the contribution of him and his firm to some of the tax issues contained in Chapter 11.

Finally, I would like to express my gratitude to the following contributors:

> Michael Boyle, who drafted Chapter 11 on valuation issues: his knowledge and experience in these matters has been invaluable. Michael is a Fellow of the Royal Institution of Chartered Surveyors and senior partner of Boyle & Co of South Kensington. He has practised in residential valuation for over 30 years and, since the 1993 Act, has specialised in leasehold reform.

Edwin Johnson QC for his thoughts on the book and for providing the Foreword. Edwin was called to the Bar in 1987 and was appointed Queen's Counsel in 2006. He is a member of Maitland Chambers. He is recognised as a leading practitioner in the field of leasehold enfranchisement and has appeared in a number of reported and important cases.

Christopher Sykes
May 2007

Table of cases

7 Strathray Gardens Ltd v. Pointstar Shipping & Finance Ltd [2004] EWCA
 Civ 1669; [2005] HLR 20; [2005] 1 EGLR 53 46
9 Cornwall Crescent London Ltd v. Kensington and Chelsea RLBC [2005]
 EWCA Civ 324; [2006] 1 WLR 1186; [2005] 4 All ER 1207 42
9–29 Wiltshire Drive Halescher RTM Co Ltd v. Sinclair Gardens Investments,
 LW 9/3/06, BIR/OOCR/LRM/2005/002) 69, 75
Arbib v. Cadogan (Earl) [2005] 3 EGLR 139; [2005] RVR 401 159
Cadogan (Earl) v. Sportelli [2006] RVR 382; EW Lands LRA/50/2005 ......34, 159
Cadogan Estates Ltd v. Morris (1999) 31 HLR 732; (1999) 77 P & CR 336
 [1999] 1 EGLR 59, CA 39, 101
Cadogan Holdings Ltd v. Pockney [2005] RVR 197; EW Lands LRA/27/2003 ...159
Campomar, De v. Pettiward's Estate Trustees [2005] 1 EGLR 83; [2005] 15
 EG 124 146
Cawthorne and others v. Hamadan [2007] EWCA Civ 6 44
Chelsea (Viscount) v. Morris see Cadogan Estates Ltd v. Morris
Dawlin RTM Ltd v. Oakhill Park Estate (Hampstead) Ltd, LVT 21/9/2005,
 (LON/OOAG/LEE/2005/0012) 63
Gaingold Ltd v. WHRA RTM Co Ltd [2006] 1 EGLR 81; [2006] 03 EG 122 64
Jassi v. Gallagher [2006] EWCA Civ 1065; [2007] PNLR 4; [2006] 31 EGCS
 88 127
John Lyon's Free Grammar School v. Secchi (2000) 32 HLR 820; [2000] L & TR
 308; [1999] 3 EGLR 49 102
Malekshad v. Howard de Walden Estates Ltd [2002] UKHL 49; [2003] 1
 AC 1013; [2003] 1 All ER 193 120
Marine Court (Paignton) RTM Co v. Gibbs LVT, 24/9/05 75
Minshull Place RTM Co v. Park Rutland Ltd LON/OOAF/LRM/2004/2005 63
Willingale v. Globalgrange Ltd (2001) 33 HLR 17; (2000) 80 P & CR 448;
 [2000] 2 EGLR 55 107

Table of statutes

Commonhold and Leasehold Reform
Act 2002 ....5, 7, 8, 24,
25, 56, 63, 64, 65, 68,
69, 72, 74, 77, 78, 81,
83, 85, 92, 95, 97,
133, 172, 177, 181
    Part 1 173
    Part 2 173
    s.20 60
    ss 71–113......................56, 57, 58
    s.72 63
    s.73 ....66, 86
    s.74 ....66, 86
    s.75 62
    s.76 62
    s.77 62
    s.78 ....67, 68
        (7) 67
    s.79 68
    s.80 69
    s.81(1) 70
    s.82 ....65, 72
    s.83 71
    s.84 74
    s.85 68
    s.86 79
    s.88 77
    s.90 67
    s.91 78
    s.92 78
    s.93 ....65, 72, 81
    s.94 81
    s.96 58
    s.97 58
    s.99 82
    s.103 ....81, 82
    s.106 92
    s.112 57
        (1) 63
    s.113 57
    s.158 177
    s.159 179
    s.164 178
    s.166 179
    s.167 183
    s.168 183
    s.170 183
    Sched.6 ....56, 63
    Sched.7 ....56, 84
    Sched.11 177
Companies Act 1985 165
Companies Act 2006 ....164, 166, 168
Financial Services and Markets
    Act 2000 178
Housing Act 1988 174
Housing Act 1996......................5, 133
    s.81 183
    s.84 177
    Sched.4 174
Landlord and Tenant Act 1927
    s.23 124
Landlord and Tenant Act 1954
    Part II 118, 120, 174
Landlord and Tenant Act 1985 .....4, 176
    s.1......................................122, 173
    s.3 175
    s.3A 175
    s.19 176
    s.20..................................179, 180
    s.20B 176
    s.21 ....176, 177
    s.21A 177

s.21B 176
s.22 177
Sched. 178
Landlord and Tenant Act 1987 ....4, 7,
8, 26, 57, 69,
84, 92, 124, 174
   Part I 174, 175
   Part II 181
   s.35(2) 182
   s.36 182
   s.37 182
   s.40 182
   s.42 176
   s.42A 176
   s.47 176
Law of Property Act 1925 4
   s.146 183
Leasehold Reform Act 1967 ....3, 4,
7, 9, 116, 117, 119,
120, 123, 125, 137,
138, 140, 141, 150,
154, 169, 173, 179
   ss.1–4 118
   s.1B 118
   s.1ZC 118
   s.2(1) 119
   s.3 119
   s.6A 139
   s.7 138
      (7) 139
   s.8 136
   s.9 132
      (1) 132, 133, 150
      (1A) 133
      (1C) 133, 158
   s.9A 132
   s.10 131
   s.11 136
   s.15 150
      (2) 150
   s.22 ....124, 127
   Sched.3 127
      para. 6 124
Leasehold Reform, Housing and
Urban Development Act 1993 ....4, 5,
7, 8, 24, 25, 26, 29,
33, 34, 37, 38, 39, 45,
46, 48, 49, 50, 54, 94,
99, 100, 106, 108,
110, 113, 131, 157,
164, 168, 170, 176
Part 1
   Chapter 1 24
   Chapter 2 95
   Chapter 7 24
   ss.1–38 24
   s.1 29
   s.3 29
   s.4 30
   s.4A 36
   s.4B 36
   s.4C 36
   s.5 ....31, 97
   s.6 110
   s.7 ....31, 97, 110
   s. 9 31
   s.10 30
   s.11 33
   s.12A 36
   s.13 112
      (3) 37
   s.15 ....34, 35
   s.16 35
   s.21 43
   s.23 ....45, 52
   s.24 52
   s.25 52
   s.26 ....32, 53
   s.27 32
   s.33 27
   s.35 51
   s.36 50
   ss 39–62 95
   s.39 97
   s.40 98
   s.41 ....99, 173
   s.42 ....40, 44, 96, 112, 113
   s.44 104
   s.45 105
   s.47 107
   s.48 108
   s.49 107
   s.50 114
   s.54 112
   s.57 110
      (3) 109

TABLE OF STATUTES

Leasehold Reform, Housing and
Urban Development Act 1993 (*cont.*)
    s.59 110
    s.76 174
    ss.90–103 24
    s.92 100
    s.93 24
    s.99 .... 24, 39, 103
    Sched.1 .... 31, 43
    Sched.2 54
    Sched.6 .... 24, 33
    Sched.7 48
    Sched.8 51
    Sched.9 50
    Scheds.11–10 24
    Scheds.11–14 95
    Sched.11 .... 102, 105
    Part II 99
    Sched.12 37
    para. 9 102
    Sched.13, para. 2 113
Places of Worship (Enfranchisement)
    Act 1920 4
Rentcharges Act 1977 136

Table of statutory instruments

Civil Procedure Rules (SI 1998/3132) 24, 95, 117, 146
Housing Association Shared Ownership Leases (Exclusion from Leasehold
   Reform Act 1967) Regulations (SI 1987 /1940) 116, 140
Landlord and Tenant (Notice of Rent) (England) (Regulations)
   (SI 2004/3096) 179
Landlord and Tenant (Notice of Rent) (Wales) (Regulations)
   (SI 2005/1355) (W.103) 179
Lands Tribunal Rules (SI 1996/1022) 148
Leasehold Houses (Notice of Insurance Cover) (England) (Amendment)
   Regulations (SI 2005/177) 178
Leasehold Houses (Notice of Insurance Cover) (Wales) (Amendment)
   Regulations (SI 2005/1354) (W.102) 178
Leasehold Houses (Notice of Insurance Cover) (England) Regulations (SI
   2004/3097) 178
Leasehold Reform (Collective Enfranchisement) (Counter-notices) (England)
   Regulations (SI 2002/3208) 24, 43
Leasehold Reform (Collective Enfranchisement) (Counter-notices) (Wales)
   Regulations (SI 2003/990) (W.139) 24
Leasehold Reform (Collective Enfranchisement and Lease Renewal)
   Regulations (SI 1993/2407) 24, 47, 95
      Sched.1 47
Leasehold Reform (Enfranchisement and Extension) Regulations
   (SI 1967/1879) 116, 125, 128, 140
Leasehold Reform (Notices) (Amendment) (England) Regulations
   (SI 2002/1715) 116, 123, 124, 127, 140
Leasehold Reform (Notices) (Amendment) (Wales) Regulations
   (SI 2003/991) (W.140).............................116, 123, 124, 127, 140
Leasehold Reform (Notices) Regulations (SI 1997/640) 116, 123, 124, 127, 140
Leasehold Valuation Tribunals (Procedure) (Amendment) (England)
   Regulations (SI 2004/3098) 24, 53, 57, 68, 93, 114, 179
Leasehold Valuation Tribunals (Procedure) (Amendment) (Wales)
   Regulations (SI 2005/1356) (W.104) 24, 57, 68, 95, 116, 182
Leasehold Valuation Tribunals (Procedure) (England) Regulations
   (SI 2003/2099) 24, 53, 56, 68, 95, 116, 145, 182
Leasehold Valuation Tribunals (Procedure) (Wales) Regulations (
   SI 2004/681 (W.69)..........................24, 53, 57, 95, 116, 145, 182

TABLE OF STATUTORY INSTRUMENTS

Right to Manage (Prescribed Particulars and Forms) (England) Regulations
(SI 2003/1988) 56, 67, 69, 70, 74, 78
   Sched.3 74
Right to Manage (Prescribed Particulars and Forms) (Wales) Regulations
(SI 2004/678) (W. 66) 56
Rights of Re-entry and Forfeiture (Prescribed Sum and Period) (England)
Regulations (SI 2004/3086) 183
Rights of Re-entry and Forfeiture (Prescribed Sum and Period) (Wales)
Regulations (SI 2005/1352) (W.100) 183
RTM Companies (Memorandum and Articles of Association) (England)
Regulations (SI 2003/2120) 56, 66, 86
RTM Companies (Memorandum and Articles of Association) (Wales)
Regulations (SI 2004/675) (W.64) 56, 86
Service Charges (Consultation Requirements) (Amendment) (No. 2) (England)
Regulations (SI 2004/2939) 179, 180
Service Charges (Consultation Requirements) (Amendment) (Wales)
Regulations (SI 2005/1357) (W.105) 179, 180
Service Charges (Consultation Requirements) (England) Regulations
(SI 2003/1987) 179, 180
   Sched.3 181
Service Charges (Consultation Requirements) (Wales) Regulations
(SI 2004/684) (W. 72) 179, 180
   Sched.3 181
Tenant's Rights of First Refusal (Amendment) Regulations (SI 1996/2371) 174

Abbreviations

1967 Act	Leasehold Reform Act 1967
1987 Act	Landlord and Tenant Act 1987
1993 Act	Leasehold Reform, Housing and Urban Development Act 1993
2002 Act	Commonhold and Leasehold Reform Act 2002
EMS	estate management scheme
LVT	Leasehold Valuation Tribunal
RTE company	right to enfranchise company
RTM company	right to manage company

PART I

Introduction

CHAPTER 1

A brief history

1.1 THE INITIAL STAGES

Practitioners commonly assume that the Leasehold Reform Act 1967 ('the 1967 Act') heralded the introduction of the law on leasehold enfranchisement. Although this statute introduced a right for tenants of houses to extend the terms of their leases or acquire the freehold interest, subject to the qualifying criteria being fulfilled, the concept of leasehold enfranchisement has been around for a lot longer. Leasehold enfranchisement was the subject of much debate during the nineteenth century, during which period one of the key reasons for its introduction was to provide working class citizens with improved housing. Although a number of bills introducing the idea were tabled during that period, none of them received royal assent.

1.2 THE RATIONALE

As mentioned, a historical rationale for leasehold enfranchisement was the provision of better housing for the working classes. However, it was the landlord and tenant power struggle and intrinsically disadvantaged position of tenants that led to the idea of leasehold enfranchisement gaining momentum. When a long lease enters the latter stages of its term its value can depreciate rapidly and ultimately would be lost altogether as would the right to live in the property. If a tenant wished to continue living in his or her leasehold property, he or she would have to do so by extending the term or buying the freehold interest but without any right to do so.

Prior to the introduction of the laws on leasehold enfranchisement, landlords would in most situations have carte blanche to deal with properties in the aforementioned circumstances and although there was legislation which might give a tenant a statutory right to occupy a property, there was nothing which might preserve any capital value in the lease. Thus, landlords could impose an unreasonable price for an extended term or freehold interest in the property or impose other unreasonable requirements. Alternatively, if a tenant wished to sell his or her property this could prove to be extremely difficult,

PART I: INTRODUCTION

partly due to potential buyers being unable to obtain a mortgage for such leases and because of the uncertainties associated with buying a short lease.

Many commentators saw the prevailing circumstances as being inherently unfair towards tenants and advocated the need to impose a statutory regime redressing the imbalance. It was these circumstances that resulted in the right to enfranchise a house under the 1967 Act.

1.3 PRE-1967 ACT LEGISLATION

It should be noted that rights of enfranchisement were also available, in limited circumstances, prior to the introduction of the 1967 Act. These rights were contained in the Law of Property Act 1925 and Places of Worship (Enfranchisement) Act 1920. However, they were seen to have limited application and thus these rights were rarely exercised.

1.4 POST-1967 ACT CONCERNS

After the introduction of the 1967 Act, a number of commentators identified that the rationale behind the introduction of a right to enfranchise for tenants of houses (see **1.2** above) also applied to tenants of flats in buildings. However, there was another reason for proposing the introduction of an enfranchisement regime in respect of flats, namely the poor or unreasonable management of buildings containing flats.

It is standard for leases of flats to make the landlord or a management company responsible for repairing common areas and external parts of buildings. A common complaint of tenants has been the mismanagement of such areas and parts or the imposition of unreasonably high service charges. Attempts were made to try to resolve this issue by introducing legislation regulating the imposition of service charges in the form of the Landlord and Tenant Acts 1985 and 1987. Critics viewed these pieces of legislation as having made little difference and argued that more drastic measures were required. Interestingly, the Landlord and Tenant Act 1987 also introduced a collective right of first refusal for tenants to enable them to acquire the freehold of their building when a landlord wished to dispose of it. This did not and does not force a landlord to sell to the tenants.

1.5 LEASEHOLD REFORM, HOUSING AND URBAN DEVELOPMENT ACT 1993

The Housing and Urban Development Bill was published on 22 October 1992 and received royal assent on 20 July 1993 in the form of the Leasehold Reform, Housing and Urban Development Act 1993 ('the 1993 Act'). It was a radical piece of legislation. The 1993 Act introduced the right for qualifying tenants of flats to have the term of their leases extended and the right for the tenants to acquire the freehold of their building (otherwise known as the 'right to collective enfranchisement').

The right to collective enfranchisement was not initially exercised as much as the proponents of the right had predicted. This was in part due to the difficulties associated with uniting tenants of buildings, with organising the exercise of the right and with funding, and the qualifying criteria were restrictive. With recent changes (see below) making it easier to exercise the right it is now becoming increasingly popular, particularly with tenants of flats in smaller buildings.

Since its introduction, the 1993 Act has been subject to some amendment, primarily with a view to making it easier for the right to be exercised. The amendments include abolishing the low rent test and the residence condition; increasing to 25 per cent from 10 per cent the amount of non-residential floor area which might otherwise exclude a building from qualifying; and removing 'marriage value' where the unexpired term of the tenancy of a participating tenant exceeds 80 years. The most significant of these changes were contained in the Housing Act 1996 and the Commonhold and Leasehold Reform Act 2002 (the '2002 Act').

1.6　IMPENDING CHANGES TO THE RIGHT TO COLLECTIVE ENFRANCHISEMENT

Significantly, the 2002 Act contains provisions relating to a 'right to enfranchise company' ('RTE company'). These provisions state that a claim for a right to collective enfranchisement can only be made through a RTE company having a prescribed constitution and all qualifying tenants have a right to become members of the RTE company. Before serving any claim on the landlord, the RTE company must first afford an opportunity to each qualifying tenant to become a participating tenant, by serving a notice on the qualifying tenants inviting them to participate. These provisions are yet to come into force, their introduction having been considerably delayed having been subject to much criticism, and are dealt with in more detail in Chapter **4**.

1.7　RIGHT TO MANAGE

The 2002 Act is also significant because it introduced a right for tenants of flats in a building to take over the management of the building (known as the 'right to manage'). The introduction of this right was mainly due to the management issues raised above (see **1.4** above). Previously, it was possible for

PART I: INTRODUCTION

the tenants to oust the landlord from the management of their block by seeking to have a manager appointed by the Leasehold Valuation Tribunal. This was difficult to achieve, particularly as it was necessary to prove mismanagement by the landlord. The right to manage is a 'no fault' one exercisable regardless of how good or bad the landlord is. The right is viewed as a viable alternative to the collective right to enfranchisement where tenants are unable to finance the acquisition of the freehold interest and their principal concern relates to the management of the building containing their flats. The qualifying rules for exercising the right to manage are similar to those for exercising the right to collective enfranchisement and the right to manage came into force in England on 30 September 2003.

CHAPTER 2
The rights

2.1 OVERVIEW

As has been seen in the brief history in Chapter **1**, the rights with which this book is concerned are all derived from statute. The primary statutes by which each of the rights were created are listed below and the following abbreviations will be used:

- Leasehold Reform Act 1967: '1967 Act' (individual right to enfranchise or extend the lease of a house);
- Landlord and Tenant Act 1987: '1987 Act' (collective right of first refusal);
- Leasehold Reform, Housing and Urban Development Act 1993: '1993 Act' (collective enfranchisement of blocks of flats and the right to extend the lease of a flat);
- Commonhold and Leasehold Reform Act 2002: '2002 Act' (collective right to manage).

The rights can be divided into those which may be exercised by tenants acting collectively and those which can be exercised individually. The word individually here generally includes corporate and similar entities.

2.2 COLLECTIVE RIGHTS

These can broadly be described as the rights of a group of tenants of long leases of a building comprising flats subject to the fulfilment of certain criteria.

2.2.1 Right to collective enfranchisement

This is the right of a group of qualifying tenants to have the freehold and certain intermediate interests conveyed to their nominee purchaser (RTE company) at a price determined by a formula contained in the 1993 Act. See Chapter **4**.

2.2.2 Right to manage

Following a procedure laid down in the 2002 Act, this is the right of a group of qualifying tenants to take over the management of their building. This includes the management functions of any management company whether or not controlled by the tenants. It is exercised through a right to manage company ('RTM company') having a prescribed constitution. The landlord has a right to membership of the RTM company in his capacity as landlord and may also have a right in respect of parts of the premises he may retain. See Chapter **5**.

2.2.3 Right of first refusal

This is the right under the 1987 Act of qualifying tenants to be offered the freehold or other superior interest of their building before the landlord can dispose of their interest to a third party. It should be noted that the landlord cannot be forced to sell the property to the tenants under this legislation so it is not strictly a right of enfranchisement. It is not intended to cover the 1987 Act in any detail in this book, but some brief information is given in Chapter **12**.

2.2.4 Miscellaneous rights

There are miscellaneous rights, for example, to appoint a manager, of which an awareness is useful. If a group of tenants exercise collective rights and takes over the management functions of the landlord, they (or rather their nominee purchaser/RTE/RTM company) will need to observe the various duties placed on landlords. These are also mentioned briefly in Chapter **12**.

2.3 INDIVIDUAL RIGHTS

2.3.1 Right to a new lease of a flat

This is the right of an individual tenant under the 1993 Act to 'extend the lease of their flat' on payment of a premium to the landlord calculated under a statutory formula. The statutory extension of rights, although commonly described as an extension of the lease, takes the form of a new lease granted in substitution for the existing lease. The new lease is for a term of 90 years in addition to the unexpired term of the current tenancy. Ground rent is reduced to a peppercorn. See Chapter **6**.

2.3.2 Enfranchisement of a house

This is the right under the 1967 Act of an individual tenant of a house to have the freehold conveyed to them on payment of a price calculated according to a statutory formula. See Chapter **7**.

2.3.3 Right to a new lease of a house

This is the right under the 1967 Act of an individual tenant of a house to 'extend their lease' by 50 years on payment of a premium calculated in accordance with that Act. It is rarely used and will not be covered in detail. See Chapter **8**.

2.3.4 Miscellaneous rights

There are a number of miscellaneous rights benefiting the tenants of flats, such as the right to information about and to challenge service charges. These are contained in various statutes. It is useful to have an awareness of them as they might be used as an alternative or in addition to the rights with which this book is primarily concerned. Brief details are given in Chapter **12**.

2.4 COMPARISON OF RIGHTS: PROS AND CONS

It is often necessary to consider which of the different rights might be appropriate to meet the concerns of the tenants. A list of key pros and cons of each of the main rights is set out below.

2.4.1 Collective enfranchisement

Possible benefits

- The tenants that participate can grant themselves very long leases without payment of a further premium and may eliminate or reduce the ground rent payable, but bearing in mind the need to fund the expenses of any nominee (RTE) company.
- There is no residence qualification or minimum period of ownership required on the part of any tenant wishing to participate.
- There is no need to invite all qualifying tenants to participate (this will change under the RTE company regime).
- Usually, but not always, the management of the building will also be acquired.

- There may be scope for the participants to extract additional value from the reversion, e.g. in respect of non-participating qualifying tenants, as there is no requirement to pay a 'marriage value' for flats of tenants who qualify but do not participate.
- It may be possible to use the process as an opportunity to rectify defects in the standard lease.
- There is, or at least is perceived to be, an enhanced saleability of flats in the building.

Possible disadvantages

- The process is more expensive and protracted than, e.g. the RTM procedure. In particular, it is necessary to fund the premium which could substantially increase if any marriage value is payable or if the commercial areas have to be acquired because the freeholder does not exercise their right to a leaseback.
- It is necessary to pay arrears of rent and service charge in addition to the price.
- The management functions where they are acquired may be more onerous than anticipated and there may be issues with enforcement against neighbours, in particular with those who have not participated.
- Contracts entered into by the landlord do not automatically cease.
- It may be more difficult to obtain the necessary number of tenants to participate, particularly in a larger building, and even if that number is obtained there could be a heavy burden on the participators where there is a fair proportion of qualifying tenants who do not participate.

2.4.2 Right to manage

Possible benefits

- It is simpler and cheaper than collective enfranchisement and is cost effective if management problems are the main issue.
- There is a shorter timescale.
- There is no need to obtain a valuation.
- There is no need to show fault on the part of the landlord and there are very limited grounds on which a landlord can object or matters which need to be argued or negotiated with the landlord.
- Management and service contracts entered into by the landlord or any manager come to an end unless the RTM company agrees otherwise with the contractor.
- There is no need to pay any arrears of ground rent or service charge in order to exercise the right although there will be a continuing liability to the landlord for those tenants in arrears.

Possible disadvantages

- The legislation does not deal adequately with all situations, in particular where there is an estate of more than one building.
- The management functions may be onerous and there will be accounting, legal and practical issues arising with regard to service and similar charges.
- The RTM company and its officers will have to comply with company and landlord legal obligations.
- Management information needed from the landlord or landlord's managing agent can be difficult to obtain even though there is a legal right for such.
- The landlord has a right to membership of the RTM company.
- Some management functions remain with the landlord, e.g. the right to forfeit and an involvement with the giving of approvals where these are required under the tenants' leases.
- There is no ability to extend the leases of participators or to enhance capital value other than through better management.

2.4.3 Right of a tenant to extend the lease of their flat

Possible benefits

- There are no organisational issues and the tenant is not dependent on others.
- It is comparatively simple.
- It is useful if the entire building does not qualify for collective enfranchisement or where it does qualify but it is not possible to get the required number of tenants to participate.
- The ground rent is reduced to a peppercorn.

Possible disadvantages/limitations

- The further period of extension is 90 years, which is adequate but is not the 999-year lease which participating tenants under the collective procedure normally grant themselves.
- There are no economies of scale, e.g. in terms of costs, as there might be under the collective process.
- It does not deal with any management issues.
- There is a requirement for the tenant to have owned the lease for at least two years prior to the date of exercising the right.

2.4.4 Rights in respect of houses

The comparison here is between obtaining an extension of the lease or acquiring the freehold. To extend the lease may be cheaper and less expensive, in terms of the price payable, but the term of the extension is only for 50 years plus the existing term. Also, the qualifying criteria can be more difficult to fulfil. Therefore for the tenant of a house this option is rarely exercised and almost invariably the tenant will be advised to seek to acquire the freehold. It should be noted that it is necessary for the tenant of a house to have owned the lease for at least two years.

PART II

Collective rights

CHAPTER 3
Managing the collective process

3.1 GENERAL

The collective rights with which this book is primarily concerned are collective enfranchisement and the right to manage. For any collective action to be successful and to minimise the risk of problems, a high degree of preparation and organisation will be required both on the part of the tenants and their advisers.

There are a number of issues to be considered in the management of a potentially large number of individuals who may need to be persuaded to participate, who require to be advised and informed, their signatures obtained and monies collected. This is in addition to the information gathering necessary to assess qualifying criteria and general feasibility. It is therefore essential that these matters are well thought out at an early stage.

Precisely how the process is organised will depend upon the particular circumstances, so no set rules can be laid down. It will depend, e.g. upon the type of right to be exercised (collective enfranchisement or RTM), the number of flats in the building and potential interest in participation in any form of action which is often triggered by dissatisfaction with the management of the building. Information should be obtained as to what the tenants want to achieve. The initial work can broadly be divided up as follows:

- obtaining preliminary information;
- assessing the potential level of interest in participation;
- assessing the options;
- binding participators to the process;
- valuation (in the case of collective enfranchisement);
- issues relating to the subsequent management of the building;
- providing information;
- communication;
- costs and contributions;
- forming a nominee RTE/RTM company;
- professional issues;
- information management.

The process is normally driven by one or two tenants, or possibly a residents' committee if one exists. These co-ordinators will collect information on the legal, financial and practical consequences of exercising the relevant rights. A solicitor might be instructed from the outset or at a later stage of the preparatory process. A solicitor might be asked to address a residents' committee or a general meeting of tenants.

In larger blocks the possibility of using the services of a professional project manager might be considered.

3.2 OBTAINING PRELIMINARY INFORMATION

More detail on the information required for particular rights is contained in later chapters. Basic information which is common to both rights includes:

- the type of building and number of flats;
- the number of flats on long leases, their terms and the identity of tenants;
- what proportion of the building, if any, comprises non-residential/commercial areas;
- the names and addresses of any relevant landlord/freeholder.

This is often a two-stage process: initial assessment and feasibility, collecting funds and gathering support in principle before undertaking a more detailed investigation.

3.3 ASSESSING POTENTIAL INTEREST

How and when this is done will depend on the circumstances, in particular on the size of the building. It will probably be an ongoing process. Unless it is a building with very few flats, at some stage a formal approach to tenants may be required and it may be necessary to persuade them to participate. This could be done, e.g. by one or more of the following: sending a circular, holding a tenants' meeting, possibly with a solicitor to answer questions on legal issues or, as is often the case, knocking on doors.

The circular might be a letter from (or drafted by) a solicitor setting out the options and explaining briefly the relevant procedures, where possible with some estimation of likely costs.

3.4 VALUATION

For the purposes of collective enfranchisement it is necessary to state the proposed price in the notice which initiates the claim. The prospective participating tenants will in any case need to have a reasonable idea of their likely contribution and whether it is affordable. The valuation formula is complex and its application will in most cases require the services of a specialist. A formal valuation will be needed in most cases. This could be expensive and will need to be funded. A decision will need to be made as to when that expense is incurred, which the co-ordinators and their advisers will probably wish to spread amongst as many tenants as possible. One possible approach is to obtain a broad informal estimate of price for the purpose of gaining support and obtain a formal valuation later in the preliminary process. See Chapter **10** for more information on valuation issues.

3.5 ASSESSMENT OF THE OPTIONS

Once some preliminary information gathering has taken place, consideration should be given as to whether one, both or neither of the primary rights should be pursued. This will depend on such factors as whether qualifying criteria are met, the cost of the process, in particular the likely price to be paid in the case of collective enfranchisement, and how best the objectives of the tenants can be achieved. See the comparison of rights in Chapter **2**.

Alternative remedies may need to be considered, e.g. if excessive service charges are an issue. These could be challenged under other legislation (see Chapter **12**) or if there is insufficient support for collective action an individual tenant may wish to seek an extension of their lease (see Chapter **6**).

3.6 COMMUNICATION AND PROVISION OF INFORMATION

An agreed system of communication should be set up between the lead tenants/residents' committee and the solicitor, and between the lead and other tenants.

It is recommended that the tenants' solicitor at an early stage endeavour to restrict communication to one or two of the lead tenants nominated for the purpose, otherwise unnecessary time and expense will be incurred dealing with enquiries from individual tenants and there is the possibility of mixed messages or confusion. It may not be possible to avoid altogether being contacted by other participators but this can to a large extent be eliminated by effective communication through the primary contacts. Email is the quickest and cheapest way of updating and gathering information.

When acting for a group, tenants' confidentiality is the key and care should be taken not unwittingly to notify the landlord (so that, e.g. the landlord is copied in on what is happening). This is a particular risk if the landlord or a nominee owns a flat in the building. With collective enfranchisement, until the RTE provisions are brought into effect the participating tenants are not obliged to invite or indeed communicate at all with all qualifying tenants, although in most instances it will be desirable to encourage as much participation as possible. For the right to manage, there is a requirement to invite all qualifying tenants to participate.

3.7 COSTS AND CONTRIBUTIONS

Funding will be necessary for:

- investigative work;
- a valuation, where relevant;
- continuing professional costs;
- the landlord's legal and valuation costs;
- the price and any arrears of rent and service charge and any consequent disbursements, such as stamp duty land tax and Land Registry fees in the case of collective enfranchisement;
- future funding after the relevant right has been exercised both for any nominee/RTE/RTM company and where management of a building is being taken over for the prompt collection of service charge contributions.

Careful thought should be given as to when these are collected, usually as a stage process. It is recommended that funds be obtained in advance of incurring the liability. See also **3.10** below.

The accounting treatment of contributions and any tax issues may need to be considered, particularly in the case of collective enfranchisement. See **3.9** below and Chapter **11**.

3.8 BINDING THE TENANTS TO THE PROCESS

It is important that at an early stage, and certainly before any notice seeking to exercise a right is served on the landlord, the tenants bind themselves to each other and to the process. There should be a disincentive to any participator seeking to withdraw. As to how detailed or complex any agreement should be will depend on the circumstances. This could be dealt with by way of a letter of intent or by a participation agreement, or both. A letter of intent is a simpler document which is particularly useful, first for covering preliminary work in collective enfranchisement matters, and secondly for RTM cases. For anything other than the simplest of collective enfranchisement matters it is recommended that there be a more detailed participation agreement. A specimen letter of intent for RTM matters is included at **A9** and a participation agreement for collective enfranchisement matters at **A2** of Appendix **A**, which will need to be adapted for the particular circumstances. If any prospective participator is being invited to enter into a binding contract, the main consequences to them of doing so should be explained with a recommendation that they should seek separate legal advice if necessary.

3.8.1 Participation agreement

Some of the issues which will need to be covered are:

- the payment of costs and indemnity for the other tenants for any shortfall;
- whether to bind tenants at the outset to pay the price once agreed or determined, or to include a commitment to pay contributions to expenses and subsequently the price in stages (this leaves the possibility that if a certain stage is reached and one or more tenants withdraw, this could bring the process to an end);
- withdrawal from the process;
- the position if a tenant sells his lease and the need to bind any assignee;
- whether the liability to contribute costs is up to a limit subject to the liability to contribute to the landlord's costs;
- the proportions of contributions as to cost and price: these could be equal but may not be depending, e.g. on the level of benefit a particular participator may obtain in collective enfranchisement matters, or e.g. according to the percentage liability for service charges of the flats of the participators (in this latter case it is fairly simple to convert those percentages to total 100 per cent so as to take into account the fact that some tenants may not be participating);
- confidentiality;
- assimilation of information;
- liability for the landlord's costs;
- indemnity to the nominee/RTM company and its officers/lead participators;
- constitution of the nominee company;
- the benefits the tenants will receive on the successful enfranchisement of the building, e.g. a very long lease with no ground rent;
- professional advisers and communication.

In enfranchisement matters, particular attention should be paid to the situation where a participator wishes to sell their flat during the process, to ensure that they are obliged to bind the buyer to the process. It is also useful to have a policy of how to deal with enquiries from sellers and buyers and their agents and advisers, which can be repetitive and time-consuming in a large block where there may be a number of sales during the claim.

A firm policy should be established at the outset to deal with any participator who refuses to pay any contribution when required.

3.9 NOMINEE/RTE/RTM COMPANY

Whilst not a requirement, collective enfranchisement at present is usually exercised through a nominee company, and it is a requirement that the right to manage be exercised through a RTM company. Consideration should be had to directors' responsibilities and other company law issues. It is not the function of this book to cover these in any detail but see Chapter **11**.

As regards the formation of a company, the RTM company has a prescribed constitution. For collective enfranchisement, until the introduction of RTE companies it could be by way of guarantee or by shares, but more commonly the latter. Officers will need to be appointed. Funding issues should be considered, e.g. is there to be any borrowing? Is a tenant's contribution to be by way of share capital or by way of loan? For further information see Chapter **11**.

Care should be taken in the preparation of the Articles of Association of the nominee purchaser. Standard Articles are available. Specimen Articles are included in **A5** of Appendix **A**. These would usually be prepared so as to ensure that membership of the company is restricted to owners of flats in the building concerned. More bespoke drafting will be required if there are special circumstances, such as one participator contributing substantially more to the price to pay for the proportion attributable to the flat of a non-participator.

A decision needs to be made as to when any corporate vehicle is formed. It would be common to delay this until a decision in principle to exercise the relevant right has been made.

3.10 PROFESSIONAL ISSUES FOR SOLICITORS

For detailed guidance reference should be made to *The Guide to the Professional Conduct of Solicitors 1999,* published by the Law Society (likely to be replaced by the Solicitors' Code of Conduct, due to come into force during 2007), but some broad issues to be considered in this context are set out below.

3.10.1 Who is my client?

The solicitor could at the outset be acting for representative individuals, assuming there is no company formed by the participators, and subsequently for any nominee/RTE/RTM company. These matters need to be thought out carefully at the outset and should be dealt with in the retainer/client care letter.

When a nominee company is formed, the solicitor should ensure that instructions are received from that company, properly minuted, and follow other procedures which would normally be undertaken when acting for a company. Care should be taken not to breach the warranty of authority.

The solicitor should consider whether to act solely for the company (which may have limited funds and no track record), or whether to continue to have a retainer with the lead individual participators.

Regardless of the strict letter of the retainer, there is a question as to whom duties are owed. It is probable that a duty will be owed to all the participators, not merely to those with whom there is a retainer.

3.10.2 Money laundering

There is an issue as to whether it is necessary to check the identity of all participators. There are clearly practical and logistical issues if there are a large number of participators in a substantial building. If the solicitor is only acting for a company, then the identity and address checking, etc, relating to the company and its officers should be followed. The solicitor will probably receive money from all the participating tenants, which could possibly trigger a requirement to obtain ID for all those participators. Consideration could be given to the lead participators collecting funds in the account of the nominee company or some trust or similar account which is set up, and then paying them on to the solicitor, but this may be difficult to implement in practice. It would be a matter for the solicitor to use his or her own judgement in the particular circumstances as to how anti-money-laundering procedures should be followed.

3.10.3 Conflicts

Whilst the interests of all participators will usually be the same, there are occasions when there may be competing or conflicting interests, e.g. in collective enfranchisement matters, if one party is paying a substantially greater proportion of the price to cover the interests of non-participators and in return is receiving a greater interest in the nominee company. Professional advisers should be aware of the potential for conflict and, even though they may continue in control of the process, where necessary ask the specified participators to seek separate advice. Particular attention should be paid to Solicitors' Practice Rule 16D (see also draft Solicitors' Code of Conduct, r.4) which contains special rules relating to conflicts. There will not normally be a conflict where there is a common interest, e.g. where (as is likely to be the case here), it would be disproportionate for the participators to instruct separate solicitors. However, where a conflict or potential conflict undermines the common purpose, it may be possible for a participant to be required to obtain separate advice on defined areas.

3.10.4 Cost information

The Solicitors' Costs Information and Client Care Code 1999 will apply (see also draft Solicitors' Code of Conduct, r.2). It may be helpful both for the purposes of obtaining instructions and to comply with the Code to have pro forma breakdowns of costs dividing the relevant process into its constituent parts, with costs parameters for each. Specimen breakdowns of costs for use with collective enfranchisement and RTM matters are included at **A3** and **A10** respectively in Appendix **A**. It will be necessary to update the information, e.g. if matters become more complex or protracted or if there is an application to the Leasehold Valuation Tribunal, and on the delivery of interim invoices and costs updates in accordance with the Code.

3.10.5 Information and costs management

The solicitor or other co-ordinator of the process will need to keep a close control of information on tenants' contributions. It is useful to have a spreadsheet to keep basic information on each participating tenant and to keep track, e.g. of the term of their lease, whether they have signed and returned their participation agreement and whether and when they have paid any required funds. A specimen spreadsheet of basic information is included at **A4** in Appendix **A**.

Solicitors will need to abide by client account rules. Funds received from participators should be identified separately on the ledger by reference to the name of the participator and the flat number.

3.11 LOOKING FORWARD

The participating tenants and those advising them will need to plan ahead to address issues which might arise during the exercise of the right concerned and afterwards, assuming there is a successful outcome.

For collective enfranchisement, consideration should be given to the benefits to be offered to participators, such as the extension of their leases and on what terms, and this will usually be addressed in the participation agreement.

For cases where the management of the building will be taken over, consideration should be given as to how and when it will be undertaken. See further Chapter **5**.

One particular issue to be aware of is insurance. In collective enfranchisement matters, arrangements should be made to put in place new insurance to take effect immediately when risk passes to the nominee purchaser, which may be on entering into a binding contract (depending on the terms of that contract) or more likely (since contracts are not often entered into in these matters) on completion. In right to manage cases, the insurance policy of the landlord will cease on the acquisition date, as will all other contracts made by or on behalf of the landlord, unless the RTM company agrees with the insurer to continue the contract.

In all instances where there is a corporate entity exercising the right, the funding and management of it must be fully addressed.

CHAPTER 4

Collective enfranchisement

4.1 OVERVIEW

The right of collective enfranchisement can broadly be described as that created by the Leasehold Reform, Housing and Urban Development Act 1993 for a group of tenants of flats under long leases to acquire freehold or other intermediate interest in their building at a price and on terms in accordance with the 1993 Act.

A timetable flowchart is included at **B1** and a checklist of preliminary matters at **B2** in Appendix **B**.

4.2 FINDING YOUR WAY AROUND THE LEGISLATION

The 1993 Act has been amended in particular by the Commonhold and Leasehold Reform Act 2002. The principal provisions are in Chapter 1 of the 1993 Act, ss.1–38. Other key provisions are in Chapter 7, ss.90–103, dealing with such matters as anti-avoidance (s.93) and notices (s.99).

Schedules 1–10 deal with various detailed matters flowing from Chapter 1, such as valuation in Sched. 6.

The Leasehold Reform (Collective Enfranchisement and Lease Renewal) Regulations 1993, SI 1993/2407 ('the 1993 Regulations') deal with some conveyancing and related procedures.

The Leasehold Reform (Collective Enfranchisement) (Counter–notices) (England) Regulations 2002, SI 2002/3208 ('the 2002 Regulations') deal with additional content of a landlord's counter-notice. Similar Regulations relating to Wales were made in 2003 (SI 2003/990 (W.139)).

Regard should also be paid to the Leasehold Valuation Tribunals (Procedure) (England) Regulations 2003, SI 2003/2099, as amended by SI 2004/3098 (SI 2004/681 (W.69) as amended by SI 2005/1356 (W.104) in Wales) ('the LVT Procedure Regulations') in the case of application to the Leasehold Valuation Tribunal (LVT), and to the Civil Procedure Rules in the case of application to the court.

4.3 KEY TERMINOLOGY

It is useful to have an understanding of some of the key terms used in the 1993 Act:

- 'relevant premises': the building the freehold of which is to be acquired;
- 'qualifying tenant': a tenant of a flat which fulfils the qualifying criteria;
- 'participating tenant': a qualifying tenant who participates in the process;
- 'reversioner': the freeholder or other intermediate landlord who has the right to conduct the claim on behalf of all landlords where there is more than one;
- 'nominee purchaser': the person or entity nominated to have conduct of the proceedings on behalf of the participating tenants (this will be changed to the 'RTE company' when and if those provisions come into effect);
- 'initial notice': the notice by which the claim procedure is commenced;
- 'other relevant landlord': a landlord other than the reversioner;
- 'relevant date': the date of service of the initial notice, e.g. the valuation date.

The 2002 Act potentially introduces the concept of a right to enfranchise (RTE) company through which any claim must be exercised, but because of perceived concerns with these provisions, there is as yet no commencement date for them. The RTE provisions are dealt with in greater detail at **4.8** below, otherwise the main workings of the 1993 Act (save where stated to the contrary) remain unchanged and for 'nominee purchaser' one can substitute 'RTE company'.

4.4 KEY FEATURES

- The right is exercised by a nominee purchaser (RTE company) on behalf of the participating and the qualifying tenants.
- The claim is initiated by an initial notice.
- No binding contract is created until one is specifically entered into by the parties or a vesting order is made by the court.
- The nominee purchaser can withdraw at any time prior to a binding contract subject to a liability for the costs of any landlord.
- Unless and until introduction of the RTE provisions there is no obligation on the prospective participators to invite all qualifying tenants to participate, although in many cases they will wish to have on board as many as possible.
- The value is based on the valuation as at the date of service of the initial notice. It is necessary to state a price in the initial notice.

PART II: COLLECTIVE RIGHTS

- Marriage value (see **4.6.9** below) is disregarded in respect of the flats of participating tenants whose leases have more than 80 years unexpired as at the relevant date and of the flats of tenants who qualify but do not participate.
- An initial notice triggers a strict timetable; if this is not followed by the tenants, they will be deemed to have withdrawn, and if it is not followed by the landlord, it would, e.g. lose its right to challenge the price proposed by the tenant. See the timetable flowchart at **B2**.
- There is no need for a qualifying tenant to have owned their lease for any period or to have occupied the flat as their residence.
- Although the primary forum for determining issues is the LVT, there are circumstances where jurisdiction is with the county court.
- The participating tenants are required to acquire certain intermediate leasehold interests and are entitled to acquire others.
- The right applies even though a considerable proportion of a building may be commercial, i.e. up to 25 per cent.
- The freeholder may be entitled to a leaseback of 'unsold' flats and commercial areas.

4.5   GENERAL COMMENTS

The right of qualifying tenants to acquire the freehold of their building is a powerful tool. It must be borne in mind that it is not a complete panacea for all issues which might arise. The tenants can only acquire the premises and ancillary rights as provided by the relevant legislation. This leaves some gaps, particularly in areas such as where there are intermediate leasehold interests. It may not necessarily resolve all management issues. For details of the pros and cons see **2.4.1** above.

4.5.1   Purchase outside the statutory regime

The tenants or any of them may seek to acquire the freehold by direct negotiation with the landlord outside of the statutory regime. This is more common in smaller buildings. There can be a saving in costs and time. Any proposed purchase is likely to be subject to the requirements of the Landlord and Tenant Act 1987 (see Chapter **12**) giving the right of first refusal for the freehold to be first offered to all qualifying tenants. A private treaty purchase would not prevent a subsequent claim by the requisite number of qualifying tenants for collective enfranchisement under the 1993 Act. In practice, it is usually the case that a majority of tenants participate in the private treaty purchase.

It would still be advisable for the tenants to obtain a valuation to ascertain that the acquisition is justified on a costs benefit analysis.

A freeholder would normally wish to ensure that their professional costs in dealing with any private treaty claim are covered. Some freeholders will not incur any costs until the initial notice is served as this will trigger a statutory liability on the nominee purchaser for certain of the freeholders' and the landlords' costs (see **4.5.2** below). Alternatively, a freeholder may ask for an undertaking from the tenants' solicitor to pay their proposal fees in any event and careful consideration will need to be given by the tenants as to the likelihood of a successful deal and whether or not costs may be wasted. A freeholder might also want an initial notice to be served in order to preserve their right to claim roll-over relief for CGT purposes. See further Chapter **11**.

If the freeholder is a company which has been dissolved in circumstances where the property has passed *bona vacantia* to the Crown it will often be possible to agree terms of purchase with the Treasury Solicitor. See also regarding absentee landlords at **4.6.7**.

4.5.2 Costs

In addition to the tenants' own professional costs which will be mainly solicitors', surveyors' and possibly accounting fees, there may also be stamp duty land tax and there will be Land Registry fees and other usual conveyancing disbursements. Where applicable there will be the costs of setting up and the management of a nominee/RTE company.

Once the initial notice is served, the nominee purchaser will be liable for the reasonable costs of the freeholder and other relevant landlord. Costs are limited to certain matters, namely investigating the claim and issues arising out of the initial notice, deducing title and conveyancing, and valuation costs (but not the costs of negotiating with the nominee purchaser's valuer) (s.33 of the 1993 Act).

If the initial notice is withdrawn or deemed withdrawn, the liability for the landlord's costs is a joint and several one of all the participating tenants. When RTE companies are introduced, the liability will be on the company and anyone who has been a participating member of the company (unless they have assigned their lease to someone who has become a member). See also regarding withdrawal at **4.15** below. There are some exceptions to the general rule.

There is generally no liability for another party's costs if an application is made to the LVT. The LVT's power to award costs is limited. If there are court proceedings, e.g. to determine the validity of a claim, then the usual rules apply and costs will often follow the event.

Those representing the tenants will normally wish to ensure that contributions to costs are collected up front. See Chapter **3**.

PART II: COLLECTIVE RIGHTS

4.6 PRELIMINARY INVESTIGATIONS

The importance of carrying out a thorough preliminary investigation and assessment of feasibility before service of the initial notice cannot be overstated. See the checklist of preliminary matters at **B2**.

The following are the key matters which need to be considered:

- whether the premises qualify;
- qualifying tenants and the sufficiency of participation;
- what additional property or rights should be included in the claim and other title issues;
- the names and addresses of the freeholder and other relevant landlords;
- valuation;
- if applicable, the formation of a corporate nominee purchaser (RTE company);
- other matters relevant for the preparation of an initial notice such as any plan which needs to be attached to it.

These matters are looked at in more detail below.

In addition, the issues relating to managing the collective process referred to in Chapter **3** need to be considered and an assessment/appreciation of the procedural timetable subsequent to the service of the initial notice is useful, in particular to anticipate/deal with key dates as they arise.

4.6.1 Qualifying criteria

The broad qualifying criteria are as follows:

- a self-contained building or part of a building;
- not more than 25 per cent of the building is non-residential;
- two or more flats are held by qualifying tenants;
- the total number of flats held by those tenants is not less than two-thirds of the total number of flats;
- the participating tenants must be those of flats comprising not less than 50 per cent of the total number of flats at the relevant date (i.e. the date the initial notice is given) with a minimum of two participators. Note that the total number of flats includes those of qualifying tenants and of all other flats in the building, e.g. if there are 23 flats in a building, at least 16 (two-thirds) must be held by qualifying tenants and at least 12 qualifying tenants (50 per cent of the total number of flats) must participate. Also note that the qualifying number needs to be rounded up where the relevant percentage is not a whole number.

4.6.2 Qualifying premises

These are defined in s.3. The self-contained building should be structurally detached but can be attached to other buildings such as one building in a terrace. There is an issue where there is an estate comprising more than one building. Enfranchisement of all buildings on an estate in one claim is not possible on a strict interpretation of the Act, although it is possible for each block to enfranchise separately. An attempt has been made to assert that an estate of six buildings was, in effect, 'one continuous building', in which claim the tenants succeeded but only as the landlord withdrew his objection. The proposition has not therefore been properly tested.

For part of a building there needs to be a vertical division of the structure which could be redeveloped independently of the remainder and where the relevant services provided are independent, or could be independent, without significant interruption to the services for the occupiers of the remainder.

There are issues with overhanging buildings and there can be buildings where the position is not clear. Buildings which at first glance might not be considered to qualify, in fact do so, and vice versa.

The right does not apply if there are non-residential parts (excluding common parts) where the internal floor area over those parts exceeds 25 per cent of the internal floor area of the whole premises. In assessing the area of non-residential parts, the communal areas are disregarded, similarly when calculating the area of the residential parts.

It should be noted that these excluded areas are not necessarily commercial *per se* and the statutory definition relates to premises not occupied or intended to be occupied for residential purposes. Care should be taken to ascertain whether or not premises are non-residential.

Residential areas will include areas (not common parts) ancillary to the use of a flat, e.g. parking spaces or storage areas which are for the use of that flat.

Careful consideration needs to be given as to what property should be included in the claim (see s.1). This falls within three types, namely:

- the premises or building itself, including communal areas within that building;
- appurtenant property which is property demised by the lease of a qualifying tenant of a flat in the premises and in the curtilage of the premises, such as a garage or garden;
- other property which a qualifying tenant is entitled to use pursuant to his lease in common with other occupiers of the premises, namely communal facilities whether or not contained in the premises, save that in this case the freeholder can elect to grant permanent rights to the nominee purchaser rather than convey the freehold of those areas.

4.6.3 Intermediate leasehold interests

The tenants are obliged to acquire:

- interests superior to the leases held by the qualifying tenants of flats in the premises (this applies to all qualifying tenants, not just participating ones).

They are entitled to acquire:

- the interests of a tenant under any other lease which demises any common parts or appurtenance of the premises where reasonably necessary for the proper management or maintenance of the common parts by the participating tenants.

The tenants are not entitled to acquire any other leasehold interest, e.g. where there is a lease of a commercial unit. If there is, e.g. a headlease of the whole building which includes as well as flats of qualifying tenants other flats not let on long leases and communal areas, then the participating tenants would only acquire the headleasehold interest insofar as it relates to the parts of the premises referred to above.

Key practice points

- Save in the simplest of buildings it is necessary to examine carefully what premises should be included in the claim.
- Consider using a surveyor/valuer and undertaking a site inspection.
- Analyse the title/legal structure of the building and obtain/study any Land Registry and other plans.
- Consider what other rights might need to be acquired over the adjoining premises of the landlord and what would be the communal areas.

4.6.4 Excluded premises

Apart from the 'non-residential' threshold being exceeded, there are the following exemptions where the premises will not qualify for the right (ss.4, 10):

(a) where there is a resident landlord (however, this is extremely limited and only relates to premises which are not purpose-built blocks and contain not more than four units, the freehold of which is owned by the same person and prior to the conversion into flats and was occupied by him or an adult member of his family as his own or main place of residence within the 12–month period ending with the date on which the resident landlord exemption is claimed to be fulfilled);

(b) where the premises include the track of an operational railway.

4.6.5 Qualifying tenants

Under s.5, a qualifying tenant is a tenant of a flat under a long lease. Section 7 sets out what is meant by a 'long lease'. The main definition is a lease granted for a term certain of more than 21 years and this will be the situation most commonly encountered. There are other definitions, but those likely to be of significance include leases granted under the right to buy legislation and shared ownership leases where the share is more than 100 per cent and renewal leases where the total renewal exceeds 21 years, including the subsequent lease.

There are exceptions where leases do not qualify; primarily business leases, charitable trust leases and subleases which have been granted unlawfully.

If the lease is other than what might be described as a standard long lease or there are any unusual circumstances, then s.7 should be considered in detail.

It should be noted that there is no requirement for a tenant to have owned the lease for any period nor for occupation of the flat as a main residence. If there are two or more long leases of the same flat, it is only the tenant in possession who is the qualifying tenant.

If one tenant (or if a company, an associated company) would be a qualifying tenant of three or more flats in the building whether or not by one or more leases and whether or not as a joint tenant or a subtenant, then there is no qualifying tenant for any of these flats. Subject to tax and commercial considerations, a determined tenant can overcome this barrier by transferring one or more of the offending flats to a friendly party. There are other circumstances where a qualifying tenant is not permitted to participate which are mainly where the tenancy is subject to notice of termination or proceedings for possession but these are rarely encountered in practice.

As part of the preliminary investigation it will be necessary to obtain office copies of the title to each flat to ascertain the details of qualifying tenants and their leases. If the superior title is registered the Land Registry entries will contain brief details of all registered leases which should include all those which qualify. Where the superior title is not registered, title details of each registered lease can be obtained on a flat-by-flat basis.

4.6.6 Who is the landlord?

The freeholder or both of all of them if more than one and every owner of a leasehold interest to be acquired, in other words, intermediate/headlandlords.

There are provisions for determining who is the reversioner for the purposes of the claim, and if there is a dispute the court can appoint (see s.9 and Sched. 1). Whilst this would normally be the freeholder, he may not be, for example, if the headlandlord has a very long lease and the freeholder a minimal reversion.

It is the reversioner who conducts the proceedings for all the relevant landlords. In some circumstances a relevant landlord can act separately, e.g. where a claim is resisted on the grounds of redevelopment, and can apply for directions in the event of dispute as to how the claim is dealt with.

Where the title of all relevant interests is registered, details can easily be obtained by obtaining office copies from the Land Registry. Care should be taken to check for pending applications. A landlord is obliged by law to provide a name and address for service on rent and service charge demands, and also to give notice of assignment on change of landlord. A most recent rent/service charge demand should be looked at and checked against title information. See also **4.6.8** below.

If there is an unregistered superior interest there can be circumstances where the landlord's identity cannot be obtained easily, and seeking the information through other lines of enquiry needs to be considered. There is the risk of service of an invalid notice if it is not served on the correct party.

Where any landlord is a company, in the case of one incorporated in England and Wales a search should be made online at Companies House to check, e.g. that it is not in liquidation or similar and for its registered office. For other corporate entities their status should be checked where reasonably feasible.

4.6.7 Absent landlord

Sections 26 and 27 contain detailed provisions for situations where a landlord cannot be found, for their identity to be ascertained. An application to the court is required.

Until the commencement of the RTE company provisions there is a different qualifying threshold for utilising the absent landlord rights than there is for exercising a standard claim. It is necessary for at least two-thirds of qualifying tenants to wish to exercise the right to collective enfranchisement as compared with one-half of all the tenants in the building as with a standard claim.

Assuming the court is satisfied that the claim of the tenants, if made, would be valid, where all relevant landlords are absent the court can make a vesting order, i.e. an order directing that the tenants are entitled to exercise the right and vesting the freehold in the nominee purchaser. Where one landlord is absent but there are others, or when the initial notice can be served, the court can dispense with service on the one missing. If that one is the freeholder, then another landlord can be appointed as the reversioner. If an initial notice is then served, the claim will proceed as normal.

When the court makes a vesting order, it refers the matter to the LVT for the terms to be determined. The LVT, in effect, stands in the shoes of the landlord, e.g. for assessing what is the correct price payable.

The court would expect to see evidence of what efforts had been made to trace any missing landlord. It may give directions as to the further steps to be taken, such as the placing of advertisements, before making a vesting order. The court can make orders as to the execution of the conveyance and payment of the price into court and other ancillary matters to give effect to the vesting order.

4.6.8 Information notice

See s.11. A notice can be given to the immediate landlord or a person receiving rent, e.g. a managing agent, to require them to give information on the freeholder or about any superior leasehold interests and also to the freeholder to require them to give other information relevant to the enfranchisement claim. There is a right to obtain copies of relevant documents containing the information on payment of a reasonable fee.

There is no prescribed form of notice. It can be signed by a qualifying tenant or on their behalf.

The landlord has a duty to reply within 28 days. Any qualifying tenant can serve a default notice requiring that the landlord give a further 14 days to comply in default of which an application can be made to the court. Clearly, there will be practical and costs implications. An assessment will need to be made whether it is absolutely necessary to obtain the information in this way.

If a landlord disposes of his interest within six months of service of an information notice he must notify the qualifying tenant who served it if within that period he receives an initial notice and that tenant is not one of the participating tenants.

4.6.9 Valuation and price

The price to be paid and how it is to be apportioned between the reversioner and other relevant landlord is set out in Sched. 6. The valuation is a complex area and in most circumstances a valuer experienced in carrying out valuations under the 1993 Act will be required for both or all parties. Valuation is covered in more depth in Chapter **10**.

The valuation date is the date of service of the initial notice.

In brief, the price payable is the aggregate of:

- the value of the freeholder's interest;
- the freeholder's share of marriage value (i.e. 50 per cent), if applicable;
- compensation for any loss resulting from the enfranchisement, if applicable.

The value of the freehold interest is based on an open market value based on certain assumptions and subject to existing 1993 Act rights. Improvements by a qualifying tenant or a predecessor are disregarded.

Where there is a leaseback to the freeholder of a flat or unit, the value relating to that unit is disregarded.

The valuation is an exercise in yields and capitalising ground rents.

Marriage value

This is an area of some ambiguity, but in essence is the increase in value when the freehold and other acquired interests are in the hands of the nominee purchaser as compared to their value when held by the reversioner/relevant landlord, e.g. the ability of participating tenants to grant themselves long leases at no premium. The marriage value is ignored in respect of the flat of any participating tenant where his lease has an unexpired term of more than 80 years at the relevant date and in respect of the flats of non-participating tenants.

Additional compensation

This would include, e.g. diminution in value of the freehold interest in other property (including additional land to be acquired by the nominee purchaser), resulting from the acquisition of the premises such as loss of development value.

Hope value

It is often asserted by landlords that the price should be increased by reference to additional value which the nominee purchaser might extract from the payments, e.g. from the price which might be charged to non-participating tenants to extend their lease. The Lands Tribunal have ruled in *Cadogan* v. *Sportelli* EW Lands LRA/50/2005 that no hope value is to be attributed in respect of the flats of non-participating tenants.

4.7 THE NOMINEE PURCHASER

The following paragraphs deal with the position prior to the proposed requirement to exercise the right through an RTE company.

The 1993 Act requires that the property must be acquired through a nominee purchaser. It does not need to be a company but for all but the smallest buildings this is recommended. Section 15 deals with the appointment of a nominee purchaser.

It is not necessary to invite all the qualifying tenants, provided there is a sufficient number of participators to qualify. In most circumstances those organising the process will wish to obtain as many participators as possible in order to spread the cost. However, there may be special circumstances, e.g.

some qualifying tenants may see the opportunity for profit which can be shared between a smaller number of them.

If a company is used as the nominee purchaser it must be formed prior to the service of the initial notice.

The constitution of the company, particularly the Articles of Association, can be finalised later, although it is better if dealt with contemporaneously with its formation. It should dovetail with the relevant provisions in any participation agreement. Consideration should be given to governing voting rights, possibly special voting rights if, e.g. one participator is contributing more. Respective rights of contribution could be solely covered in a shareholders/participation agreement, but bear in mind the question of how to make these binding on the transferee of a member's share. There are pro forma Articles of Association for a tenants' company and these would normally contain regulations requiring the transfer of the share of a qualifying participator/member on the disposal of their interest in the flat concerned so as to keep ownership within the building. Specimen Articles of Association are included at **A5** in Appendix **A**.

For other corporate issues see Chapter **11**.

Where there is in existence a management company where the shares are owned by participating tenants it is recommended this not be used. The shareholders/members of the management company may include persons who are not participators and there can be accounting complications.

If a participating tenant assigns their lease, the assignee must within 14 days notify the nominee purchaser of the assignment and whether he elects to participate in the proposed acquisition. He is then a participating tenant as from the date of the assignment.

Note that for the benefit of the assignor and of the assignee there should be secured the assignment of rights under any participation agreement and an indemnity. The nominee purchaser will wish to secure any assignee to be bound by the obligations under the participation agreement. This should be covered in the participation agreement itself.

A qualifying tenant other than an assignee who did not participate originally can seek to participate but only if all other participators agree.

4.7.1 Death of a participator

The personal representatives have 56 days from the date of death to notify the nominee purchaser of that fact and whether they wish to withdraw. If no notification of withdrawal is given, then they will become the participating tenant for the deceased's flat.

Within 28 days of being notified of any change in the identity of the participating tenant or of the death of that tenant, the nominee purchaser must notify the reversioner with a copy to other relevant landlords.

PART II: COLLECTIVE RIGHTS

There are provisions for the replacement of the nominee purchaser which are contained in ss.15 and 16.

4.8 RTE COMPANIES

As previously mentioned, the provisions relating to RTE companies are not yet in force and are to be introduced by secondary legislation. Key points to note are as follows:

- The right must be exercised through an RTE company which might be onerous in terms of cost and administration, particularly in small buildings.
- It will be necessary to invite all qualifying tenants to participate by means of service of the prescribed notice of invitation to participate. The prescribed form has not yet been published.
- All qualifying tenants must be invited, and this may include the landlord or its nominee holding a flat under a qualifying tenancy and therefore make the landlord privy to the tenants' tactics and valuation.
- The company must be limited by guarantee with members' liability limited to contribute up to a certain amount if the company is wound up.
- There is a prescribed Memorandum and Articles of Association which is inflexible, e.g. it does not cater for situations where there are unequal contributions to price or interest.
- The RTE company can be also an RTM company but cannot be a commonhold association.
- The company, being one limited by guarantee, cannot have different classes of shares, which is a common way of dealing with unequal interests.
- The notice of invitation to participate has to include an estimate of costs and a price, which is difficult to ascertain until it is known how many tenants will participate.

Regulations will provide for the content of the prescribed constitution. Provisions in the constitution which are inconsistent with the regulations will be of no effect. Only one RTE company can exist for any building while a notice of claim is in force.

The primary requirements of RTE companies, their membership and regulation are found in ss.4A, 4B and 4C.

4.8.1 Notice of invitation to participate

The membership must satisfy the same qualifying criteria as for a nominee purchaser but if there are only two qualifying tenants in the building, both must be members.

Prior to service of the initial claim notice, the RTE company must give notice to any qualifying tenant who has not agreed to become a member of it. The notice is not prescribed but must contain certain particulars (s.12A), include an estimate of costs and price and the rights and obligations of participating members. The Memorandum and Articles of the company must be attached or details given as to how they can be inspected or copies obtained. The notice is not invalidated by inaccuracy in the particulars.

The notice must be given by the RTE company at least 14 days before the initial notice is served.

A recipient of the notice, assuming that they are a qualifying tenant, can elect to become a member of the RTE company by serving a participation notice. This is simply a notice in writing stating that the tenant wishes to be a participating member. There is no prescribed form.

The participation notice can be given to the RTE company before the claim notice or during the participation period. This is the period between whichever is the first of the date of the claim notice and six months thereafter (or such other period as regulations may specify) or prior to the RTE company entering into a binding obligation to purchase, if earlier. If given after service of a claim notice and before a binding contract has been entered into, it is of no effect unless a copy is also given to the reversioner.

An assignee of a lease of a participating member can within 28 days of assignment (if entered on the execution of the conveyance to the company) elect to participate and the personal representatives of a deceased participating member can do so at any time before the execution of such conveyance.

The initial notice is deemed withdrawn if the RTE company is wound up, struck off or there are similar acts of insolvency.

4.9 INITIAL NOTICE

This is the first step to exercise a claim to collective enfranchisement. It does not create a binding contract but it does initiate a strict timetable which must be followed. Failure to follow particular steps in the timetable can have serious consequences for the defaulting party, as many of the time limits cannot be varied by agreement. In the case of a tenant a failure to comply may lead to the initial notice being deemed withdrawn. In the case of a landlord, default can lead to loss of rights. Consequences of specific failures are set out below.

There is no prescribed form of initial notice. It is recommended, however, that the use of a form obtained from a law stationers best avoids the chance of missing key information. A check should be made that the form is of the latest version. A specimen notice is included at **A6** in Appendix **A**. The 1993 Act specifies what the notice must contain (see s.13(3)). Supplementary provisions in respect of the initial notice are in Sched. 12. A checklist is as follows:

- Specify the freehold premises to be acquired.
- Specify any additional premises to be acquired.
- Specify any premises over which rights are to be granted.
- Attach a plan showing the premises to be acquired and those over which rights are to be acquired. It is suggested that colouration be used to differentiate between the different areas.
- State the grounds on which the claim is based. These must be set out in detail rather than by broad assertion, i.e. the total number of flats and how many of them are owned by qualifying tenants and that they comprise two-thirds of the total, etc.
- Specify any intermediate leasehold interest to be acquired and any flat considered to be subject to mandatory leaseback to the freeholder.
- Specify the proposed purchase price of the freehold of the specific premises, of additional premises and of any leasehold interest to be acquired.
- Specify the names of the qualifying tenants and the addresses of their flats (there is no need to state the qualifying tenants' home or usual addresses if different) and particulars of the leases, i.e. the date and term and commencement date.
- Specify the name and address of the nominee purchaser.
- Specify the date for the reversioner to serve a counter-notice, being a date not less than two months after service of the initial notice.
- Specify if copies need to be sent to any other relevant landlord.

The initial notice must be signed by all participating tenants, including both where there is a flat with joint tenants. It cannot be signed on their behalf or by an agent. When the RTE provisions are in force this will change so that the notice can be signed by an agent.

An inaccurate notice may be invalid. Great care should be taken both in the preparation and in the service of the initial notice. The notice should be accurate and complete. The 1993 Act contains a saving provision that the initial notice is not invalidated by any inaccuracy in the particulars or of any description of the property to be acquired. In these circumstances the court can amend the notice. Also, where details are given of a participating tenant when that person is not a qualifying tenant or prohibited from participating, then provided there are still sufficient participating tenants who are qualifying tenants, the notice will not be invalid.

Nevertheless reliance should only be had to the saving provision as a last resort; there is debate as to the extent of the contents of the initial notice to which it applies and giving a landlord the opportunity to challenge a notice will cause uncertainty in the minds of the participating tenants as well as increased costs, not to mention the risk of an invalid notice. It is important to note that the saving provision does not cover other defects in the notice such as failure to attach a plan.

A common point of prospective challenge is an allegation that the price/valuation is wholly unrealistic. An initial notice is potentially invalid if the price given is so low that it cannot be said to be a genuine amount. This does not mean to say that one cannot for negotiating purposes specify a figure which is slightly on the low side, but at the very least the price should be such as can be properly supported by a sensible argument from an expert valuer. See *Cadogan Estates Ltd* v. *Morris* [1999] 1 EGLR 59, CA, where a notice was held invalid as the tenant had stated a nominal price when they knew a realistic price was considerably higher.

4.9.1 Service of the notice

See s.99. Briefly, the notice may (but need not necessarily) be served by post and must be served:

- on the freeholder and if there are intermediate interests to be acquired, on any other relevant landlord (if the freeholder cannot be found or their identity cannot be ascertained, service on a relevant landlord will suffice);
- at an address in England and Wales specified by the recipient as the address for service;
- if the recipient is the immediate landlord who has not specified an address for service for the purposes of the 1993 Act, at the address provided to a tenant as the landlord's address for service or, if there is no such address, the address provided in the last ground rent or service charge demand.

Allow sufficient time between the period after which service is deemed to have taken effect (e.g. if service is by post, service is the working day after posting), and the specified time for the landlord to serve a counter-notice. As with the service of all critical notices, some days' margin for error should be allowed wherever possible.

The notice should be registered, in the case of registered reversionary titles, as a unilateral notice at HM Land Registry or in the case of unregistered titles as a land charge at the Land Charges Registry. Registration is important as it triggers various restrictions on a reversioner's ability to dispose of their interest (see **4.9.2** below) and on a disposal of the freehold the new owner will not be bound by the notice if it is unregistered.

As stated above, copies of the notice are to be sent to all those known or who are believed to be relevant landlords. The recipient of a notice must give a copy to any relevant landlord who is not specified as having been served by the nominee purchaser. If a relevant landlord who has responded to an information notice (see **4.6.8** above) is not served with the initial notice before the end of the time specified to serve the counter-notice, then the initial notice will be invalid.

PART II: COLLECTIVE RIGHTS

Service by recorded delivery, whilst seemingly attractive, runs the risk of the notice being returned undelivered. If recorded delivery is used, an additional method, e.g. by hand or by ordinary post, should be considered. A 'belt and braces' approach is most likely to avoid disputes about service of the notice.

> **Key practice points**
> - Make sure that a plan is attached and accurately defines all property to be included in the claim.
> - Have the notice and the plan(s) checked by the surveyor/valuer.
> - Leave the landlord's response date blank until the notice is signed by all participators and it is ready to be served.
> - The notice must be signed by all participating tenants.
> - Unless the address for service of any landlord, particularly the freeholder, is clear, consider serving the notice on more than one address and by more than one method. There is no penalty for this.
> - Once served, register the notice at HMLR/HMLC.
> - Diarise critical dates.

4.9.2 Effect of service of initial notice

- The freeholder must not sever any interest in any appurtenant premises.
- The freeholder and the relevant landlords must not grant a lease which would otherwise have been liable to be acquired by virtue of the claim. (Note that the freeholder and other relevant landlords can still dispose of the whole of their interests.)
- A purchaser of the relevant freeholder/relevant landlord's interest will be bound by the initial notice and any other notices served on or steps taken by the disposer.
- If at the date of service of the initial notice there is a binding contract for the disposal of a reversionary interest then the contract is suspended until the termination of the tenants' claim and if a binding contract is entered into by the nominee purchaser the obligations of the parties will be discharged. This does not apply if the contract provides for the eventuality of the service of an initial notice.
- There are restrictions on the landlord terminating the lease of a participating tenant during the continuance of the initial notice.
- If there is a current s.42 notice (claim by a tenant to extend their lease) this is suspended.
- A further initial notice cannot be served whilst a valid one is in force. This does not prevent a nominee company from serving a notice which is without prejudice to the first, e.g. where the landlord disputes the validity of the first notice.

COLLECTIVE ENFRANCHISEMENT

4.10 TIMETABLE AND PROCEDURE FOLLOWING SERVICE OF INITIAL NOTICE

As has been stated, the service of the initial notice triggers a procedural timetable. This is both in terms of the main steps needed to be taken but also in terms of investigative matters, particularly for the reversioner preparing for service of the counter-notice. See also the timetable flowchart at **B1**.

1. Within 21 days of service of the initial notice, the reversioner can serve a notice on the nominee purchaser to deduce the title of any participating tenant.
2. Within 21 days of the service of the landlord's request the nominee purchaser must comply.
3. At any time after service of the initial notice the reversioner and any other relevant landlord have a right of access to the premises or any appurtenant property for valuation or any other purpose arising out of the claim. There is a reciprocal right of access given to the nominee purchaser. The right is exercised by giving not less than 10 days' notice in writing to the occupier or to the person entitled to occupy.
4. Within two months of the initial notice the reversioner must give a counter-notice to the nominee purchaser.
5. Within two months of the counter-notice, if the reversioner disputes the tenants' right to collective enfranchisement the nominee purchaser can apply to the court for a determination of the issue.
6. If the landlord admits the right to collective enfranchisement then not earlier than two months nor later than six months from service of the counter-notice the nominee purchaser must apply to the LVT to resolve any issues in dispute and at any time after such admission can require the reversioner to deduce title to the freehold and other interests to be acquired.
7. If all material terms are agreed between the parties, a further timetable is triggered. See **4.10.5** below.
8. If no counter-notice is served, then within six months of the date when a counter-notice should have been served, the nominee purchaser must apply to the court for determination.
9. If a landlord opposes the claim on the basis of an intention to redevelop the premises, then unless the right of the participating tenants to exercise the right is also disputed, the landlord must apply to the court for a determination within two months of service of the counter-notice or lose the right to dispute the claim on that basis.

4.10.1 The landlord's response

The freeholder and other relevant landlord will need to consider how best to respond to the initial notice. This will be driven by legal issues and perhaps more importantly by commercial factors. Save in cases of smaller blocks with no marriage value where a pragmatic approach might be better, a landlord will probably wish to undertake a fairly detailed investigative process bearing in mind that there is a liability on the part of the participating tenants to pay the reasonable costs incurred as a consequence of the initial notice and the potentially large amounts at stake.

The usual cost/benefit analysis should be undertaken if there is a possibility of challenging the right. This would include issues such as whether there may be a technical defect with the initial notice; whether there is a tactical benefit to be gained by raising the issue or whether this would simply lead to increased and possibly irreplaceable costs and a delay between the date of valuation if a claim is ultimately successful (fixed at the date of service of the initial notice) and the date of receipt of the price; or the likelihood that making matters more difficult for the participating tenants would cause them to break ranks and abandon the claim.

Just as care should be taken by the tenants on appurtenant property and rights, so should care be taken on these issues from a landlord's perspective, including such matters as whether to exercise any right to a leaseback and what restrictive covenants it may wish to retain/impose.

An investigation of the tenants' claim should be undertaken using the rights to investigate title and to inspect the premises referred to briefly above.

There is no prescribed form of notice for requesting title which will often be in the form of a letter.

From the tenants' perspective, proof of title in the case of registered title is satisfied by producing office copy entries. It is possible to use ones obtained prior to the service of the initial notice if these only predate that notice by a short period. To avoid any argument the nominee purchaser could consider obtaining up-to-date office copy entries.

The nominee purchaser has 21 days from service of the notice to deduce title as requested. This cannot be extended and failure to comply will lead to the initial notice being deemed withdrawn.

Key practice point

- Those representing the participating tenants should prepare title ahead of service of initial notice in anticipation of the landlord's request.

Key for the landlord will be instructing an appropriate valuer and ascertaining the price for the purposes of the counter-notice and for any negotiations. Unlike with the initial notice, a gross overstatement of the price will not invalidate the counter-notice as there is considered to be no prejudice to the tenants. See *9 Cornwall Crescent London Ltd* v. *Kensington and Chelsea* [2005] EWCA Civ 324, CA.

The nominee purchaser has a duty to notify the landlord of any agreement between the nominee purchaser and any person other than the participating tenant for the disposal of a relevant interest, or any interest in the specified premises or other property to be acquired entered into prior to the date of the initial notice as soon as possible. Failure to do so could render the nominee purchaser and participating tenants liable for any increase in the price had this been disclosed. An issue for the nominee purchaser and its advisers is whether to defer any binding agreement with a third party until after the date of service of the initial notice. The reversioner should raise enquiries as to whether there is any such agreement or proposal for agreement. There is no obligation on a nominee purchaser to reply but if there is failure to do so the landlord should consider as to whether to press the point in the negotiations or with the LVT in the context of any determination of the price.

The reversioner must liaise with the other relevant landlords and take into account their views before serving a counter-notice. As far as possible the reversioner should ensure that all parties' requirements are dealt with. Schedule 1 to the Act deals in detail with the conduct of the proceedings by the reversioner on behalf of the landlords and, as previously mentioned, in the event of a dispute the court can decide who is to be the reversioner and determine issues between landlords.

The reversioner acts on behalf of other relevant landlords, can act in their name and bind them to the terms of the acquisition including as to price. If he acts in good faith and with reasonable care, he will not be liable to the other landlords for his acts or omissions. In practice, a prudent reversioner will no doubt wish to seek the agreement of other landlords before committing them to any binding agreement and in the event of dispute, to refer the matter to the court so as not to expose himself to the risk of claim.

4.10.2 Counter-notice

The reversioner must serve the notice by the date specified in the initial notice, which is a date not less than two months after service of the initial notice.

There is no prescribed form but as with the nominee purchaser's initial notice, it is recommended that a preprinted notice be used to minimise the risk of errors and omissions. It is also recommended that the notice be checked against the statutory criteria (s.21 and the 2002 Regulations).

Contents of counter-notice

It must:

- state whether the reversioner admits the right to exercise the claim in respect of the specific premises;

- if it does not admit that right, then state for what reason;
- state whether a relevant landlord intends to oppose the exercise of the right on the ground of proposed redevelopment of the whole or a substantial part of the premises;
- specify an address for service in England and Wales;
- state whether the premises are in an area of an estate management scheme.

Failure to comply with any of these requirements is likely to render the purported counter-notice invalid.

If a claim is admitted, the counter-notice must also contain details of the following:

- which proposals are accepted and which are not, specifying counter-proposals (note in particular the position on price, see **4.10.1** above);
- if the freeholder requires a leaseback of any unit in the premises, in circumstances where he is entitled to such, his specification of that requirement and his leaseback proposals (it was thought that a freeholder might be able to serve a separate notice in this respect at a later date, but the Court of Appeal have decided that a freeholder cannot do so, and must specify any leaseback proposals in the counter-notice; if the freeholder fails to do this, the right to a leaseback will be lost: see *Cawthorne and others v. Hamadan* [2007] EWCA Civ 6);
- whether a landlord requires a nominee purchaser to acquire other property not specified in the initial notice (this can only be property which will cease to be of practical use once the interest in the specified premises has been acquired);
- where the tenants have sought to acquire the freehold of other properties over which they require rights, whether the freeholder wishes to make a counter-proposal to grant permanent rights instead, if so giving details;
- those rights which the freeholder seeks to retain, any covenants to be imposed/continued and other matters which the reversioner wishes to see included in the conveyance;
- any s.42 notice (lease extension) received and any counter-notice given in response.

Landlord disputes the validity/form of the initial notice

There is no mechanism laid down in the legislation for dealing with this situation. The reversioner could take court proceedings to challenge the notice or it could wait for the nominee purchaser to make any application to the LVT for a determination of the claim or to the court if no counter-notice is served.

It is likely to be dangerous for a reversioner not to serve a counter-notice save in a case where an initial notice is blatantly defective or has not been properly or timeously served. See **4.10.3** below. It is preferable for a counter-notice to be served but without prejudice to the contention that an initial notice was invalid.

Landlord disputes right to collective enfranchisement

The onus is on the nominee purchaser to apply to the court (not the LVT) for determination. Failure to do so within two months of service of the counter-notice would render the initial notice invalid.

If the court is satisfied that the nominee purchaser is entitled to enfranchise it can declare the counter-notice to be of no effect and require the reversioner to serve a further counter-notice, i.e. one which contains counter-proposals. There is an exception if there are objections on the basis of redevelopment.

Landlord's intention to redevelop

If the landlord intends to redevelop the premises or a substantial part of them, and successfully establishes this, then there is no right to enfranchise. However, this objection is fairly limited in practice, in particular as one of the criteria for a landlord to satisfy is that two-thirds of all long leases in the premises must terminate within five years of service of the initial notice. Therefore it is not proposed to cover this objection in detail. The relevant landlord then has to apply to the court for determination within two months of a counter-notice but the application is on hold if the landlord has also disputed the right to enfranchise and the nominee purchaser has applied for a declaration (s.23).

Landlord admits the claim

If the landlord admits the claim the parties are expected to, and in practice usually do, negotiate. It is unlikely that the reversioner will agree with all terms proposed in the initial notice. There is a specified two-month period from service of the counter-notice for negotiation to take place. This is a short period and is normally insufficient in all but the simplest cases. If any terms of the acquisition are not agreed within that period the nominee purchaser may apply to the LVT to determine the terms in dispute. The tenant must apply not earlier than two months and not later than six months after service of the counter-notice. This is an absolute time limit and failure to comply will lead to the deemed withdrawal of the initial notice.

Agreement in this context does not mean a binding contract nor does it need to be written. The parties should make sure that any proposed agreement is recorded in writing with a statement as to whether it is intended to comprise an agreement within the meaning of the 1993 Act.

The 1993 Act envisages a negotiated agreement or an LVT determination and then a binding contract incorporating those terms. When terms are agreed or determined, the parties have two months from that date to enter a binding contract or such other date as may be specified by the LVT for that purpose (this period being known as 'the appropriate period') and if there is no binding contract, the nominee purchaser must apply to the court before the expiry of a period of two months beginning with the end of the appropriate period. In effect the nominee purchaser has four months from the date on which all terms are agreed to enter into a binding contract (or complete) or to apply to the court. Again, there is a deemed withdrawal of the initial notice if this is not done.

Key practice points

- The landlord will often propose a very high price in the counter-notice. Tenants and their advisers should not be intimidated by this provided they are satisfied that their own valuation is reasonably accurate.
- Tenants should be wary of challenging the validity of the counter-notice unless the prospects of success are very high. Whilst such challenge can be tempting in view of the potential benefits if successful, there have been a number of instances where tenants have spent a lot of time and money on lengthy challenges which have ultimately proved to be unsuccessful. See e.g. *7 Strathray Gardens Ltd* v. *Pointstar Shipping & Finance Ltd* [2005] 1 EGLR 53, CA. It must be remembered that, with court proceedings, costs follow the event, making it a high risk area, generally more so for tenants than landlords as there is often a mismatch of resources.

Care should be taken:

- from the tenants' perspective to control when the terms are agreed as this triggers the time limit in which to agree a binding contract or to apply to the court;
- from both parties' perspectives with 'without prejudice' offers, as if accepted they cannot be resiled from.

4.10.3 No counter-notice served by landlord

The court must make an order declaring the terms of the acquisition in accordance with the proposals in the initial notice. The nominee purchaser must apply to the court within six months of the time when the counter-notice should have been served. The tenants must still establish they have a right to enfranchise and that the initial notice has been properly served. There are severe consequences for the reversioner landlord as, for example, the price specified in the initial notice would be the price set by the court. The only safety net for a landlord would be to challenge the validity of the initial notice if, e.g. the proposed price was greatly understated.

If the court has determined terms but no binding contract is entered into within the appropriate period, the court may make a vesting order in similar terms as in **4.13** below.

4.10.4 Conveyancing timetable and conveyance

Whilst the 1993 Act envisages the conveyancing being a two-stage process, namely a binding contract followed by a transfer/conveyance, in practice it is common to move straight to the terms of a conveyance. It should be noted that as certain time limits are dependent upon there being a binding contract, the consequences of omitting this step should be considered.

As stated above, the nominee purchaser has the right to require the reversioner to deduce title to the interests to be acquired. This can be done at any time after service of a counter-notice admitting the claim or if no counter-notice is served. If not done previously, then this should be done as soon as possible once the terms have been agreed. The timetable for delivery of the reversioner's title is in Sched. 1 to the 1993 Regulations. The time limits need to be carefully observed.

- The reversioner must comply within 28 days by the delivery of Land Registry entries or if an interest is unregistered, an epitome of title.
- The nominee purchaser has 14 days thereafter to raise requisitions.
- The reversioner has 14 days to reply to requisitions.
- Where a relevant landlord is acting independently, the nominee purchaser should deal directly with that landlord in relation to that landlord's interest.

The timetable for the drafting and agreement of the contract is also contained in the 1993 Regulations and is as follows.

Once terms are agreed or determined:

- within 21 days the reversioner must submit a draft contract to which a draft transfer would be attached;
- within 14 days thereafter, the nominee purchaser must amend or approve the draft or is deemed to accept it as drawn;
- within 14 days thereafter, the reversioner must re-amend or approve the revised draft or is deemed to accept the nominee purchaser's amendments.

On a binding contract the nominee purchaser can be required by the reversioner by notice to pay a deposit on exchange of £500 or 10 per cent of the price, whichever is the greater. This is to be held as stakeholder.

It is common practice for the detailed terms to be negotiated even though a price has not been agreed and for the conveyancing process to run alongside the negotiations between the respective valuers. One issue which may come to light during the negotiations and should be raised by the nominee purchaser is the extent of any arrears of ground rent or service charge which the reversioner will wish to collect on completion. Service charges in particular are a common source of dispute, and potential issues which may impact on the enfranchisement process should be identified early. If unresolved, in extreme cases this may cause there to be no binding contract and hence an application to the court for a vesting order may be required. See also at **4.12.4** below regarding the vendor's lien.

A situation may be encountered where there are issues to be resolved which fall outside the remit of the legislation or where gaps are left. For example, there may be an intermediate/headlandlord whose interest is acquired for the specified premises but which remains in place for other parts of the premises such as 'unsold' flats. This could lead to an unsatisfactory structure for service charges or other management issues. It should be noted that this is not covered by the leaseback provisions. Another example is an estate of more than one block where only one enfranchises. From the perspective of all interested parties these issues are often resolved by negotiation outside the statutory framework but there is no guarantee that this can be achieved.

4.10.5 Contents of the conveyance

The contents of the conveyance are governed by Sched. 7.

The conveyance must contain mandatory statements referring to the fact that the acquisition has been made under the 1993 Act.

The title is such as the relevant landlord has, plus a limited title guarantee.

Rights to be included

These are such as are necessary to secure such rights as existed prior to the conveyance or such additional rights as are necessary for the reasonable engagement of the premises and only insofar as the reversioner can grant them. They relate to support, access, services and the like.

Right of air is not specifically referred to in the 1993 Act but the freeholder may seek to exclude this right if it is excluded in a relevant lease. The nominee purchaser may wish to oppose this, as if the right is excluded and the nominee purchaser subsequently wishes to build on the premises, it would need the freeholder's permission. There are some interesting technical points on the issue of whether the freeholder can exclude the right.

The reversioner is entitled to reserve for the benefit of other property the same rights to which the premises are already subject and any further rights as necessary for the reasonable enjoyment of other premises in which the freeholder has an interest.

The reversioner is entitled to the continuation of restrictive covenants other than those imposed by the leases or agreements subject to which the relevant premises are acquired and are still enforceable.

It is important that either the freeholder or the nominee purchaser may require the continuation of restrictions contained in the leases or agreements subject to which the premises are acquired, in particular in the leases of the qualifying tenants: in the case of the freeholder, only such as materially enhance the value of other property and in the case of the nominee purchaser, such as materially enhance the value of the premises.

In addition, such further covenants may be imposed as will not interfere with the reasonable enjoyment of the premises and which materially enhance the value of other property of the freeholder.

Key practice points

The extent to which rights are included or excluded or covenants imposed can affect the value of the premises or adjoining property. Therefore careful attention should be paid to:
- the rights to be included or reserved to make sure that the premises and any adjoining property can be fully enjoyed and managed effectively;
- the covenants to be included as these can impact significantly on the use of the premises.

Those advising tenants should not be slow to dispute onerous covenants or the exclusion of key rights.

Other encumbrances and rentcharges

Encumbrances and rentcharges capable of being overreached are overreached by the conveyance but the conveyance is subject to rentcharges which are not overreached. There are detailed provisions relating to rentcharges in s.34 to which reference should be made should a rentcharge be encountered.

Management schemes

It is for practical purposes no longer possible to create new management schemes, but there are a number which do exist, particularly in the large traditional estates, e.g. in Central London. These schemes, authorised under the 1993 Act, broadly are those where a common landlord wishes to impose a uniform scheme of management and covenants to ensure the consistent standard of maintenance and appearance. These schemes are only binding on a property once a landlord has disposed of their interest in it. There is no need for them to be mentioned specifically in the conveyance but the landlord must specify in the counter-notice whether such a scheme exists. Upon acquisition of the freehold the nominee purchaser of the relevant premises will be subject to the scheme. Although they are a burden, they can also be seen as a benefit in terms of keeping up standards in the area.

Intermediate interests

Whilst not strictly necessary to have a separate conveyance/transfer of any intermediate interests, this is sometimes convenient in practice, particularly where there are more complex provisions agreed between the nominee purchaser and an intermediate landlord who is retaining an interest in the premises.

4.11 LEASEBACKS

In certain circumstances the 1993 Act gives a right to a freeholder to a leaseback of certain parts of the premises. In some instances the leaseback is mandatory; in others it is to be granted at the option of the freeholder. This is only relevant to the freeholder and not to an intermediate landlord. Section 36 and Sched. 9 govern the position.

4.11.1 Mandatory leasebacks

These apply to:

- flats let under a secure tenancy where the freeholder is the tenant's immediate landlord and the freeholder and any intermediate landlord is a public sector landlord;
- flats let by a housing association under a tenancy (even if not secure) not being a qualifying tenancy.

The mandatory leaseback provisions do not apply to vacant flats or where units are let on, e.g. assured shorthold tenancies and commercial tenancies.

4.11.2 Optional leasebacks

The freeholder can ask for a leaseback of a unit not being a flat let to a qualifying tenant which could encompass vacant flats or those let on assured shorthold tenancies or on commercial tenancies.

The freeholder must give notice to the nominee purchaser. This must be in a counter-notice (see **4.10.2** above).

Where the freeholder is a resident landlord and the freeholder is also a qualifying tenant of the flat, the freeholder can require a surrender of the qualifying lease and a regrant.

4.11.3 Terms of the leaseback

Terms of leasebacks:

- a term of 999 years at a peppercorn;
- there are provisions for the incorporation of appropriate rights, obligations and covenants;
- there can be no prohibition or restriction on assignment or subletting unless there is a business unit where alienation must be subject to consent, not to be unreasonably withheld;
- there can be no break notice and no forfeiture on insolvency.

An application can be made to the LVT to depart from the specified terms where it is reasonable to do so or can be agreed between the nominee purchaser and the freeholder. It should be noted that where there is a mandatory leaseback, any amendment to the terms must be approved by the LVT even if they have been agreed.

There are special provisions for local authorities and leasebacks. Broadly, the idea is to maintain the rights of public sector tenants.

4.12 COMPLETION

If there is a binding contract, the process of completion will follow the provisions of the contract. Where there is no binding contract, in practice completion will follow the usual completion procedures.

4.12.1 Discharge of mortgages

See s.35 and Sched. 8. The conveyance of the freehold under a collective enfranchisement claim discharges the interest under any mortgage. If the price is insufficient to pay off the mortgage in full, the lender will retain a right to claim the balance from the mortgagor.

It is the duty of a nominee purchaser to apply the consideration first to redeem any mortgage. In practice this will be dealt with by an undertaking from the reversioner's solicitor following standard conveyancing procedures. Care should be taken where there are mortgages of an intermediate landlord. There are provisions for ascertaining the identity of a person entitled to the benefit of a mortgage or if there is difficulty in ascertaining the amount due under a mortgage. Payment can be made into court in these circumstances.

4.12.2 SDLT returns

The nominee purchaser must complete the appropriate Land Transaction Returns for stamp duty land tax purposes. See also Chapter **11**.

4.12.3 Costs

These are dealt with in more detail in **4.5.2** above. There is a liability on the nominee purchaser to pay certain of the landlord's reasonable costs. It is common for costs to be agreed prior to completion but there is no requirement on the tenant to pay before completion. If the landlord's reasonable costs cannot be agreed, they can be determined by the LVT.

PART II: COLLECTIVE RIGHTS

4.12.4 Vendor's lien and service charges

The freeholder and relevant landlords have a lien over the premises for any price payable and for:

- amounts due at the date of the conveyance from any of its tenants, e.g. rent and service charges;
- any amount due to failure of the nominee purchaser to disclose agreements with non-participating tenants;
- costs due from the nominee purchaser.

The lien can be protected by a notice at the Land Registry.

As referred to above, the reversioner will want to collect arrears of rent and service charge on completion and any issue arising, particularly with services charges, will probably come to light during the negotiations. If unresolved, the nominee purchaser will need to apply to the court for a vesting order. The court may make a vesting order on such terms as it thinks fit. In this connection this could be on terms that the vesting order takes place immediately with the landlord's entitlement protected by a lien or by the vesting order being deferred until the dispute has been resolved. Where there is a defined amount the court could require payment of the sum into court. Any dispute as to service charges needs to be resolved by way of a separate application based on other rights. See Chapter **12**.

4.12.5 Insurance

The nominee purchaser should ensure that adequate buildings insurance is in place on the date when risk passes to it, which will usually be on the completion date.

4.13 APPLICATION TO THE COURT

The primary circumstances for an application to the court are where:

- the landlord intends to redevelop (see **4.10.2** above);
- terms have been agreed or determined by the LVT (s.23) but no binding contract has been entered into within the specified period (see **4.10.4** above); in this case the court can vest the property on terms either as agreed or determined or subject to certain modifications or provide for the initial notice to be deemed withdrawn at the end of the appropriate period (s.24);
- there is no counter-notice, assuming that the participating tenants can satisfy the court of their entitlement and proper service of the initial notice, and the court may make a vesting order on the terms contained in the initial notice (s.25) (see **4.10.3** above);

COLLECTIVE ENFRANCHISEMENT

- where the freeholder or other relevant landlord cannot be found (s.26) (see **4.6.7** above).

For the purposes of making an application to the court, a Part 8 claim form is used.

4.14 APPLICATION TO THE LVT

An application to the LVT is made if terms cannot be agreed. See **4.10** above. This is the most common form of application in these matters.

There is no prescribed form for the application to the LVT. The LVT Procedure Regulations specify the information which is to be included. A specimen application is included at **A8** in Appendix **A**. In addition to information which is to be included in all types of LVT applications, the following additional information is required for collective enfranchisement applications:

- a copy of the initial notice;
- the name and address of the freeholder and any intermediate landlord;
- the name and address of any mortgagee of an interest of the freeholder or other landlord.

It is recommended that the application includes all documents and information which might be helpful to the tribunal, going beyond the statutory requirements, e.g. by attaching the counter-notice and relevant title documents.

The application can be signed by the solicitor or agent for the nominee purchaser.

For the procedure of the LVT see Chapter **9**.

4.15 WITHDRAWING FROM THE PROCESS

Withdrawal by the tenants can be either voluntary or deemed. With voluntary withdrawal, the participating tenants may withdraw from the process at any time prior to there being a binding contract. It could, e.g. encompass a situation where a price has been determined by the LVT which the participating tenants are unable or unwilling to pay.

Withdrawal is effected by giving written notice. There is no prescribed form. It should be noted there is a slightly different process when the RTE company provisions come into effect. Prior to the RTE provisions, notice must be given to the nominee purchaser, the reversioner and other known relevant landlords. Post-RTE provisions, notice must be given to all qualifying tenants in the building, the reversioner, and to any other relevant landlord who has given notice that it is acting independently of the reversioner.

Deemed withdrawal occurs if the nominee purchaser fails to make an application to the court or the LVT within the relevant time limits (see above) or there is a failure to deduce title in time; also where the nominee purchaser's appointment is terminated or it has retired and without another being appointed in its place.

Under the RTE provisions there will be deemed withdrawal on the winding up or insolvency or similar of the RTE company.

4.15.1 Costs

Wherever there is a withdrawal or a deemed withdrawal there is a liability for payment of the costs of any landlord down to the date of withdrawal. If withdrawal is by notice, then there is a joint and several liability of the participating tenants or under the RTE provisions, of the RTE company and all of its members. Under a deemed withdrawal there is a similar liability but where there is a nominee purchaser, it is also jointly and severally liable.

The possibility of withdrawal should be contemplated and covered in any participation agreement.

4.16 OTHER ISSUES

There are special circumstances covered by the 1993 Act but as these are not commonly encountered, it is not proposed to deal in detail with these. They include, e.g. where there is a compulsory purchase procedure affecting the property or the property is a qualifying property so designated under IHT legislation where the initial notice is of no effect. There are also provisions for special categories of landlord in Sched. 2, such as ecclesiastical landlords.

4.17 EXTENDING THE LEASES OF PARTICIPATING TENANTS

Following conclusion of satisfactory acquisition of the freehold, the participating tenants will often wish to grant themselves long leases and reduce or eliminate ground rent. Ideally, these matters should have been addressed in the participation agreement to minimise scope for potential argument. It is not common for the participators to pay an additional premium as this will usually have been factored into the contributions payable to take into account, e.g. any differentials in unexpired terms, size of flat or what may be considered other relevant criteria. It is a matter for the participators in each situation to consider what is fair and appropriate in their circumstances. The most common scenario is the straightforward case where all participators have similar leases, where their contributions would usually be the same.

In a reasonably-sized block and as with the process itself, good preliminary organisation will pay dividends. In this regard, many of the principles referred to in Chapter 3 of organising the collective process should be followed.

It must be remembered that it will be administratively easier for the nominee purchaser if as many participators as possible take up the option of varying their leases at or about the same time. One possibility may be to offer an incentive to those who take up the offer within a set period, e.g. to offer to subsidise their costs. Some key issues to be considered are as follows:

- the amount/length of the extended lease: an extension to 999 years is common;
- whether to reduce or eliminate ground rent for the participators (particular consideration should be given to the income which is required by the nominee purchaser to meet its ongoing expenses, e.g. whether there is sufficient income from the ground rent from any non-participating tenant or from any vacant flat or commercial unit which has been acquired);
- whether there are any other terms of the lease which the tenants may wish or need to be varied, e.g. to correct defects or make covenants less onerous (however, great care should be taken that a consistent management structure is not prejudiced and that any variation is not in breach of any obligation, e.g. of covenants given by the landlord in the leases of those tenants not participating);
- the costs of the exercise and whether the nominee purchaser can subsidise some of the legal fees;
- the usual conveyancing formalities relevant to a deed of variation must be observed, e.g. obtaining consent of any mortgagee;
- compliance with the Land Registry formalities for the deed;
- carrying out of the property and bankruptcy searches;
- Land Registry fees, SDLT and Land Transaction Returns.

A solicitor co-ordinating the exercise will no doubt wish to send a circular letter to the participators identifying the due process, the relevant costs and disbursements. It is easier if that solicitor acts for all parties subject to compliance with Solicitors' Practice Rule 6 and Rule 16D (draft Solicitors' Code of Conduct, rr.3 and 18) but it is recommended that each participator be invited to use separate solicitors if they so wish. A separate ledger will need to be maintained for each participating tenant for which the solicitor acts in the process and for the nominee purchaser.

CHAPTER 5
Right to manage

5.1 OVERVIEW

The right to manage can broadly be described as the right given to a group of tenants of flats held under long leases to take over the management of their building subject to fulfilment of the statutory criteria.

It is a new right created by the Commonhold and Leasehold Reform Act 2002. The relevant provisions came into force in England on 1 September 2003 and in Wales on 30 March 2004. It is not without its faults, but in practice works reasonably well. It is a relatively inexpensive method for tenants to take over the management of their building but the obligations of management need to be carefully considered.

A timetable flowchart is included at **B3** and a checklist of preliminary matters at **B4** in Appendix **B**.

5.2 FINDING YOUR WAY AROUND THE LEGISLATION

Sections 71 to 113 of the 2002 Act contain the primary provisions.

Schedule 6 to the Act deals with premises excluded from the right and Sched. 7 with various ancillary matters such as covenants not to assign, defective premises and other instances where modification of other statutes is required.

The Right to Manage (Prescribed Particulars and Forms) (England) Regulations 2003, SI 2003/1988 ('the 2003 Regulations') (similar regulations, SI 2004/678 (W.66), were made in respect of Wales) contain requirements as to the additional content of key notices served in connection with the right and annexes prescribed forms of the notice of invitation to participate, the claim notice and the counter-notice.

See also the RTM Companies (Memorandum and Articles of Association) (England) Regulations 2003, SI 2003/2120 ('the RTM Companies Regulations') (SI 2004/675 (W.64) in Wales).

Regard should also be paid to the Leasehold Valuation Tribunal (Procedure) (England) Regulations 2003, SI 2003/2099, as amended by SI

2004/3098 (SI 2004/681 (W.69) as amended by SI 2005/1356 (W.104) in Wales) ('the LVT Procedure Regulations') in the case of application to the Leasehold Valuation Tribunal (LVT), and to the Civil Procedure Rules in the case of application to the court.

5.3 KEY TERMINOLOGY

It is helpful to have an understanding of some of the key terms used in the 2002 Act:

- 'claim notice': the notice by which the right is exercised;
- 'RTM company': the right to manage company through which the right is exercised;
- 'notice of invitation to participate': the notice which must be served on qualifying tenants prior to the service of the claim notice;
- 'relevant date': the date when the claim notice is given;
- 'acquisition date': the date on which the RTM company takes over the management of the premises;
- 'manager party': the landlord, any party to a lease other than the landlord or the tenant, e.g. a management company or a Landlord and Tenant Act 1987 manager;
- 'premises': the building or part of a building to which the right applies;
- 'appurtenant property': other property in addition to the premises over which management functions are sought to be acquired.

For more detailed information on definitions, reference should be made to ss.112 and 113.

5.4 KEY FEATURES OF THE RIGHT

- There is no need to prove fault on the part of the landlord.
- Provided that the tenants meet the qualifying criteria and the correct procedure is followed, there is very limited scope for the landlord to object or to hold up the process.
- The qualifying criteria are broadly the same as those for collective enfranchisement.
- The claim is exercised through an RTM company, a company limited by guarantee with a prescribed constitution.
- The right is triggered by the service of a claim notice specifying an acquisition date which, in effect, is a date not less than four months later.
- It is a requirement that all qualifying tenants be invited to become members of the RTM company prior to service of the claim notice.

PART II: COLLECTIVE RIGHTS

- On the acquisition date, management contracts (whether relating to the appointment of a managing agent or for specific services or otherwise) entered into by the landlord terminate unless the RTM company elects to continue them.
- Accrued but uncommitted service charge funds have to be paid to the RTM company.
- The landlord is entitled to be a member of the RTM company and will retain an involvement in certain management functions, e.g. in connection with the granting of approvals.
- If there is a dispute as to the entitlement, the LVT has jurisdiction, although in certain other aspects the court has jurisdiction.

Further details of these matters are considered below.

5.5 GENERAL COMMENTS

As one would expect, the desire to exercise the right is usually prompted by problems with the management of the building concerned and possibly also disputes over service charges. There are a number of other remedies available to tenants to deal with these issues. Tenants and advisers should be aware of these rights and they may need to be considered as an alternative or in addition to exercising the right to manage. The 2002 Act also contains radically revised and extended rights of protection given to tenants, some of which are yet to come into force. See Chapter **12**. The possibility of collective enfranchisement often arises. See the comparison of rights at **2.4** above.

By exercising the right, the RTM company takes over the management functions of the landlord or other party to a lease of the premises. These are those relating to services, repairs, maintenance, improvements, insurance and management. Sections 96 and 97 deal with management functions.

It should be borne in mind that the duties of proper management will also be owed to qualifying tenants who do not participate and others who have an interest in the management of the building, such as the landlord.

The RTM company will be inheriting the existing management structure in terms, in particular, of the relevant covenants contained in the leases affecting the premises, e.g. relating to what services are to be provided or how service charges are to be collected. That structure may be defective or inadequate, e.g. it might not cover the setting up of a reserve fund. To the extent that it is possible or cost effective to do so, an analysis of the legal management structure of the building should be undertaken. Practitioners should point out to the company the desirability of carrying out this exercise.

The right can be exercised regardless of whether collective enfranchisement has taken place or whether there is a tenants' management company which is a party to the tenants' leases and is responsible for management of the building. If there is a tenants' management company this may or may not be controlled by the tenants, as e.g. the landlord may hold controlling shares, but if the tenants do have control there may be no need to exercise the right. However, it could be that certain key management functions are controlled by the landlord which are not within the control of the management company but which would pass to the RTM company, e.g. the right/obligation to insure. Certain functions will remain with the landlord or require the landlord's involvement despite the exercise of the right to manage, see **5.22** below.

The right must be exercised through an RTM company. This is a company limited by guarantee. The landlord is entitled to be a member of the company, and so may others. There is a potentially complicated voting entitlement.

As with a right to enfranchise claim, in order to bind the participators to each other and to the process, it is suggested there be a participation agreement or a letter of intent. A specimen letter of intent is included at **A9** in Appendix **A**. However, there may be practical difficulties in getting possibly large numbers of tenants to sign a complex legal agreement (see further **5.6.2** below).

5.6 PRELIMINARY INVESTIGATIONS

As with other collective enfranchisement action, care, planning, good organisation and preliminary investigation are required. See managing the collective process in Chapter **3** for general guidance on these issues.

The key matters to be considered are as follows:

- whether the premises qualify;
- qualifying tenants and sufficiency of participation;
- what 'appurtenant premises' should be included in the claim;
- formation of the RTM company;
- the identity and address of any landlord or other manager party;
- other matters relevant to the preparation of the claim notice;
- the choice of acquisition date;
- future management.

As there is a statutory requirement to invite all qualifying tenants to participate it will be necessary to identify all qualifying tenants and details of their leases. It is not necessary to ascertain their usual residential addresses, although for the practical purposes of participation this is helpful. It is recommended that office copy entries of all flats are obtained. The primary participators would normally initially prepare a circular letter, preferably drafted by a professional adviser setting out the reasons for the RTM claim, giving details of the basic procedure, benefits and potential costs. A meeting of tenants is often called with, if possible, a solicitor and prospective managing agent present to answer questions.

Consideration should be given to future management. In all but the smallest blocks it is likely that, and indeed highly desirable for, professional managing agents to be appointed. It is unlikely that the residents themselves, even if they have the expertise in their ranks, will (at least after an initial period) have the time or inclination to take on the future management, particularly if the key participators move or decide that they have had enough. It is also advisable for the directors of the RTM company to distance themselves, as far as is practicable, from direct contact with their neighbours in dealing with recovery of service charges and other areas of potential dispute. See s.20 for further information on management after the acquisition date.

5.6.1 Managing agent

In appointing a managing agent, residents should obtain recommendations and references and estimates of charges. The agent should be a member of a professional association, e.g. ARMA or RICS. A managing agent's advice will be needed in terms of what is required for the information on the current management and service charges to enable a smooth transition of management from the landlord's agent to the RTM company and any agent appointed by it. The managing agent would also liaise with the company or its solicitors regarding the request for information which it is usually necessary to serve on the landlord.

Some examples of other issues to be looked at when appointing a managing agent are as follows:

- What is their track record?
- Insurance: the managing agent may be better placed to obtain specialist cover. What commission will they earn and should this be credited for the benefit of the tenants?
- How would they appoint contractors?
- What are their arrangements for managing reserve funds?
- Do they have the capability and resources?
- What will be their charges for carrying out other administrative functions, such as supplying management/service charge information to tenants wishing to sell their flats or dealing with changes of ownership/membership of the RTM company?
- What are the arrangements for dealing with emergencies?
- What are the systems for effective communication of information with the RTM company and tenants generally?
- Are they proactive rather than reactive?
- Do they have adequate professional indemnity insurance?

LEASE/ARMA have a leaflet entitled 'Appointing a Managing Agent' which is worth looking at and can be downloaded from the LEASE website, see Appendix C.

If it is not proposed to appoint a managing agent, information as to the qualifications and expertise of the members of the company undertaking the management duties has to be given in the notice of invitation to participate.

The RTM company will need to comply with the usual statutory and other obligations of landlords, such as those for the protection of tenants, e.g. the consultation procedure for major works. See **5.22** below and Chapter **12**.

5.6.2 Participation

With the potentially large sums of money involved in collective enfranchisement matters with consequent potential benefits and probably more serious costs liabilities, both in the exercise of the right and to the landlord, a full participation agreement is usually justified. However, with the right to manage it may be necessary to take a more pragmatic approach and balance the wish to cover fully the legal consequences of participation with the need to encourage sufficient tenants to participate and to make matters as simple and as cost effective as possible.

Where the tenants do not wish to have a full participation agreement they should be advised of the desirability of such in an ideal world. Each situation must be looked at on its merits and a judgement made as to the extent to which the arrangements between participators are contained in any formal agreement.

All participators will need to be members of the RTM company once formed and will be bound by the prescribed constitution. Agreements which conflict with the prescribed constitution will have no effect to the extent that they are inconsistent.

5.7 QUALIFYING CRITERIA

The qualifying criteria with regard to participating tenants and premises are broadly the same as the right to enfranchise. For ease of reference these are:

- the premises must be a self-contained building or part of a building;
- two or more flats are held by qualifying tenants;
- the total number of flats held by those tenants is not less than two-thirds of the total number of flats;
- the participating tenants must be those of flats comprising not less than 50 per cent of the total number of flats at the relevant date (i.e. the date the initial notice is given) with a minimum of two participators. Note that

PART II: COLLECTIVE RIGHTS

the total number of flats includes those of qualifying tenants of all other flats in the building. A 'rounding up' exercise should be applied where necessary. See the example at **4.6.1** above.
- A tenant can participate regardless of the number of flats they own in the building.
- Not more than 25 per cent of the building can be non-residential/commercial.

5.7.1 Qualifying tenants

The qualifying tenant is one who holds the flat under a long lease. A definition of 'qualifying tenants' is in s.75. There are exclusions primarily where the lease held is a business tenancy or where there is a sublease granted in breach of the terms of the superior lease where the breach has not been waived. A flat may only have one qualifying tenant so that if there is more than one relevant long lease it is the tenant under the most inferior one who will qualify. If there are joint tenants they are jointly the qualifying tenant.

The definition of 'long lease' is in ss.76 and 77 and is broadly the same as that for collective enfranchisement. The primary definition is a lease granted for a term of years certain exceeding 21 years whether or not it is terminable before the end of the term. As with collective enfranchisement matters, if a lease is encountered which is other than what can be described as a straightforward long lease, the wording of the relevant provisions should be considered carefully. See **4.6.5** above.

The qualifying criteria need to be met on the relevant date. It does not matter if subsequently they cease to be met, e.g. if the number of participators falls below the requisite minimum.

As with the right to enfranchise, there is no requirement for a qualifying tenant to occupy their flat as their residence for any period of ownership. However, unlike the right to enfranchise, there is no limit on the number of flats which can be held by a qualifying tenant.

5.7.2 Requisite number of participators

It is necessary to invite all qualifying tenants. See further at **5.9** below. This can be a time-consuming process for those organising the claim. It is usual to obtain support informally and only where enough tenants show an interest are matters progressed to the next stage.

Qualifying tenants who do not participate are not members of the RTM company and have no direct say in the management. They still have the practical benefits which the exercise of the right brings about. Also a qualifying tenant may join the RTM company at any time. There appears to be no requirement to pay the same or any contribution to the costs of the exercise or other sum paid by the original participators. The officers of the company may seek to take a pragmatic approach and try to insist that later participators do so contribute.

> **Key practice points**
> - Obtain office copy entries of all relevant titles including of all flats which have registered titles and of superior titles.
> - Obtain a specimen flat lease and check its key terms.

5.7.3 Qualifying premises

The right applies to the premises themselves and any appurtenant property. The definition is in s.72. The building must be structurally detached, although this does not mean that it cannot be physically connected to other buildings. See **4.6.2** above.

If an estate has more than one block, it is necessary to have a claim for each block, not one for the whole. However, there can be circumstances where two blocks which are joined might be considered as one. See *Minshull Place RTM Co.* v. *Park Rutland Ltd*, LON/OOAF/LRM/2004/2005. Also, one RTM company can make a claim in respect of two blocks provided that the qualifying criteria are met for each. See *Dawlin RTM Ltd* v. Oakhill Park Estate (Hampstead) Ltd, LVT 21/9/2005, (LON/OOAG/LEE/2005/00012). There can also be issues, e.g. where an estate comprises a number of blocks of flats and also freehold houses. The 2002 Act does not properly address these situations.

5.7.4 Appurtenant property

This is defined in s.112(1) as any garage, outhouse, garden, yard or appurtenances belonging to, or usually enjoyed with, the building or part of it or a flat. This is potentially quite wide-ranging. If there is an estate with more than one block there could well be a situation where property appurtenant to a block seeking to exercise the right could also be appurtenant to another block.

5.7.5 Exempt premises

Premises which are exempted from the right are referred to in Sched. 6. These are as follows:
- if the internal floor area of non-residential parts exceeds 25 per cent of the internal floor area of the whole building. Common parts are disregarded in the computation and cannot be regarded as non-residential. Premises used in conjunction with a particular flat, e.g. a designated

PART II: COLLECTIVE RIGHTS

parking space or storage space, are treated as residential. For an analysis of some issues arising in respect of whether parts of premises are non-residential, see *Gaingold Ltd* v. *WHRA RTM Co. Ltd*, [2006] 03 EG 1222;
- where there is a resident landlord, but as with collective enfranchisement claims this exemption is extremely limited since it only applies if the premises are not a purpose-built block and contain not more than four flats. The resident landlord must be a freeholder of the premises and there are residency requirements which must be fulfilled;
- if the local housing authority is the immediate landlord of any qualifying tenant;
- if the freehold of different parts of the premises are owned by different persons, then the right does not apply if any of these parts is a self-contained building;
- if those premises are already managed by an RTM company, subject to certain exceptions.

Key practice points

- Great care should be taken when considering and checking if the building qualifies.
- A site inspection by the solicitor and/or surveyor is recommended, particularly in more complex situations, e.g. an estate of several buildings or if there is an issue as to the extent of non-residential premises where accurate measurements will be required.
- Consider whether there are other areas which might be treated as residential under the 2002 Act, e.g. parking spaces if these might tip the balance where the non-residential parts might otherwise appear to be over 25 per cent.
- Analyse what can be included as appurtenant property and look to include as much as possible, e.g. if there is an estate, assuming that this is what is desired.

5.7.6 Information from and about the landlord

In order to serve the claim notice it is necessary to ascertain the names and addresses of the freeholder and intermediate landlord. Sources of this information could be rent and service charge demands, office copy entries, etc. See **4.6.6** above.

Formal request for information

Consideration needs to be given as to whether any contact, either formal or informal, is made with the landlord prior to the exercise of the right. This may give a landlord the opportunity to try to undermine the proposed exercise, e.g. by dissuading tenants from participating. There are legal constraints on the extent to which a landlord can levy increased service charges and e.g. undertake major works, but regardless of the letter of the law, a landlord may try to bring pressure to bear.

A landlord will receive prior notification, e.g. if it holds a flat as a qualifying tenant or if the lease of a flat has been granted to a connected party, when the notices of invitation to participate are served, although by then it is likely that the RTM company will have sufficient participating members.

Apart from the rights given to an RTM company under the 2002 Act there are also rights given to an individual tenant to obtain information as to the name and address of the landlord. See Chapter **12**.

There are two statutory rights to obtain information under the 2002 Act:

- a pre-claim notice under s.82;
- a post-claim notice under s.93.

Pre-claim notice

Service of a pre-claim notice is a right given to the RTM company (note, therefore, it can only be used once the RTM company is formed) to require any person to provide it with information in his possession or control which the RTM company requires for ascertaining the particulars and details to be included in the claim notice; also to allow the RTM company to inspect the documents in which that information is contained and to obtain copies on payment of a reasonable fee.

There is no prescribed form for the notice which could be, e.g. by letter.

The notice can be served on any person, not only the landlord. Therefore it could be served, e.g. on the landlord's managing agents, solicitors, accountants, even on caretakers and contractors.

The notice is limited to information necessary for the claim notice and therefore does not extend, e.g. to obtaining general information about the management of the building such as details of maintenance contracts and the like.

The recipient of the notice has 28 days to provide the information.

Careful consideration has to be given as to whether to serve this notice. It will often be possible to obtain the formal information required for the claim from other sources. There is also an issue as to whether the landlord could be required to disclose the usual residential address of a qualifying tenant as this information is not necessary to complete the notice but the information would be useful, e.g. if the RTM company is seeking to get in touch with a tenant who has sublet their property.

There is no immediate sanction for failure to comply with the notice. An application to the court must be made. The RTM company may be faced with a decision whether to go ahead based on the information it has. An assessment will need to be made as to the risk of a notice being invalid if not correctly served.

PART II: COLLECTIVE RIGHTS

Post-claim information notice

The RTM company can serve this on the landlord or a manager party. The information is that reasonably needed in connection with the right to manage. This right is far wider than the right to serve a pre-claim information notice and is discussed in greater detail at **5.14** below.

5.7.7 Information about management contracts

There is no obligation on the landlord to provide information on management contracts or other practical matters prior to service of the claim notice. There may be informal sources such as the knowledge of participators and caretakers, or gleaned by the proposed new managing agent from the old one. It is important to build up as complete a picture as possible. It is necessary, therefore, to assess management, service charge and any other practical issues which may arise once the claim has been exercised.

5.8 THE RTM COMPANY

To exercise the right, the participating tenants must form an RTM company. It must:

- be a private company limited by guarantee;
- have a Memorandum and Articles of Association which comply with the RTM Companies Regulations and state that it has as its object or one of them to exercise the right to manage the relevant premises.

Sections 73 and 74 specify the requirements for an RTM company and its membership and regulations.

There cannot be an RTM company if it is a commonhold association or if another company is already an RTM company in relation to the premises. If an RTM company acquires the freehold it ceases to be an RTM company.

Under the RTM Companies Regulations the constitution of the company is prescribed.

The only persons who are entitled to be members are the qualifying tenants and, from the date of acquisition, any landlord.

The liability of a member to contribute to the assets of the company is limited to £1. The company cannot distribute any profits to its members.

5.8.1 Formation of the RTM company

It is simplest to buy the company through a formation agent as a number of these have a specific RTM company package. It should be noted that the

RIGHT TO MANAGE

company and its officers have a number of responsibilities and statutory duties which are referred to in more detail at Chapter **11**.

See also **5.23** below for information on membership, meetings, directors and voting rights which will be of more significance after the acquisition date.

5.9 NOTICE OF INVITATION TO PARTICIPATE

Unlike collective enfranchisement where (at least until the RTE provisions are brought into effect) it is not necessary to seek participation of all qualifying tenants, it is a mandatory requirement that before a claim notice is served the RTM company gives notice to all qualifying tenants who are not members or who have not agreed to become members of it.

The notice is in a prescribed form and contains prescribed particulars. Reference should be made to s.78 and to the 2003 Regulations. A specimen notice is included at **A15** in Appendix **A**. It must be served at least 14 days prior to the exercise of the right. The form requires a considerable amount of information and care should be taken in completing it. It is not proposed to list all the contents. In broad terms it states that the company intends to take over the landlord's duties of management and include details of names and addresses of relevant parties. Some key points about the notice are as follows:

- It must make clear that there is a potential personal liability for the landlord's costs.
- It must state whether the RTM company intends to appoint a managing agent and if so the details. If no managing agent is to be appointed, then details should be included of the property management experience and qualifications of the relevant members of the RTM company.
- A copy of the Memorandum and Articles of Association of the company must be attached or facilities offered for inspecting and taking copies of them.
- The notice is not invalidated by any inaccuracy in its particulars (see s.78(7)). It can be served on a qualifying tenant at their flat unless that tenant has notified the company of a different address for service.

5.10 ACQUISITION DATE

The acquisition date defined in s.90 is the date on which the right to manage takes effect assuming that it has been validly exercised. Where there is no dispute about entitlement it is the date specified in the claim notice, which is not less than three months after the date specified for service of the landlord's counter-notice which is in turn a date not less than a month from the service of the claim notice. Therefore, the minimum period from service of the notice of claim to the acquisition date is four months.

Where the claim is disputed and either the RTM company applies to the tribunal and a determination is made in its favour or an agreement with the landlord is made as to the RTM company's entitlement, then the acquisition date is three months after the determination or agreement as appropriate.

5.10.1 Timing of the acquisition

In many instances the participating tenants will wish the management of the premises to be taken over as soon as possible. However, there are practical, commercial and financial issues which should be considered and the following particular points are likely to be of relevance:

- Will the RTM company have sufficient information and will it be sufficiently prepared in terms of arranging contracts and the like to take over the management on the relevant date?
- Without causing undue delay, can it be made to coincide with the financial year end for the current service charge regime?
- Have arrangements been made or considered for the funding of the company such as for the collection of service charges so that it has sufficient resources to pay bills as soon as it takes over the management?
- When is the date of buildings insurance renewal?

5.11 ABSENT LANDLORDS

The 2002 Act in s.85 deals with the position where the RTM company cannot find or ascertain the identity of any of the persons or where the claim notice is required to be given. It follows, e.g. that if the freeholder cannot be found but there is a management company which is a party to a relevant lease then the notice could be given to that party.

The RTM company must fulfil the relevant criteria and must be otherwise in a position to give a valid claim notice.

Application is made to the LVT for an order that the company is entitled to acquire the right. Notice of the application must be given to all qualifying tenants. The 2002 Act does not specifically require the service of notices of invitation to participate but the LVT Procedure Regulations require the application to contain a statement that the applicant has complied with the requirement of ss.78 and 79. Section 78 requires the giving of notices of participation, and accordingly such notices need to be given. In terms of compliance with the provisions of s.79 which relate to the claim notice, clearly this cannot be served as this is the whole point of the application to the LVT, but it is assumed that it means that the company would otherwise be in a position to serve a valid claim notice.

In addition the application must attach a copy of the notice of the application given to all qualifying tenants and state that such notice has been served.

It would be advisable to have taken reasonable steps to have traced the landlord and be able to demonstrate this to the LVT. The LVT may require the company to undertake further steps to trace the absent person.

If an absent person is subsequently traced, the LVT cannot make an order that the company acquire the right to manage but the application is treated as though it were a claim notice duly given and the LVT will make directions to give effect to the parties' rights and obligations.

5.12 CLAIM NOTICE

The claim is made by the RTM company serving a claim notice.

The qualifying criteria above must be met on the relevant date, which is the date that the notice is served. As previously stated, it does not matter if subsequently, e.g. the number of qualifying tenants who are members of the company falls below the relevant threshold.

It must be given at least 14 days after service of the notices of invitation to participate.

There is a prescribed form of notice which has specified contents. See s.80 and the 2003 Regulations. A specimen claim notice is included at **A13** in Appendix **A**.

5.12.1 Service of the claim notice

The claim notice must be served on:

(a) anyone who is a landlord under a lease of the whole or part of the premises; this would include intermediate landlords having a superior interest to a qualifying tenant and the freeholder;
(b) a party to a lease otherwise than as landlord or tenant, e.g. a tenant's management company;
(c) a manager appointed under the Landlord and Tenant Act 1987.

A copy must be given to all qualifying tenants. The 2002 Act does not state when it must be given and it has been held in the LVT that it is not necessary for this to be done at the relevant date (*9–29 Wiltshire Drive Halescher RTM Co. Ltd* v. *Sinclair Gardens Investments*, LW 9/3/06, BIR/OOCR/LRM/2005/ 0002) but prudence suggests it is better to send copies at the same time as the service of the claim notice on the landlord.

For the position where a landlord cannot be traced, see **5.11** above.

5.12.2 Contents of the claim notice

The claim notice must contain:

- details of the premises and a statement of grounds;
- full names of each qualifying tenant who is a member of the RTM company, the address of his flat (as with the right to enfranchise there is no requirement to give the usual residential address, if different);
- particulars of the lease of each participating tenant, the date, the term and term commencement date;
- name and registered office of the RTM company;
- the date for service of the counter-notice, being not earlier than one month after the date the claim notice was given;
- the acquisition date, being a date at least three months after the date for service of the counter-notice;
- a statement that if the recipient does not dispute the RTM's entitlement and is a manager party (under a management contract) he must give the relevant contract notices (see **5.20** below);
- a statement that as from the acquisition date, any landlord of the premises is entitled to become a member of the RTM company (see **5.23** below re voting rights);
- a statement that the notice will not be invalidated by inaccuracies in its particulars and inviting any recipient who considers there to be an inaccuracy to identify it with reasons;
- a statement that a recipient should seek legal advice;
- the information notes contained in the 2003 Regulations.

There is a saving provision that the claim will not be invalidated by any inaccuracy in the particulars (s.81(1)) but a recipient who considers there to be inaccuracy should notify the RTM company. There is a lot of detail in this notice and it is an area where errors could easily be made. It would be unwise for the RTM company to give the landlord any opportunity to raise a technical objection on the content or service of the claim notice. Even if the argument is tenuous it may leave doubt in the minds of the members and may cause delay and add to the costs.

A claim notice in respect of the same premises cannot be served while an existing claim notice remains in force. If the landlord does object on technical grounds, the RTM company can consider serving a further notice without prejudice to the first or withdraw the first claim notice and serve another claim notice, but there can be an issue with liability for the landlord's costs and also with the timing of the acquisition of the right and potential disaffection amongst the participating tenants.

RIGHT TO MANAGE

> **Key practice points**
> - Use a pre-printed form or precedent claim notice.
> - Make sure that the dates for service of the counter-notice and given as the acquisition date comply with the minimum period requirements. Avoid having to rely on the 'corresponding date' argument by allowing for appropriate days of clearance.
> - Diarise these dates with appropriate forward review.
> - Take care with service of the notice and see the guidance given in **4.9.1** above.

5.13 POSITION FOLLOWING SERVICE OF THE CLAIM NOTICE

5.13.1 Timetable

Service of the claim notice triggers a timetable, the primary steps in which are as follows:

1. The relevant parties can exercise a right of access to any part of the premises.
2. Within one month, or such later date as specified in the claim notice, the landlord may serve a counter-notice and if it does not do so will be deemed to have admitted the right.
3. Within two months of the counter-notice, if the landlord disputes the right the RTM company must apply to the LVT for a determination and if it does not do so the claim is deemed withdrawn.
4. Once the claim is admitted, deemed admitted or determined in the company's favour, the provisions for contractor notices are triggered.
5. The company may serve an information notice (but see **5.14** below on timing).
6. On the acquisition date, if the claim is successful the RTM company acquires the right to manage the premises.

5.13.2 Right of access

The RTM company, the landlord and other parties have a right of access to any part of the premises if reasonable in connection with matters arising out of the claim (s.83). The following are key points in connection with this right:

- It can be exercised once the claim notice has been given.
- It is on 10 days' written notice at any reasonable time.
- There is no prescribed form.
- It may be exercised by any person authorised to act on behalf of the RTM company, the landlord and other manager parties, e.g. it could be exercised by the proposed managing agent to be appointed by the RTM company.

- It is given to the occupier of the relevant premises or if unoccupied to the person entitled to occupy.

From the landlord's perspective, it would normally have access to communal areas and to relevant parts of the building. There is an issue as to whether they would have a right to access individual flats and whether this is reasonable. From the RTM company's perspective, it may require access to areas which are under the landlord's control to establish the state of repair and maintenance and the nature and routes etc. of the communal facilities. As the RTM company will assume the liabilities under relevant leases for structural and other repairs, it will need to assess the state of repair. The RTM company may want to consider the possibility of the tenants making a disrepair claim against the current landlord, although ideally this should have been looked at prior to the service of the notice.

5.14 INFORMATION NOTICE

In order to be in a position to take over the management in the most effective way, the RTM company will need to obtain as much information as possible about the current management regime. Unlike the pre-claim information notice under s.82, s.93 provides at least in theory a mechanism for the RTM company to obtain extensive information about the management of the building by service of an information notice. Some key points relating to this are as follows:

- It can be given at any time where the right to manage premises is to be acquired by the RTM company. There is some ambiguity here as to whether this entitles the RTM company to serve the notice after service of the claim notice or only if the right is admitted or deemed admitted or determined. There is similar wording in the sections of the 2002 Act relating to contractor notices which might indicate that the latter interpretation is more likely to be correct. From a practical point of view the RTM company will want to obtain information as soon as possible. The company may wish to serve an information notice as soon as the claim notice has been served, then possibly serve the information notice again when and if the right is admitted or determined, e.g. when a landlord serves their counter-notice admitting the right.
- It can be served on the landlord or other manager party.
- It relates to information in the recipient's possession, power or control. Therefore, e.g. a landlord would have to provide information held by its agents, such as the managing agent or solicitors or accountants.
- The information is that reasonably required in connection with the exercise of the right. This is very wide-ranging and would include management

RIGHT TO MANAGE

contracts, service charge information, insurances and practical matters relating to the block. It should be noted that under the contractor notices procedure (see **5.18** below), in theory, details of relevant contracts should be given or provided by the landlord as a matter of course but it would be prudent to include all relevant information required in the information notice.

- There is no prescribed form or contents. A specimen notice is included at **A12** in Appendix **A**. This is fairly comprehensive and should be adapted according to the particular circumstances. A notice which is too onerous, whatever the legal obligation may be on the landlord, may possibly be counter-productive. Consider the type of building and likely ability of the landlord or its agents to deal with replies.
- Where information is contained in a document, the recipient can be required to permit the company to inspect the document and to supply a copy of it.
- The time for compliance is whichever is the later of 28 days after service of the information notice or the acquisition date. It should be noted that the landlord cannot be compelled to provide information prior to the acquisition date and this could be a practical problem, as clearly the RTM company needs the information ahead of that date in order to prepare.
- There is no specific requirement to pay the landlord's costs for providing information. There is a possible argument that this could be recouped as part of the landlord's entitlement to the costs of dealing with the claim. See **5.17** below.
- This is a critical document and care should be taken in its preparation. It is recommended that it be prepared with the assistance of any proposed new managing agent.
- It is possible to serve more than one notice but bear in mind that service has to be prior to the acquisition date.
- In practice information is often provided on an ad hoc basis rather than by a formal reply to an information notice. A pragmatic and flexible approach is helpful.

Key practice points

- Consider serving an information notice immediately after service of the claim notice even though there is an issue as to whether this may be premature; it may speed up matters by giving the landlord earlier notice of what the RTM company requires and may be useful in prompting discussion with the landlord if the landlord does not provide the information required. The information notice should be re-served after the right has been admitted or determined.
- Use informal methods of obtaining information such as direct contact between the new and existing managing agents.

PART II: COLLECTIVE RIGHTS

5.15 LANDLORD'S POSITION FOLLOWING SERVICE OF CLAIM NOTICE

On receipt of a claim notice, a landlord party will need to give consideration to legal, commercial and tactical issues, including the following:

- whether or not to admit the claim;
- its obligations and position in respect of contracts;
- issues with regard to contractor notices;
- the general approach to take in dealing with the RTM company;
- the treatment of service charges;
- costs.

5.15.1 Counter-notice

The formal position in respect of the counter-notice is as follows:

- It must be served no later than the date specified in the claim notice, being not less than one month after the service of the claim notice.
- It must be in a prescribed form with required particulars.
- It must either admit the claim or dispute it.
- Where the landlord disputes the claim, the RTM company has two months from the date of the counter-notice (or if more than one from the last of them) to apply to the LVT.
- If the landlord admits the claim or no counter-notice is served, the RTM company acquires the right to manage on the acquisition date.
- If there is a dispute the RTM company does not acquire the right to manage until after determination by the LVT or the landlord agrees.
- There is no provision for one landlord to act on behalf of other landlord/manager parties so each can act independently.

There is no obligation on the landlord to serve a counter-notice but if it does not do so there is deemed to be no dispute.

5.15.2 Contents of the counter-notice

The requirements for a counter-notice are contained in s.84 and the 2003 Regulations, with a prescribed form annexed at Sched. 3 to the 2003 Regulations. A specimen counter-notice is included at **A14** in Appendix **A**. The counter-notice must:

- either admit the right or allege that the RTM company was not entitled to exercise it;
- if the right is disputed, give reasons by reference to provisions of the 2002 Act and state that the right will not be acquired until so determined by the LVT or agreed by the landlord(s);

- if the right is disputed, state that the RTM company may apply to the LVT for a determination of the matter within two months;
- contain the information provided in the notes to the prescribed form.

As with other notices, particularly prescribed ones, a pre-printed form or a precedent should be used.

The notice should be served at the address for service of the RTM company given in the claim notice.

5.15.3 Landlord's considerations

The basis for dispute is limited. This is a no fault process, therefore a landlord cannot object, e.g. because it does not think the RTM company is competent or there are disputes about arrears of service charge. It can only do so on technical grounds, e.g. that the qualifying criteria are not met or there is some substantial defect in the claim notice or its service (but see below as to the general view taken by the LVT).

A landlord will investigate the qualifying criteria in the same way as the RTM company should have done so. There is no right for a landlord to obtain information from the company and it is assumed that the landlord could check from his own records, from office copy entries and details of leases it has in its possession. Inspection of the premises and any appurtenant property may be required. The right of access can be exercised (see **5.13.2** above).

When considering whether to object on technical grounds, reference should be made to the saving provision concerning inaccuracies in particulars. It should be said that in the decided cases so far under this relatively new right, the LVT have been reluctant to rule that notices are invalid on technical grounds, particularly where there is no prejudice to the landlord. See e.g., the *9–29 Wiltshire Drive* case referred to at **5.12.1** above. However, if there a serious defect in the claim notices, e.g. a failure to specify an acquisition date or failure to give the names of all participating members of the RTM company (see *Marine Court (Paignton) RTM Co.* v. *Gibbs*, LVT 24/9/05), then an objection on one of those grounds is likely to succeed.

There is no specific provision for the LVT to award costs to the RTM company should a landlord unsuccessfully object to the claim, but if the landlord adopts an unreasonable approach or if it withdraws its objection at the eleventh hour, the LVT may well penalise it in costs. There is a specific provision which permits the LVT to award costs to the landlord if it successfully opposes the exercise of the right.

Regardless of potential technical objections, the landlord would need to consider whether or not it should object; the extent to which it will wish to incur costs which may be irrecoverable either in part or in whole; also whether it wishes to get involved in a dispute with the RTM company or whether it is simpler to accept the right and to take a pragmatic approach. Are there any benefits in disputing the claim even simply for the purposes of delay and what benefit is to be gained? The answer to these questions will, of course, depend on the particular circumstances. A landlord may have a substantial interest in the remainder of the premises, there may be potential development value on other parts of any estate of which the premises form part which are not included in the claim but which may be affected by it. The landlord will be concerned about the insurance position. Where there is no real prospect of any technical opposition and no major prejudice to the landlord, it may decide not to contest the right. It may be better to co-operate with the company and the process. Although this process will often have been started after dissatisfaction or a dispute with the landlord or the managing agent, nevertheless the practical issues, particularly where there is an estate or mixed use premises will normally force there to be a discussion between the parties. It is also in the landlord's interest that the premises be managed properly by the RTM company.

Key practice point

- The landlord should consider carefully what premises are included in the claim, particularly appurtenant premises, which may well be an issue with an estate where there are also premises not subject to the right. The claim notice may not specify precisely what appurtenant premises are included and, in this case, clarification should be sought from the RTM company. In cases where the extent of appurtenant property to be acquired may prejudice the landlord, a formal dispute on this issue should be considered.

5.16 RTM COMPANY'S POSITION IF THE RIGHT IS DISPUTED

If a counter-notice is served disputing the right there should be considered:

- whether the notice has been served in time and whether it complies with the statutory criteria;
- whether it raises any valid objection to the exercise of the right and if so what are the likely chances of the claim succeeding;
- the effect on the timing of acquisition and any practical issues affecting the management of the building.

If it is considered that the landlord is unlikely to succeed with its objections, particularly if based on alleged minor technical defects, or if the landlord raises a substantial point but the company is keen to press on with the claim, an application to the LVT should be made by the company as soon as practical.

As has been previously stated, the application must be made within two months of the date of service of the counter-notice or the claim is deemed withdrawn.

For the application to the LVT see Chapter **9**. The application must contain in addition to the standard requirements for such applications:

- the name and address for service of the RTM company, of the freeholder and any intermediate landlord or manager;
- a copy of the Memorandum and Articles of Association of the RTM company;
- copies of the claim notice and counter-notice.

As with all LVT applications, it is recommended that as much information as possible be given with it.

5.17 COSTS

There is the liability of the RTM company to pay a landlord/manager party's reasonable costs in connection with the claim notice (s.88). If costs are not agreed the landlord will need to apply to the LVT for a determination. This exercise in itself will incur costs which may not be recoverable. The LVT adopts a fairly critical and conservative approach to the assessment of costs. In practice some landlords may adopt a minimal involvement approach in terms of professional fees.

If a claim ceases, is withdrawn or deemed withdrawn there is a joint and several liability on the members of the RTM company for costs incurred. See further **5.19** below.

As stated above, the landlord can ask the LVT to award costs in its favour if it successfully opposes the claim.

5.18 MANAGEMENT CONTRACTS

Management contracts are those whereby a person agrees to provide services or to do anything relating to a management function. A management function is one relating to services, repairs, maintenance, improvements and insurance or the management of the premises but excludes functions relating to part of the premises other than a flat or unit not held under a lease by a qualifying tenant. In effect, this covers unsold flats and commercial premises.

It is important to note that management contracts determine on the acquisition date unless agreed otherwise between the RTM company and the contractor. The 2002 Act does not specify that contracts terminate on the acquisition date. It is assumed that they are frustrated by the exercise of the right.

PART II: COLLECTIVE RIGHTS

The 2002 Act provides a mechanism for the service of notices on contractors and then from contractors on to subcontractors and so on with provision of the information back to the RTM company. Reference should be made to ss.91 and 92 and to the 2003 Regulations.

Notice is given by a manager (if one of the landlord parties) to a contractor and by any contractor receiving a notice to a subcontractor. The manager or contractor giving such a notice must at the same time give to the RTM company a contract notice.

There is no prescribed form of contractor or contract notice, but there are required contents set out in s.92 and in the 2003 Regulations. There is no obligation to supply a copy of the contract concerned, though in practice it may be the easiest way of providing the information. The RTM company should be able to obtain copies using the information notice procedure, see **5.14** above.

5.18.1 Contents of contractor notice

A contractor notice must state:

- sufficient details to identify the contract;
- that the right to manage is to be acquired by the RTM company;
- the acquisition date;
- that if the contractor or subcontractor wishes to continue with the services, they are advised to contact the RTM company.

5.18.2 Contents of contract notice

A contract notice must:

- contain particulars of the contract and of the contractor or subcontractor; and
- advise the RTM company to contact the contractor if it wishes the contract to be continued.

There is no requirement to tell a contractor that their contract will end. However, from a landlord's perspective it would be prudent to include such a statement and possibly also to serve a formal termination notice. There are practical and commercial considerations and it will partly depend on what contractual arrangements there are between the parties and also on what their commercial relations are as to how the matter is handled. There are other possible issues, e.g. where major works have been contracted for.

5.18.3 Service of contractor notice

The timing of contractor notices relates to the determination date. This is defined as when the claim is admitted, deemed admitted or determined. With contracts existing before that date, notice must be given on the determination date or as soon as reasonably practicable thereafter and where contracts are entered into between the determination date and the acquisition date, on the date they were entered into or as soon as reasonably practicable thereafter.

There is no sanction for failure to comply and it would be necessary for an application to be made to the county court to enforce compliance. In many cases this may not be justified on a cost/benefit analysis and here efforts should be made to obtain the information in other ways.

5.19 WITHDRAWAL OF CLAIM NOTICE

Withdrawal by the RTM company can be either voluntary or deemed. A voluntary withdrawal is by written notice under s.86. It can be given at any time prior to the acquisition date and is served on all relevant parties and on all qualifying tenants whether or not members of the company. Deemed withdrawal would occur if no application was made to the LVT within two months of a counter-notice disputing the right (see **5.16** above) or if an application is made and withdrawn, and also on the winding up, insolvency or similar of the RTM company.

There is a liability to pay the costs of the landlord which is joint and several between the RTM company and its members past and present, although if a member's lease is assigned to a person who becomes a member, the former member is not liable. The liability is for costs up to the date of the withdrawal. There may be a question as to whether the term 'costs' could, e.g. include increased service charges caused by disruption to contractors.

5.20 MANAGEMENT AFTER THE ACQUISITION DATE

As has been previously mentioned, the acquisition of the management function by the RTM company requires consideration of a number of legal, practical, commercial and accounting issues. Whilst there will be far more issues for the RTM company to address, than for the landlord, it is also important from the landlord's point of view that it understands what rights it will retain or involvement it will have in the continuing management of the building, particularly where it has a substantial interest to protect. As part of the planning process, the RTM company and the participating tenants should have obtained an appreciation of the rights and duties of the RTM company. At exactly what stage each element should be looked at in detail will depend upon the circumstances.

Some of the issues include the following:

- general management of the premises;
- compliance with company legislation and the running of the company;
- service charges and accounts, including compliance with other relevant landlord and tenant legislation;
- accounting issues;
- buildings insurance;
- directors' insurance;
- consideration of lease obligations;
- approvals;
- monitoring and enforcement of covenants;
- possible defects in the service charge regime;
- duties towards non-participating leaseholders;
- communications with tenants, both members and non-members;
- landlord's involvement.

5.20.1 General management

A well organised RTM company will put in place suitable structures to ensure the smooth running of the administration of the building. Where there is a managing agent this will be done in conjunction with them. It would include matters such as:

- the allocation of particular specialist roles for the officers of the company;
- the lines of responsibility and decision-making and the extent to which day to day decisions can be dealt with by the managing agents;
- the lines of communication with tenants and other occupiers and also with any landlord party;
- the appointment of accountants, and defining their role.

In general terms, the intention should be to keep on board the goodwill of all the tenants in the building.

5.20.2 Service charges

It is, of course, key that the RTM company can be funded going forward so that in particular it can meet the running costs of the premises. Funds will primarily come from one of the following sources:

- accrued but uncommitted service charge funds held by a landlord;
- contributions from tenants;
- contributions from landlords.

Under s.94 of the 2002 Act, uncommitted service charge funds held by the landlord or other manager parties as at the acquisition date must be paid to the RTM company. Uncommitted funds are to be paid on the acquisition date or as soon as possible thereafter. Uncommitted funds are those service charge monies which are held, together with any interest accrued on those sums, less sums required to meet costs incurred prior to the acquisition date.

The LVT can determine the amount payable. In this connection either party can apply.

There may be a number of instances where it is difficult to obtain the necessary information from the landlord or to procure an early payment of sums. To obtain information, the s.93 notice procedure should be used. See **5.14** above. This should be used early in the proceedings to try to gauge the likely level of uncommitted service charge funds as at the acquisition date, but of course the service charge accounting process is a moving feast with expenses being paid and receipts coming in.

For contributions from tenants and, indeed, any other persons liable to contribute towards service charges the company must abide by the contractual provisions contained in any relevant lease as to matters such as the timing of service charge demands, what type of expenditure is recoverable and what sums may be demanded. Any demand must comply with any statutory requirements. Subject to these matters, the company should be advised to submit service charge demands as soon as practicable following the acquisition date.

It should be noted that the company has no power to send out a service charge demand prior to the acquisition date, so the tenants cannot pay the RTM company sums which were due to the landlord prior to the acquisition date. The 2002 Act prohibits the RTM company from receiving such monies. The possibility of diverting payments in this way is a question which often arises in practice and care should be taken not to encourage any tenant to breach their contractual obligations to the landlord. However, the tenants or some of them can make loans to the RTM company which can then be credited against service charge demands issued to those tenants. This may lead to some accounting and administrative expenses but may be the practical way of making sure that the RTM company has enough money until it is able to collect in the necessary funds from service charge demands.

There is potential liability on the landlord to contribute towards service charges under s.103. This arises where there is a flat or other unit which is not subject to a lease of a qualifying tenant and the aggregate of the service charge proportions of the qualifying tenants is less than 100 per cent. The appropriate person is then liable to pay the difference for these 'excluded units'. If there is more than one excluded unit, the charge is apportioned according to relative floor areas. The appropriate person is the one who has the lowest intermediate landlord interest or if there is no lease of that unit then the liability is that of the freeholder.

There is the possibility that there may be an unsatisfactory or unfair service charge regime regardless of (or because of or despite) s.103 which may prejudice the landlord, the RTM company or particular tenants. It may be necessary to consider whether an application should be made to the tribunal to vary leases: see Chapter **12**. Where there are unsatisfactory service charge proportions there may also be other defects or inadequacies with the lease or with the legal and service charge structure, which might also be dealt with under the variation procedure.

5.20.3 Management functions and lease covenants

As has been stated, on the acquisition date the management functions of the landlord under the relevant leases are passed to the RTM company. The landlord for these purposes includes other parties to any lease who are not the landlord or the tenant.

Certain functions which do not pass to the company are:

- the right of re-entry or forfeiture;
- matters concerning only part of the premises being a flat or other unit not held under a lease by a qualifying tenant (if a matter concerns such a part of the premises and also other parts of the premises, then it will not be excluded).

A landlord is not entitled to do anything the RTM company is entitled to do unless the RTM company agrees. Notwithstanding this, the landlord is permitted to insure the building if it so wishes.

There are functions with regard to approvals where a landlord may retain an involvement. The position here is as follows:

- Where the landlord has functions in relation to approval, this passes to the RTM company but the landlord is entitled to notice prior to it being exercised.
- An approval is a consent or licence and it should be noted that this includes approval for the purposes of complying with a restriction at HM Land Registry, e.g. such as is commonly imposed on the title of a qualifying tenant which requires a certificate from the landlord or management company that certain lease covenants have been complied with before a new owner can be registered.
- Approvals which relate to alienation, structural alterations and improvements, and change of use require 30 days' notice. All other cases require 14 days' notice.
- A landlord can object to the approval being given or seek to make it subject to certain conditions (s.99). If the landlord objects during the period of notice, the RTM company can go ahead either with the agreement of the objector or if the LVT approves. Application needs to be made by the affected party to the LVT.

- When considering approval, the RTM company needs to exercise the usual care as might be taken by a prudent landlord such as to comply with the contractual obligations and any relevant statutory provisions, e.g. not unreasonably to withhold or delay consent to assignment of a lease, also, not to grant consents which might prejudice the structure of the building or adversely affect other tenants or occupiers. The system for dealing with approvals and the issuing of consents, particularly in formal matters, such as the transfer of ownership, should be established with the managing agent, if applicable.

Covenants other than those relating to management functions are called 'untransferred covenants'. These are the covenants in any lease of the whole or part but do not include the right of forfeiture or to receive rent. They would therefore include covenants in e.g. a lease of any commercial unit.

The RTM company may enforce untransferred covenants as well as the person who is entitled to enforce them. The RTM company can exercise any right of entry to determine compliance.

It is important to note that the RTM company has a duty to review whether tenants' covenants are being complied with and to report to the landlord if it notices any non-compliance. This must be done within three months of a breach coming to the notice of the RTM company. Notice need not be given if the breach is remedied, reasonable compensation is paid regarding the failure or the landlord has notified the RTM company that it need not report failures of that type.

This duty to review whether or not covenants are being complied with is a potentially onerous obligation on the RTM company. The extent to which this is likely to be a practical or legal issue is not yet clear. It would be prudent to have a system arranged with the managing agent, if there is one, for monitoring breaches of covenant. In many cases a landlord will not be particularly concerned but they might be if, e.g., there was an illegal subletting or use of a commercial unit forming part of the premises. Analysis of relevant lease covenants should be undertaken to identify those which are likely to be of significance in this context. The landlord would also probably be keen to monitor the enforcement of covenants, particularly those affecting any commercial units.

Key practice points

- The landlord should be approached by the company to see whether it will agree that the review and/or enforcement of particular covenants need not be undertaken by the RTM company where this is of no benefit to the company.
- The RTM company should also seek to discuss management issues with the landlord such as those relating to insurance with a view to reaching agreement where there is ambiguity or where otherwise the 2002 Act does not provide a satisfactory solution.

5.20.4 Insurance

The position relating to buildings insurance requires particular consideration in view of the potentially disastrous consequences if no adequate cover is in place. There is a risk that the landlord's policy will determine on the acquisition date if no action is taken by the RTM company. The RTM company should either arrange for a new policy/cover to be effected as from the acquisition date or to agree with the landlord's insurer that the existing policy will continue. For practical reasons, the latter may often be preferred, to avoid issues such as funding the new premium and apportionment of the premium, at least until the next renewal date. It is an area of potential confusion between the RTM company, the landlord and insurers. Insurers may need to be persuaded of the legal position and the RTM company's right/obligation to insure.

Insurance arrangements should be clearly recorded with confirmation of cover obtained from the insurer.

5.21 ANCILLARY ISSUES FOR THE RTM COMPANY

5.21.1 Modification of statutes

The RTM company needs to be aware that there are various other landlord and tenant covenant statutes which have been modified to take into account the fact that the RTM company is standing in the shoes of the landlord. Some of these are listed in Sched. 7. Many of these are self-evident, e.g. making the statutory provisions for the collection of service charges applicable to the RTM company. It is not proposed to list these in detail here save to mention a couple which may be of particular interest:

- the RTM company has a duty of care regarding defective premises;
- under the 1987 Act the landlord must also give a copy of the right of first refusal notice to the RTM company.

5.21.2 Company issues

The RTM company will need to abide by the various statutory provisions applicable to limited companies, primarily as contained in the Companies Acts. The RTM company will also need to be run in accordance with its constitution. The officers, and particularly the directors, have statutory duties and potential liabilities. As mentioned previously, the RTM company is entitled to take out directors', officers', advisers' and accountants' insurance and this should be considered carefully. It may be tempting to overlook this issue but this should be resisted. RTM company directors' duties carry with them potential risks such as being sued for trading whilst insolvent and similar, just as with the directors of any other business.

Reference should be made to Chapter **11** where more information is given about corporate issues and to **5.23** below on the constitution of the company. A practitioner may wish to offer the directors of the RTM company further advice on directors' responsibilities and the like.

5.21.3 Audit/accounts

The company will need to maintain accurate accounts, both for its own purposes of compliance with company law, but also for the purposes of providing proper service charge information to the tenants. In almost every instance it is difficult to see how this can be done without professional assistance. An accountant should be appointed using a similar due diligence procedure to that undertaken when investigating the appointment of a managing agent. Indeed, the managing agent may well be able to assist with an appropriate accountant who is familiar with tenants' management companies. The accountant will also need to ensure that any contributions made by the members of the RTM company are correctly recorded in the books of the company.

5.22 ISSUES FOR THE LANDLORD

Depending on the extent of the landlord's retained interest in the premises and the size of the building and other commercial issues, the landlord will want to consider carefully how they will be affected by the RTM company. Some issues such as dealing with contractors have been dealt with above. Reference should be made to the various subject areas covered in this chapter. To summarise in general terms the key issues, these are as follows:

- the extent to which management functions will pass to the RTM company and whether and if so how these will affect any parts of the premises or the parts of an estate of which the premises forms part in which the landlord retains an interest;
- assessment of the likely liability for the landlord to contribute towards service charges for excluded parts and whether this will burden the landlord unduly;
- the effect on any contract entered into by the landlord and whether such contract, e.g. relates to other premises or functions which are not being taken over and where there might be a question as to whether the contract continues in part;
- insurance is an area where the landlord is likely to have a keen interest to see that cover and, indeed, adequate cover is maintained by the RTM company. Whilst the 2002 Act permits the landlord to undertake its own insurance, in many cases this is likely to be uncommercial, since the landlord will not be able to recover the premium from any other party. The

landlord should ensure that a system is in place to obtain a copy of the policy and up-to-date schedule and to review the renewal of the policy at each renewal date;
- the extent to which it would wish the RTM company to become involved in the monitoring and enforcement of untransferred covenants, particularly in respect of flats or units of non-qualifying tenants.

No matter how bad the landlord's previous relationship with the tenants may have been, in many cases it would be advisable for the landlord to adopt a pragmatic approach and to work with the RTM company to agree matters insofar as possible.

As regards unpaid service charges, as previously stated the RTM company is under no obligation to pay arrears of service charges owed to the landlord which are unpaid by the tenants as at the acquisition date or, indeed, at all. The landlord should take this as an opportunity to collect in the service charge arrears which may be due to it at an early stage in the process. Regardless of the legal position, the practical position is that the tenants may feel less incentive to pay arrears to the landlord once the RTM company takes over and they are paying service charges under the new regime.

5.23 RTM COMPANY: MEMBERSHIP, VOTING AND MANAGEMENT

As previously mentioned, the constitution of an RTM company is prescribed and reference should be made to ss.73 and 74 and in particular to the RTM Companies Regulations which annex the prescribed form of Memorandum and Articles of Association. It is not intended here to cover all of the articles in detail but to concentrate on some key aspects.

5.23.1 Membership

The persons entitled to be members of the company are:

(a) a qualifying tenant of the premises;
(b) a landlord under a lease of whole or part but only as from the acquisition date.

Joint tenants of a flat are a joint member for that flat so that there is only one membership per flat.

Application for membership is in a form in or in similar terms to that contained in Article 7. If the directors are satisfied as to entitlement they must register the applicant. If a member ceases to satisfy the membership criteria then they cease to be a member, e.g. if a qualifying tenant sells their flat, although then the new owner would be entitled to join.

A member can withdraw from membership of the company on seven days' notice but cannot do so in the period between the giving of the claim notice and the acquisition date or the date of withdrawal or deemed withdrawal.

There are provisions governing the position where persons become a qualifying tenant or a landlord jointly and with the position on death, bankruptcy and similar changes of circumstance on the part of a member. In these circumstances it is necessary for any person entitled to membership in substitution to the previous person to apply within a specified period (which depends on the circumstances) otherwise membership ceases. However, where membership has lapsed in this way it is possible for the person fulfilling the membership criteria to re-apply for membership.

5.23.2 Meetings

The quorum for general meetings is 20 per cent of those entitled to vote or two, whichever is the greater. Voting may be in person or by proxy.

AGMs and EGMs where there is a special resolution or a resolution appointing a director are on 21 days' notice. All other EGMs are on 14 days' notice. General meetings may be called on shorter notice if it is agreed in the case of an AGM by all members or in the case of any other meeting by 95 per cent of the membership. There are detailed provisions for the calling of meetings and the proceedings at them.

5.23.3 Voting

The allocation of voting rights can be a little intricate depending on whether or not there is a poll or if there are any landlord members.

If voting is on a show of hands, every member present has one vote.

If voting is on a poll and there are no landlords who are members of the company then one vote will be available in respect of each flat and can be cast by the member who is the qualifying tenant of that flat.

If voting is on a poll and any member of the company is a landlord, it is necessary to undertake the following exercise:

- Work out how many votes are to be allocated to each residential unit/flat in the premises (this includes flats not held by qualifying tenants). Each flat then is potentially entitled to the same number of votes as there are landlord members of the company, e.g. if there are two landlords and 30 flats then there are potentially 60 votes available for the flats; two per flat. This does not mean that 60 votes can in fact be cast since this depends on whether there is a member entitled to vote in respect of a particular flat and the votes are in effect 'earmarked'.
- If there are non-residential parts of the premises, votes are allocated to any non-residential/commercial areas. Work out the proportion of non-residential to residential by dividing the former by the latter to get a

fraction or percentage. Multiply that fraction by the votes allocated to the residential units/flats. Note that the assessment of floor areas is to be determined in the same way as when determining whether the premises qualify for the right.
- It is the immediate landlord of any non-residential part who is entitled to the vote in respect of that part. If there is no lease of a non-residential part then the vote goes to the freeholder for that part. Where there is more than one person entitled to vote for a non-resident part then the votes are divided according to the proportion of internal floor areas of those parts.
- The votes for flats are cast by the member who is the qualifying tenant of the flat but if, and only if, there is no qualifying tenant of a flat then the member who is the immediate landlord of the flat can cast the votes for it.
- If a residential unit is not subject to any lease no votes can be cast in respect of it. Therefore if the freeholder has retained a flat but has not granted any lease for it, it would not be able to exercise voting rights for the flat.
- If there is a landlord member of the company who does not receive any votes using the above allocation method, then it is entitled to one vote.

To explain the voting provisions in a different way, it is helpful to look at an example:

Voting provisions

There is a building with 30 flats: 26 are let to qualifying tenants, 20 of whom are members of the company. There is a headlease of the whole of the premises which includes the four flats not held by qualifying tenants. There is 30,000 square feet of residential property and 3,000 square feet of non-residential property. The freeholder and the intermediate landlord are members.

As there are two landlords who are members therefore each flat has potentially two votes, i.e. 60 votes in total.

The relevant fraction for determining the votes allocated to the non-residential parts is 3,000 ÷ 30,000, i.e. 1/10th. Multiply 1/10th by 60 (total votes allocated to the residential units). Six votes are therefore allocated to the non-residential areas. These would be allocated to the intermediate landlord who would be the immediate landlord of those parts.

Under the above allocation the freeholder is a landlord who is a member of the company but is not entitled to any votes under the above arrangements and therefore receives one vote.

To summarise, there would be 67 available votes broken down as follows:

- 60 for the residential units, of which 40 (two for each flat) would be utilised by the qualifying tenant members;
- 12 would be uncommitted and would be available for non-participating qualifying tenants but could not, in fact, be used unless and until those tenants applied for membership;
- 8 which would be allocated to the intermediate landlord by virtue of the fact that there are four flats for which there is no member who is a qualifying tenant and the votes are exercisable by the member who is the immediate landlord;

RIGHT TO MANAGE

> - 6 votes for the non-residential parts in this scenario, also exercisable by the intermediate landlord, assuming that there is no further subletting of those parts;
> - 1 vote for the freeholder.
>
> The voting power would be 40 for the qualifying tenants and 15 for the landlord parties.

On the basis of the formula the qualifying tenant members of an RTM company will always have a majority.

If there is a dispute as to the extent of the non-residential parts or to the allocation of voting rights between landlords of those parts then there is a mechanism for reference to an independent chartered surveyor selected by agreement or in default by the President of the RICS. The surveyor acts as an expert and his decision is final.

5.23.4 Directors

At the first AGM all directors are required to retire from office and at every subsequent AGM one-third of all directors are subject to retirement by rotation based on those who have been the longest in office. There are provisions for the deemed re-election of retiring directors if a vacancy is not filled.

Directors can only be remunerated if this is approved at a general meeting but they are entitled to be paid their expenses for attending meetings or otherwise incurred in connection with the discharge of their duties. Pensions and similar benefits can be paid to directors who are no longer in office.

Non-members can be directors but if a member director ceases to be a member then his office is vacated. Non-member directors with an interest in a matter, or if there is a matter where they have a conflict of interest, may not vote on that matter. They are treated as not being present for the purposes of quorum of a board meeting at which such a matter is raised. A member director with an interest can attend and vote even though they have an interest in a matter or a conflict although it would be wise for any such interest to be declared.

There are various other provisions for the appointment of alternate directors and for the way in which board meetings are conducted. A quorum for a meeting is whichever is the greater of 50 per cent of the directors, or two. Whilst directors have powers generally in line with general company law, in light of the nature of this type of company the directors will probably want to pay particular regard to the wishes of the members and to consult where possible, particularly on major issues regardless of whether or not this is strictly required by law. Directors are entitled to indemnity from the company in respect of their liabilities sustained in relation to the exercise of their duties. There is power to obtain the necessary directors' and auditors' insurance and this is recommended.

The company make further byelaws for the running of it provided these are not inconsistent with the prescribed constitution, e.g. it would not be possible to change the voting formula.

5.23.5 Memorandum of Association

The Memorandum contains the objects of the company. It is widely drawn. There are no particular practical issues arising from the Memorandum save to note that it provides that all income for the company must be used to promote its objects so there can be no distribution to the members other than on a solvent winding up. If the company is wound up whilst a person is a member or within a year of them ceasing to be a member, there is an obligation to contribute to the liability of the company limited to £1.

5.24 CESSATION OF RIGHT TO MANAGE

The right to manage of an RTM company will cease in the following circumstances:

(a) if the RTM company is wound up and an administrator or receiver is appointed or in other similar insolvency situations;
(b) if a Landlord and Tenant Act 1987 manager is appointed;
(c) if the RTM company ceases to be an RTM company, e.g. if it acquires the freehold of the premises.

There is no clear provision as to what happens on cessation. This will largely depend on the reason for such cessation. If, e.g. the freehold were to be acquired by the RTM company then the contractual provisions under the leases of the buildings would re-apply. This might also be the case if the RTM company were struck off. However, the original contractual positions may not be workable, e.g. if previously management was undertaken by a tenants' management company, this might have been allowed to be struck off. In this instance it may be necessary to restore it by application to the court.

5.25 MISCELLANEOUS

There are other miscellaneous provisions, the most important of which, in brief, are as follows:

- anti-avoidance provisions in s.106 which in general terms make void provisions relating to leases which purport to exclude the right of a tenant to become a member of an RTM company or impose a penalty if he does so;

- provisions for the enforcement of any breach of obligation, e.g. under the 2002 Act the failure of the landlord to reply to an information notice; 14 days' prior written notice of default must be given;
- a provision that all notices given under the 2002 Act must be in writing;
- special provisions relating to the Crown and trustees.

PART III

Individual rights

CHAPTER 6
Right to extend the lease of a flat

6.1 OVERVIEW

The right can be described as the right of a tenant of a flat holding a long lease to acquire a new lease on payment of a premium subject to the fulfilment of the statutory criteria.

The right is exercisable by corporate bodies as well as by individuals. It is probably the most commonly exercised of the enfranchisement rights and adds and/or restores considerable value to a leasehold flat.

The Commonhold and Leasehold Reform Act 2002 considerably extended the scope of the right by abolishing some of the original qualifying criteria such as the residence condition.

For a comparison of this right with others and the pros and cons see Chapter **2**.

A timetable flowchart is included at **B5** and a checklist of preliminary matters at **B6** in Appendix **B**.

6.2 FINDING YOUR WAY AROUND THE LEGISLATION

The right is contained in the Leasehold Reform, Housing and Urban Development Act 1993. Part 1 Chapter 2, ss.39 to 62 are the primary provisions. Schedules 11 to 14 contain supplemental provisions.

The Leasehold Reform (Collective Enfranchisement and Lease Renewal) Regulations 1993, SI 1993/2407 ('the 1993 Regulations') contain regulations governing the conveyancing procedure for the grant of the new lease including such matters as the payment of a deposit and deducing title.

Regard should also be paid to the Leasehold Valuation Tribunal (Procedure) (England) Regulations 2003, SI 2003/2099, as amended by SI 2004/3098 (SI 2004/681 (W.69) as amended by SI 2005/1356 (W.104) in Wales) ('the LVT Procedure Regulations') in the case of application to the Leasehold Valuation Tribunal (LVT), and to the Civil Procedure Rules in the case of application to the court.

6.3 KEY TERMINOLOGY

Some of the key terms are as follows:

- 'tenant's notice': the notice which initiates the claim; it is often referred to in practice as a 's.42 notice';
- 'relevant date': the date on which the tenant's notice is given and which is, e.g. the valuation date for the purposes of calculating the premium payable to the landlord;
- 'competent landlord': the landlord who conducts all proceedings on behalf of all landlords if there is more than one;
- 'qualifying tenant': a tenant who is entitled to exercise the right.

6.4 GENERAL

If successful the tenant will obtain a new lease in substitution for their existing lease. Indeed, on service of a valid tenant's notice the landlord is bound to grant and the tenant bound to accept a new lease subject to compliance with the 1993 Act and to the tenant's right to withdraw. The term of a new lease is 90 years plus the remainder of the existing term, i.e. if 70 years remains on the current lease, a term of 160 years will be obtained and the ground rent is, in effect, extinguished by reducing it to a peppercorn.

The right may be exercised ad infinitum, therefore there is no bar to further applications to extend.

The price payable to the landlord is calculated according to a formula laid down in the 1993 Act; it also compensates the landlord for the loss of ground rent. It is important to note that the marriage value is payable where the lease has 80 years or less as at the relevant date. This is significant, particularly for higher value flats. Advisers should be alert to situations where an expired term is getting near the 80-year mark.

The exercise may also be used as an opportunity to make changes to the lease to benefit both the landlord and the tenant. The landlord may want to modernise the lease; the tenant may wish to remedy any possible defects. There are statutory restrictions on the variations which can be ordered by the LVT (see **6.6.4** below). It may be worthwhile considering negotiations outside the statutory framework, e.g. by endeavouring to negotiate a 999-year lease, although as with negotiations for collective acquisition of the freehold, a landlord may wish to ensure that their professional fees are covered by the tenant either by a solicitor's undertaking or by requiring the tenant to serve a tenant's notice which triggers a liability for costs.

There is a liability on the tenant to pay the reasonable costs of any landlord subject to certain limitations (see **6.17** below).

Unlike with collective enfranchisement it does not matter how many flats in a building are owned by the tenant.

If the landlord does not admit the tenant's right to a new lease, the onus is on the landlord to apply to the court (see **6.9.3** below).

The benefit of a tenant's notice served by a tenant can be assigned to a new owner of the flat (see **6.14** below).

If a notice of claim for collective enfranchisement is served the tenant's claim is suspended (see **6.15** below).

6.5 QUALIFYING CRITERIA

The qualifying criteria for exercising the right can be summarised as follows:

- the tenant must hold the property under a long lease;
- the property must be a flat;
- the tenant must have held the lease for a continuous period of two years prior to the relevant date.

6.5.1 Long lease

The definition is similar to the collective enfranchisement and right to manage. See Chapters **4** and **5** for more detail. In most cases it will be where there is a lease with a term when granted of more than 21 years. As with the other rights, if anything other than a 'standard' long lease is encountered the lease should be examined carefully as against the relevant criteria. See s.39 which cross-references to s.5 and then to s.7.

6.5.2 Length of ownership

For calculating the period of ownership, this starts with registration of the tenant as proprietor at HM Land Registry and not the date on which ownership of the flat was transferred. The period of ownership requirement was introduced in the 2002 Act and applies to claims made since 26 July 2002. For claims made prior to that date there were more qualifying criteria such as a requirement to have occupied the flat as a main residence.

Following on the death of a tenant who is entitled to exercise the right, the right may be exercised by his personal representatives.

6.5.3 What is a flat?

It will normally be self-evident as to whether or not a property constitutes a flat. However, there may be unusual situations where a property which one might ordinarily consider to be a house is a flat and vice versa. The definition of 'flat' includes garage, grounds and other appurtenances, e.g. a parking space which is let to the tenant.

There may be circumstances where there is a lease of a flat and other premises or where there is more than one lease for the flat. It is provided that in this situation it is as though there were a single lease of that flat.

6.6 PRELIMINARY INVESTIGATIONS

As with other rights, good preparation is important.
Key issues include an assessment of the following:

- whether there is any critical date for service of the tenant's notice, particularly if the threshold for payment of a marriage value is looming;
- the qualifying criteria;
- the identity and address for service of the competent and other landlords;
- the premium likely to be payable;
- the adequacy of funds to pay the likely premium and costs;
- whether the terms of the existing lease need revision;
- whether there is any collective action ongoing or proposed which may impact on the proposed exercise of the right.

For assessment of the qualifying criteria, the lease, the title of the tenant and of any superior title absolute should be considered. Office copy entries should establish the period of ownership. Enquiries should be made to see whether there are supplemental leases, deeds of variation, licences or ancillary agreements.

It is usually relatively easy to determine whether the qualifying criteria are met. Care is often required when checking for ancillary matters, such as other premises which can be included within the definition of a flat and/or whether there is a question as to whether the 'flat' is in fact such. An inspection of the flat together with consideration of the lease and other plans is likely to be of assistance.

6.6.1 The landlord

By s.40, the competent landlord is the first landlord above the interest of the tenant who has a sufficient reversion to be able to grant a new lease with a 90-year extension. The competent landlord should conduct the claim on behalf of the other landlords. This will often be the tenant's immediate landlord, but if there is a headlease and the immediate landlord has only a short reversion, the competent landlord would be the freeholder, e.g. if a tenant has a lease with an unexpired term of 60 years, and there is an intermediate landlord, then that landlord would need to have a lease with an unexpired term of 150 years to be the competent landlord. If the immediate landlord is the competent landlord then any other superior title holder is not included in the process.

Part II of Sched. 11 deals with the conduct of proceedings by the competent landlord. Notices given and agreements made by the competent landlord and determinations of the court or LVT are binding on the other landlords.

If the competent landlord acts in good faith with reasonable care it is not liable for any loss or damage caused to other landlords for its acts or omissions. However, the competent landlord would be well advised to seek the approval of any other landlord before taking any step which might prejudice the interests of that landlord.

Other landlords can by giving notice to the competent landlord and to the tenant elect to be represented in proceedings in which its title is in question, or relating to the determination of any amounts payable to it, and also to elect to receive payment of such amounts direct rather than via the competent landlord. There is a duty on other landlords to co-operate with the competent landlord and provide relevant information. They have to contribute to the costs of the competent landlord which are not recoverable from the tenant. Note the election to act independently can only be made after service of the landlord's counter-notice. Any other landlord should therefore liaise with the competent landlord to make sure that their interests are protected in the counter-notice.

The steps to ascertain the identity of the landlord are much the same as for collective enfranchisement or the right to manage (see e.g. **4.6.6** above). Briefly, these include obtaining office copy entries of the superior titles and the last ground rent/service charge demands as well as use of a notice under s.41 (see **6.7.2** below). If the immediate landlord is not the competent landlord then the relevant details of any superior landlord should be obtained up to the level of the one who is the competent landlord.

There is a requirement that the tenant's notice should also be served on any other party to the tenant's lease, e.g. a management company in a tripartite lease. The address for service of that party should be ascertained.

Where a superior title is not registered then clearly one avenue of investigation is not available. This is more likely to be a problem where the landlord concerned is not the tenant's immediate landlord. A land charges search may reveal useful information or, if the identity is known but not the address, then other lines of enquiry, such as a company search on a corporate landlord, can be undertaken. It is recommended that where there is any doubt about the identity or address of a relevant landlord the procedure in the following paragraph should be used.

Under s.41 a qualifying tenant can give to their landlord or a receiver of rent a notice requiring details of relevant landlords and the freeholder of their respective interests. If the immediate landlord is not the freeholder, the tenant can serve a similar notice on the freeholder. The notice also requires other information, namely as to whether the landlord has received an initial notice of collective enfranchisement claim and details of that notice. Information is to be provided within 28 days.

In the event of failure to comply with an information notice, the tenant can make an application to the court after service of a default notice under s.92. The tenant will need to make a careful cost/benefit analysis before taking such a step.

In cases where there is an absent landlord, see **6.20** below.

6.6.2 Evaluating the premium

The price is calculated according to a statutory formula (see **6.19** below and Chapter **10**). There is no requirement to have a formal valuation but this is recommended. A specialist valuer should be used. The premium has to be split between landlords, where there is more than one, according to the respective interests. It is necessary to state the price and how it is allocated in the tenant's notice.

6.6.3 Other costs

In addition to the premium there will be the tenant's own professional costs, the administrative costs of any mortgagee (where consent will be required but will almost certainly be forthcoming as it will enhance the value of the security), the landlord's costs, Land Registry fees and Stamp Duty Land Tax, where appropriate.

Where the likely premium is substantial, funding issues are more critical. The tenant may wish to use the exercise as an opportunity to remortgage the flat on better terms.

6.6.4 Terms of the lease

This is covered in more detail at **6.12** below. As stated above, the new lease must be on similar terms (other than as to ground rent and length of term) as the existing lease. The LVT does have some scope to order a variation of existing terms under the claim. The lease should be checked for any defects and e.g. whether it complies with the requirements of the Council of Mortgage Lenders.

6.6.5 Urgency

The need for urgent action will arise if the unexpired term of the lease is approaching 80 years, at or below which a liability to pay a marriage value is triggered. Since the difference in price if the notice is served before such time and if it is served afterwards could be substantial, particularly with expensive flats, it is an issue which should be identified at the outset of the investigation.

> **Key practice points**
>
> - The tenant's solicitor should seek to ascertain the length of the unexpired term of the lease as soon as possible following the instruction or potential instruction and where the critical 'marriage value date' might be an issue, to bring this to the attention of the tenant and diarise the critical date.
> - Check carefully to see whether there is any ancillary property which might be included in the claim and ascertain whether there are deeds of variation, supplemental leases and the like.
> - Check for defects in the lease.
> - Obtain a professional valuation in all but the very simplest of cases.

6.7 TENANT'S NOTICE

The claim is initiated by the service of a tenant's notice under s.42.

Key points regarding the tenant's notice are as follows. The notice must:

- contain the contents specified in the 1993 Act but there is no prescribed form; it is recommended that a pre-printed form or precedent be used to minimise the risk of omission of required particulars (a specimen notice is included at **A16** in Appendix **A**);
- be served on the competent landlord and on any other party to the tenant's lease (e.g. a management company) with a copy sent to any other known relevant landlord;
- be signed personally by the tenant or all of them if more than one;
- be registered at the Land Registry or as a land charge; it is not binding on any purchaser of the freehold if it is not registered by the time of purchase.

6.7.1 Contents of tenant's notice

The tenant's notice must:

- specify the name of the tenant and the address of the flat;
- give particulars of the flat and of the lease. It is necessary to identify the extent of the flat. It is recommended that a plan be attached although this is not strictly required. Care should be taken to ensure that any additions to the flat and any other relevant property, e.g. a garage, is included. The information needed concerning the lease is its date, term and commencement date of the term;
- specify the premium and apportion this between landlords if more than one; note that stating an unrealistically low price may invalidate the notice (see *Cadogan Estates* v. *Morris* referred to at **4.9** above);
- state whether copies are being given to other landlords;

- specify the terms to be contained in the new lease;
- specify a date for service of the counter-notice by the landlord, being at least two months after the date of service of the tenant's notice;

State the name and address of the tenant's representative for service of notice. It is not strictly necessary to state the date on which the tenant became the owner of the lease, but precedent notices usually contain a statement that the tenant has owned the lease for two years.

There is a saving provision in Sched. 12 para. 9 that the notice is not invalidated by inaccuracy in the particulars or by any misdescription of the property. Also if the claim includes property which should not be included or omits property which should be included, the court can give leave to amend the notice. However, as discussed in connection with collective enfranchisement, reliance on this should only be had as a last resort and there are technical arguments as to what falls within the meaning of the word 'particulars'.

There is a particular issue where there is a third party to the tenant's lease who must be served with the tenant's notice. If they cannot be found or, e.g. it is a management company which has been dissolved, the 1993 Act does not provide for this situation which is not covered by the absent landlord procedure. Until a notice is served on such a party it is not validly served: *John Lyon's Free Grammar School* v. *Secchi* [1999] 3 EGLR 49, CA.

There are certain circumstances where notice cannot be given or, if it is given, is not valid. In broad terms these situations arise where there is action to terminate a lease other than by effluxion of time, e.g. where the lease is being forfeit or a notice has been served terminating the lease or if there is a court order for possession.

6.7.2 Service

Schedule 11 contains additional matters relevant to the service of the tenant's notice. Notice is to be served on the competent landlord but if the identity or address of the landlord is not known, it is effective if given to another landlord. It is still necessary to give a copy to any other person believed to be a competent landlord but regard should also be had to the absent landlord procedure (see **6.20** below). A recipient who is a landlord must forthwith give a copy of it to any person believed to be a competent landlord or another landlord whose details are not stated in the tenant's notice. The landlord must also, if it knows who is or believes itself to be the competent landlord, give notice to the tenant stating the name and address of the landlord concerned and give a copy to that other landlord, if not itself.

Method of service

See s.99. The notice may be given by post but as with the exercise of other rights, consideration should be given to service by hand as well (see **4.9.1** above).

Service may be effected on the immediate landlord at the address notified for that purpose or by the address for service last given if a rent demand. It is clearly simpler if the landlord's solicitor has agreed to accept service.

Key practice points

- Since the notice must be signed personally by the tenant or all of them if more than one, leave the date for service of the counter-notice blank until the notice is ready to be served.
- Check the contents of the notice carefully and if necessary also let the surveyor/valuer check it with particular reference to the premium stated, the extent of the property and the accuracy of any plan attached.
- Register the tenant's notice against the landlord's title at the Land Registry or as a Land Charge.
- Diarise the date for service of the landlord's counter-notice.

6.7.3 Effect of service of tenant's notice

The service of the tenant's notice has the following consequences.

- No further notice can be served in respect of the same flat whilst one is in force but this does not prevent the tenant from serving another notice without prejudice to the assertion that the earlier one is valid, if the validity of the earlier notice is disputed.
- The notice is withdrawn, deemed withdrawn or is otherwise unsuccessful. No further notice may be given for a period of 12 months from the date of withdrawal or when the claim otherwise fails.
- There is a restriction on the landlord's ability to terminate the lease.
- Save in limited circumstances, if the lease would otherwise determine by effluxion of time it continues during the claim until three months afterwards.

6.8 PROCEDURE FOLLOWING SERVICE OF TENANT'S NOTICE

The competent landlord has until the date stated in the tenant's notice, i.e. one which is not less than two months after service, to serve a counter-notice.

Any landlord has the right of access to the flat for valuation purposes.

The competent landlord may require the tenant to pay a deposit and/or to deduce title.

Whether the landlord serves a counter-notice or if he does so, whether he admits or disputes the claim will determine the subsequent procedure.

6.8.1 Right of access

This can be exercised by a landlord with not less than three days' written notice to the tenant. It may be exercised on more than one occasion. If the tenant fails to comply there is no immediate sanction but the landlord can serve a default notice and ultimately apply to the court (s.44).

6.8.2 Deposit

Any time during the continuance of the tenant's notice, the competent landlord can give written notice to the tenant requiring payment of a deposit. This is the greater of £250 or 10 per cent of the premium or other sums payable as proposed in the tenant's notice. Again, there is no immediate sanction should the tenant make default and the default notice procedure would have to be followed.

6.8.3 Title

The landlord, if it wants the tenant to deduce title, must give written notice to that effect within 21 days if it wishes. The tenant has 21 days to comply. There is no sanction on the tenant for not complying. A landlord would wish specifically to check the name of the tenant serving the notice, the relevant details of the lease and the period of ownership. The time limit on the landlord is strict and if no request is made within the 21-day period the landlord will lose that right. However, in practice, most tenants' titles will be registered and the relevant details will be on the office copy entries, which can be obtained direct from the Land Registry.

Key practice points

- There are no prescribed forms of notice for requiring access, payment of the deposit or requiring deduction of the tenant's title and although there are precedents available, requests by letter are sufficient.
- The exercise by the landlord of the rights referred to does not prejudice its right to dispute the validity of the tenant's claim and the landlord should in particular request payment of the deposit and deduction of title as soon as possible following service of the tenant's notice.
- Key dates should be diarised on receipt of the tenant's notice since failure to observe time limits could have severe consequences.

RIGHT TO EXTEND THE LEASE OF A FLAT

6.9 COUNTER-NOTICE

Key points to note regarding the counter-notice include:

- failure to serve a counter-notice by the specified date will mean the landlord loses the right to dispute the tenant's entitlement; the tenant can therefore apply to the court for a new lease on the terms proposed;
- only the competent landlord can serve it;
- there is no prescribed form; use of a pre-printed stationer's form to ensure compliance with required content is recommended (a specimen notice is included at **A17** in Appendix **A**).

6.9.1 Contents of counter-notice

Reference should be made to s.45 and Sched. 11 which deal with the content of the counter-notice, which must:

- specify any other landlords on whose behalf the competent landlord is acting;
- state whether the landlord admits or does not admit the tenant's notice and if applicable whether it intends to apply to the court to declare that the right is not exercisable by virtue of the landlord's intention to redevelop the premises;
- if it admits the right, state what proposals are accepted or not accepted, and if not accepted, specify the landlord's counter-proposals;
- specify an address in England and Wales for service.

There is no saving provision for failure to include any of the required particulars. Special care must be taken to ensure that the counter-notice is accurate and complete.

6.9.2 Landlord's considerations

There will be legal and tactical and commercial matters for consideration on the part of the landlord as to what stance to take in respect of the counter-notice. Its choices are to:

- admit the claim and make the appropriate counter-proposal;
- not admit the claim on the ground that there is no right to acquire on the date of service;
- dispute the validity of the tenant's notice by virtue of a technical defect or inadequate service;
- oppose the claim on the ground of proposed redevelopment of the premises of which the flat forms part.

6.9.3 Not admitting the right

Surprisingly, the onus is on the landlord to apply to the court within two months of the date of service of the counter-notice. In practice there are unlikely to be many circumstances where it is not clear whether or not the tenant has the right. If the application to the court is not made or is withdrawn, it is as though no counter-notice has been served. This is potentially dangerous for the landlord; therefore, if the landlord decides to withdraw its objection it must issue proceedings in order to obtain consent to an order dismissing the claim, because the court will then permit the landlord to serve a further counter-notice in which the claim would be admitted. In this way, the landlord can then object to the proposals in terms of price, etc.

6.9.4 Disputing validity of the tenant's notice

It is risky for the landlord to rely on this basis of opposition and not serve a counter-notice unless it is absolutely clear that there is a fundamental flaw in the tenant's notice or, e.g. that the period specified for service of the counter-notice is inadequate. The recommended method of dealing with this circumstance, if there is likely to be some dispute, would be for a counter-notice admitting the right to be served without prejudice to the landlord's contention that the tenant's notice is invalid. In that way the landlord will maintain their right to contest the specific proposals in the landlord's notice if the landlord is wrong on the point of principle concerning the validity of the notice.

The landlord and his advisers would need to consider the commercial aspects, such as whether disputing the notice is justified on a costs/benefit analysis or whether, if there is some suspected defect, is it simply better to take a pragmatic view and get on with negotiating the best terms with the tenant? Disputing the validity of the notice can put pressure on the tenant and could help with negotiations. There may also be instances where disputing the notice could have a significant impact, e.g. in particular in higher value cases with shorter leases where the delay in the tenant's exercise of the right could be of significant benefit to the landlord. From the tenant's perspective if there is a prospect that his notice is not valid then it would be usual practice to serve a second notice without prejudice to the contention that the first one was valid. Alternatively, subject to time and cost considerations, the first one could be agreed to be ineffective and a fresh notice served but care should be taken that there is no deemed withdrawal of a valid first notice which would prevent the service of a fresh notice for 12 months.

The validity of the notice could be of great significance where the tenant's notice has been served close to the period where a marriage value would otherwise be payable.

6.9.5 Redevelopment

The circumstances where the landlord can object on redevelopment grounds will rarely arise as in essence it only applies where the tenant's lease has less than five years unexpired at the date of its notice. The landlord must apply to the court for an order within two months of the date of the counter-notice. If the claim is dismissed, the landlord will be required to serve a further counter-notice (see s.47).

6.9.6 Admitting the right

In most cases in practice the landlord will be satisfied that the tenant has made out the right and will serve a counter-notice admitting it. In the same way as the tenant should consider carefully issues such as other premises to be included, the term of the lease, price and other proposals, so should the landlord and its advisers. The primary focus tends to be on price/valuation as perhaps one might expect.

Admission of the right triggers a timetable for negotiation and application to the LVT to determine matters in dispute (see **6.10** below).

6.9.7 Valuation

In most instances the landlord will wish to obtain a professional valuation. The tenant is obliged to pay the reasonable fees of the valuer so there is no reason for the landlord not to obtain this professional advice. It will be essential in higher value cases. The valuer would wish to inspect the flat and would also usually conduct the negotiations as to premium on behalf of the landlord. There is no sanction on the landlord for proposing an unreasonably high premium, but if the issue is referred to the LVT this could affect the credibility of the landlord's valuer in the absence of appropriate substantiating evidence.

6.9.8 No counter-notice served

If the landlord fails to serve a counter-notice then it loses the right to dispute the terms proposed in the tenant's notice (see s.49). This includes a situation where a landlord serves a counter-notice which is not valid.

The tenant must apply to the court within six months of the date when the counter-notice should have been served. The court must make an order to give effect to the tenant's proposals provided it is satisfied that the tenant has made out the right. There is no discretion in this respect. See *Willingale* v. *Globalgrange Ltd* [2000] 2 EGLR 55, CA.

If the court makes an order, there is a timetable for agreeing and completing the form of the lease and in default for application to the court. Careful regard should be had to the timetable to avoid the tenant's claim being deemed withdrawn.

6.10 TIMETABLE FOLLOWING SERVICE OF THE COUNTER-NOTICE

If the landlord disputes the validity of the tenant's notice (as distinct from disputing the tenant's right), the landlord or the tenant could issue court proceedings to determine the issue. Alternatively, the validity of the notice could be determined in the LVT following an application made by the tenant to determine the terms of his exercising the right but it is likely to be unsatisfactory to leave the validity of the notice open in this way.

If the landlord does not admit the right or opposes the claim on redevelopment grounds, the onus is on the landlord to apply to the court (see above).

If the right is admitted, there is a two-month period allowed by the 1993 Act for negotiation and either party can make an application to the LVT after two months and before six months after the service of the counter-notice. If there are any terms which have not been agreed, in practice it is the tenant who will make the application and in default the tenant's notice will be deemed withdrawn. Note that agreement of terms does not mean agreeing the form of lease.

The tenant may serve notice on the landlord to deduce title. The landlord is to respond within 28 days. There is no sanction for default. The tenant must follow the default notice procedure and apply to the court if necessary.

6.11 CONVEYANCING PROCEDURE

See s.48 and the 1993 Regulations. The landlord prepares the lease within 14 days of the terms being agreed.

The tenant has 14 days to respond. The landlord has a further 14 days to re-amend or is deemed to accept the tenant's amendments.

If the lease is not entered into by the end of the 'appropriate period' either the landlord or the tenant can apply to the court within two months beginning immediately after the end of that period, in other words within four months of the terms being agreed or determined. If no application to the court is made within that period the tenant's notice is deemed to be withdrawn.

The 'appropriate period' is, where terms in principle have been agreed, at the end of two months thereafter and where they have been determined by the LVT, two months after the determination or such other date as the LVT may fix.

See **6.12** below regarding the terms of the new lease.

6.11.1 Completion

Once the terms have been agreed or approved, notice to complete may be served by either party requiring the other party to complete on the first working day 21 days after service of the notice. This cannot be done if the date of completion falls after the 'appropriate period'. The completion date will then be as agreed or as ordered by the court.

Care should be taken about deemed withdrawal. This would have the effect that no further tenant's notice could be served within 12 months of the date of withdrawal, which could have a significant impact on the price.

To complete the new lease the tenant pays:

- the premium (apportioned if necessary between relevant landlords);
- rent due under the old lease;
- any costs payable to the landlord;
- any service charges;
- any other sums due to the landlord.

Where any of the costs, such as service charges or landlord's costs, are disputed or are not fully ascertained, the tenant can offer reasonable security. For example, if costs are not agreed it is possible that these could be held in a solicitor's client account until the issue has been resolved by the LVT.

On completion of the new lease the tenant loses any right to security of tenure at the end of the new lease but would be able to make a further claim for a new lease prior to its expiry.

Key practice points

- As with collective enfranchisement claims, the practitioner should be alert as to when all terms are agreed for the purposes of triggering the conveyancing timetable and the time limit for applying to the court and to avoid doubt by making matters clear in correspondence, e.g. as to whether agreement on one issue is without prejudice to agreement on others, and when agreement is to be treated as 'open' and binding.
- Diarise the timetable including permutations depending on whether or not agreement is reached.

6.12 NEW LEASE

6.12.1 Terms of the new lease

The length is fixed by statute, otherwise it is on terms the parties agree and the starting point will be the same terms (see s.57(3)). As mentioned above, opportunity is often taken to substitute a 'modern' satisfactory lease in place of an older, possibly defective, or out-of-date one.

If the parties cannot agree the terms the matters in issue can be determined by the LVT. The LVT has only limited powers to vary the terms of the existing lease, again contained in s.7, namely to take account of the following circumstances:

- the omission of other property that was included in the existing lease but not comprised in the flat;
- alterations/additions demised since the grant of the existing lease;
- issues arising where the demise derives from more than one lease;
- where the landlord is obliged to provide services, repairs and the like (see below);
- to remedy certain defects (see below).

There is specific provision in the 1993 Act, where services are provided and the lease does not include a provision for payment or includes payment for a fixed amount, for making of payments relating to the cost the landlord has incurred and for enforcing those as if they were rent. It should be noted that this does not provide a complete panacea for providing a comprehensive service charge regime. There will be issues such as tying in the provisions with other leases and the management structure of the building. It would be hoped from a practical perspective that the parties will co-operate to end up with a lease which reasonably reflects the relevant interests of the parties and has an effective service charge structure. The effect on the general service charge structure of the building needs to be considered.

A separate application for variation of the lease may be considered, see Chapter **12**.

An agreement collateral to the new lease can continue with suitable adaptations.

There is also power to modify the lease to:

- remedy a defect (but this has been given a fairly limited interpretation);
- take into account changes since the date of the grant of the existing lease which affect the suitability of the lease provisions, e.g. a change in the law.

However, although in practice the procedure is often used to modernise the lease, there is no entitlement simply to substitute a modern lease per se.

The lease must contain the following:

- a provision which makes it clear that any long lease created by way of sublease from the tenant's lease does not confer on the subtenant any right to acquire a new lease under the 1993 Act (see ss.57 and 59);
- a statement that 'this lease is granted under section 6 of the Leasehold Reform, Housing and Urban Development Act 1993';
- a statement to reserve the right of the immediate landlord to apply to the court at any time during the last 12 months of the existing lease or the first

five years of the new lease for a possession order on the grounds of redevelopment.

6.12.2 Exclusion of certain terms

Certain terms are to be excluded from the new lease:

- rights of pre-emption or options to purchase;
- any right to renew the lease;
- any right for the landlord to terminate the lease prior to its expiry other than for breach of covenant.

Third parties who are a party to the existing lease cannot be forced to undertake any function after its expiry, e.g. a management company. If it is necessary for someone to carry out a discharged function of a third party after the expiry of the existing lease then the new lease must provide for another person to undertake that function, which will normally be the landlord. This is also a situation where a negotiation outside the scope of the legislation may lead to a more practical solution with the third party management company which may, in practice, undertake those functions beyond the date by which they would otherwise be obliged to comply.

6.12.3 Other landlords

There is a deemed surrender and regrant of any intermediate lease. The intermediate lease continues as a concurrent lease. For any value in the lease the intermediate landlord would be compensated as part of the process.

6.13 MORTGAGES

If the flat is subject to a mortgage, that mortgage applies to the new lease and the mortgage. In practice, it would be usual for the tenant's mortgagee to be notified in advance of completion and arrangements made with them to transfer the mortgage to the new lease by agreement. The process is often used as an opportunity to remortgage, particularly if the tenant needs to borrow to fund the premium and/or costs.

The lease binds any mortgagee of the landlord who is deemed to authorise the lease. Note this is not the position if the existing lease was granted after 1 November 1993 and would not otherwise bind the mortgagee. The landlord must make all reasonable efforts to ensure that the lease is not defeated by a mortgagee.

Reference should also be made to the Land Registry Practice Guide (November 2006).

PART III: INDIVIDUAL RIGHTS

6.14 ASSIGNMENT OF THE RIGHT

The benefit of a tenant's notice can be assigned to a subsequent purchaser of the flat. This must take place at the same time as the assignment of the lease. Whilst this can be done in a separate document, it is recommended that it is incorporated in the transfer. If the flat is assigned without the benefit of the notice, there is a deemed withdrawal.

If acting for the assignee/buyer the notice or the draft notice (if it has not been served prior to the start of the conveyancing process) should be checked and approved and appropriate clauses inserted in the sale contract, e.g. to ensure due service of the notice and warranties from the seller. Generally, the assignee/buyer's solicitor should 'shadow' the seller to make sure that the buyer will obtain the benefit of a notice which complies with the 1993 Act and has been validly served.

Notice of assignment should be given to the landlord and any other party as to when the tenant's notice was served.

6.15 COLLECTIVE ENFRANCHISEMENT

Where a tenant serves a s.42 notice after an initial notice for collective enfranchisement ('s.13 notice') has been served in respect of the building containing the flat, or if the collective enfranchisement notice is served after the s.42 notice, the s.42 notice for a new lease is suspended whilst the collective enfranchisement claim continues.

A landlord receiving a s.42 notice while the collective enfranchisement claim is in progress must notify the tenant of the suspension and give details of the s.13 notice. When the collective enfranchisement claim ceases to be current, the s.42 procedure continues.

Where a s.42 notice is served before a s.13 notice and the landlord has not served a counter-notice due to the automatic suspension, it then has the whole of the period specified in the s.13 notice in which to serve the counter-notice and not just the period lost by the suspension. The landlord has the right to give notice of recommencement although the tenant can do so.

Reference should be made to s.54 for more details of the restart procedure.

6.16 WITHDRAWAL

Withdrawal from the process can either be express or deemed. For the former, the tenant must give written notice to all landlords and to any third party to his lease. This can be done at any time prior to completion of the new lease.

There is a deemed withdrawal if the tenant fails to apply to the LVT or the county court within the required time limits, the lease is assigned without the benefit of the notice or the court orders it deemed withdrawn.

6.16.1 Effect of withdrawal

The tenant can require their deposit returned, although the landlord can deduct their reasonable costs from the deposit.

The tenant can be required to cancel any registration of the notice.

The tenant can give no further s.42 notice within 12 months of the date of withdrawal.

6.17 COSTS

The tenant is liable for the reasonable costs of the competent and other landlords and of any other party to the lease once the tenant's notice has been served.

The liability ceases if the tenant's claim fails because the landlord succeeds on the basis of proposed redevelopment of the building or if there is compulsory acquisition of the flat.

As with other rights, the type of costs recoverable by the landlord parties are limited. In this instance, it is limited to the costs of investigating the tenant's claim of valuation and the conveyancing costs relating to the grant of the new lease. Costs of negotiation or of an application to the LVT are not recoverable.

6.18 REDEVELOPMENT COMPENSATION

Compensation is payable to the tenant when an order for possession is made. The possession order cannot take effect earlier than the expiry date of the existing term. Compensation is such as agreed between the parties or fixed by the LVT. It is calculated according to the basis laid down in the 1993 Act (Sched. 13 para. 2).

6.19 PRICE

The price or premium payable is calculated as at the relevant date, i.e. the date on which the tenant's notice is served. It is calculated by reference to the following matters:

- the diminution in value of the landlord's interest;

- the landlord's share of marriage value (where relevant);
- compensation for any loss the landlord may suffer in respect of any diminution in value of other property resulting from the grant of the new lease and the loss of any development value in relation to the tenant's flat.

As with the exercise of other enfranchisement and similar rights, there are various assumptions and disregards. There are provisions against anti-avoidance artificial structures which may be set up by the landlord to try to increase the value. As mentioned previously, marriage value only applies where there is 80 years or less unexpired term under the existing lease as at the date of the tenant's notice.

For further information on valuation and a worked example see Chapter **10**.

6.20 ABSENT LANDLORD

Section 50 deals with the situation where the landlord or other party on whom the tenant's notice needs to be served cannot be found or their identity cannot be ascertained. In many respects the procedure is similar to that in respect of an absent landlord under the collective enfranchisement procedure discussed in Chapter **4**. Broadly speaking, the procedure is as follows:

- If one landlord or other party to the tenant's lease cannot be found, but another landlord party is known, then the court can dispense with service on the missing party. The tenant's notice can then be served on the known party and the claim proceeds in the usual way subject to any directions the court may have given.
- If there is no landlord party on whom the notice can be served, the court can make a vesting order.
- The court must be satisfied that the tenant has made out their right to a new lease.
- It can give directions, e.g. to require further steps to be taken to trace the missing party. Clearly, before making the application to the court the tenant should have made a thorough investigation and will present evidence of such to the court.
- A vesting order is one for the surrender of the existing lease and the grant of the new lease on terms to be decided by the LVT on the statutory basis, as in the case of a standard claim.
- The price and other monies payable once determined by the LVT are paid into court and the lease executed by a person designated by the court.

6.21 SPECIAL CATEGORIES OF LANDLORD

The 1993 Act makes provision for special categories of landlord such as the Crown, ecclesiastical landlords, landlord's mortgagee in possession and landlord under a disability. If on preliminary investigation it appears that the landlord is or might be in a 'special' category, further enquiry should be made as to whether or how a claim should be made.

CHAPTER 7

Right of a tenant to acquire the freehold of their house

7.1 OUTLINE OF THE RIGHT

The right is of a tenant under a long lease of the whole of the lease of a house, to acquire the freehold of that house and ancillary premises at a price calculated in accordance with the legislation.

A timetable flowchart of the procedure is included at **B7** and a checklist of preliminary matters at **B8** in Appendix **B**.

7.2 FINDING YOUR WAY AROUND THE LEGISLATION

The relevant Act for the purposes of this right is the Leasehold Reform Act 1967. It has been substantially amended since it was first introduced; in particular, the qualifying criteria have been simplified.

The Leasehold Reform (Enfranchisement and Extension) Regulations 1967, SI 1967/1879 ('the Enfranchisement Regulations') contain e.g. the conditions of the statutory contract which is created when the right is exercised.

The Leasehold Reform (Notices) Regulations 1997, SI 1997/640 (as amended by SI 2002/1715 (for England) and SI 2003/991 (W.140) (for Wales)) ('the Notice Regulations') contain prescribed forms for use in connection with the right.

The Housing Association Shared Ownership Leases (Exclusion from Leasehold Reform Act 1967) Regulations 1987, SI 1987/1940 contain ancillary provisions relating to shared ownership leases.

Regard should also be paid to the Land Tribunal Rules 1996 and their Practice Directions 2001, the Leasehold Valuation Tribunal (Procedure) (England) Regulations 2003, SI 2003/2099, as amended by SI 2004/3098 (SI 2004/681 (W.69) as amended by SI 2005/1356 (W.104) in Wales) ('the LVT

Procedure Regulations') in the case of application to the LVT, and to the Civil Procedure Rules in the case of application to the court.

7.3 KEY TERMINOLOGY

Some of the key terms are as follows:

- 'tenant's notice': the description given to the notice which initiates the exercise of the right; it is also known as the 'notice of tenant's claim';
- 'claimant': the tenant who makes a claim, including a subtenant who serves a tenant's notice;
- 'reversioner': the landlord who has the conduct of proceedings on behalf of all landlords where there is more than one.

7.4 KEY FEATURES OF THE RIGHT

- It only applies to entire houses and not to flats.
- Service of the tenant's notice creates a binding statutory contract.
- Unlike with the exercise of other rights, there is no set time limit by which a tenant must apply to the court or the LVT to enforce the right.
- There is no right to obtain information from the landlord as a preliminary step before serving the tenant's notice.
- The right includes a right to acquire the freehold of premises appurtenant to the house such as a garage which are also let on a long lease.
- In the vast majority of cases there is no residence requirement, although there is a requirement for the tenant to have held the lease for at least two years.
- The right can be assigned together with the tenancy.
- The valuation process is complex, with different methods depending on how the house qualifies.
- The qualifying criteria as originally created by the 1967 Act included a low rent and financial limit test. These are generally no longer relevant as qualifying criteria but can be relevant in determining the basis of valuation.
- The tenant has the right to withdraw at any time until one month after the purchase price has been agreed or determined.
- Where there is more than one tenancy which might qualify for the right, it is the most inferior one tenancy which qualifies.

7.5 QUALIFYING CRITERIA

There are primary criteria and additional criteria which only apply in special and limited circumstances. These are contained in ss.1–4 of the 1967 Act.

7.5.1 Primary criteria

- The property must be held under a long tenancy.
- The lease must be of a whole house.
- The tenant must have held the lease for a period of two years leading up to the date of service of the tenant's notice. Note this period is calculated in the case of registered land from the date the tenant is registered as proprietor, not from the date of transfer.

7.5.2 Special criteria

- Where the tenancy is one to which Part 2 of Landlord and Tenant Act 1954 applies then the lease must be for a term of at least 35 years and the tenant must have occupied the house as their main residence for the last two years of periods totalling two years in the previous 10 years (ss.1ZC and 1B).
- Where part of the house is a flat let to someone who is a qualifying tenant for the purposes of the legislation governing collective enfranchisement or the right to a new lease of a flat (see Chapters **4** and **6** above) the tenant of the house must also meet a residency test.
- Where there are two or more tenancies of the whole house which would both qualify, only the most inferior will have the right.
- Where the tenancy is an excluded tenancy (i.e. of a house in a rural area or designated as such and subject to certain other criteria) or if it is a renewal tenancy, a 'low rent' test must be met (see **7.5.7** below).

7.5.3 Other points to note

There are no residency requirements for most tenants exercising their right after 26 July 2002.

Some tenancies are excluded, namely those in areas designated as rural. Certain agricultural holdings are also excluded.

There are some cases of special landlords, where particular rights and special exclusions apply, but these are quite limited in their scope.

The right can be exercised by corporate bodies and trustees as well as by individuals.

7.5.4 Long tenancy

Section 3 contains the definition of a long tenancy. It is one where the original term granted was for more than 21 years. Consecutive terms when added together come to more than 21 years do not qualify but where there has been a statutory extension including renewal or continuation tenancies, these will qualify.

A provision for early termination of the lease, e.g. landlord's right to terminate the lease prior to 21 years, is not relevant. There was an exemption for termination on marriage or death but this has now been severely restricted in its scope.

There are special provisions relating to certain types of lease, e.g. shared ownership leases. As stated in connection with other rights, if the lease concerned is anything other than a 'standard' long lease, the wording of the 1967 Act should be carefully considered.

7.5.5 What is a house?

It is helpful to refer to the statutory definition in s.2(1) which states as follows:

> For the purposes of this Act, 'house' includes any building designed or adapted for living in and reasonably so called, notwithstanding that the building is not structurally detached, or was or is not solely designed or adapted for living in, or is divided horizontally into flats or maisonettes; and
>
> (a) where a building is divided horizontally, the flats or other units into which it is so divided are not separate 'houses', though the building as a whole may be; and
> (b) where a building is divided vertically the building as a whole is not a 'house' though any of the units into which it is divided may be.

Each constituent part is subject to judicial scrutiny and scholarly debate. Key aspects are as follows:

- It must be a permanent structure, so a moving one such as a houseboat would not qualify.
- 'Designed or adapted for living in': this does not necessarily mean purpose built, it could be, e.g. a converted barn. The question to be asked is: could it be lived in as a residence?
- 'Reasonably so called' could include mixed use. The broad phrase gives considerable scope for judicial interpretation but does exclude, e.g. a block of flats.
- It does not need to be structurally detached, and therefore includes terraced and semi-detached houses (but see below re overlapping). It does not matter if it is divided horizontally into flats.

PART III: INDIVIDUAL RIGHTS

- No material part must be below or above part of the structure not included in the house.
- Individual flats or houses or units inside a house are excluded.
- Issues often arise as to the extent of overlap or overhang with other premises. Whether this would be material depends on the circumstances of the particular case: 2 per cent of the overall area of the premises is unlikely to be material whereas 10 per cent is likely to be. See *Malekshad v. Howard de Walden Estates Ltd* [2002] All ER 193, HL.

7.5.6 Residency test

For claims made after 20 July 2002, in most cases there is no longer any requirement for the tenant to show that he has occupied the house as his main residence. As stated in **7.5.2** above there is a residence test where the tenancy falls under Part 2 of the 1954 Act or where a flat forming part of the house is let to a qualifying tenant for collective enfranchisement and lease extension purposes.

Where this is relevant there are a number of evidential matters which will need to be carefully examined to establish whether the tenant has occupied the house as his residence and if so for what periods.

7.5.7 Low rent test

One of the qualifying criteria in the 1967 Act in its original form was that the tenancy had to fulfil a low rent test. Simply put, this involves a comparison between the annual rent under the lease and either the rateable value of the letting value or a specified amount depending on when the tenancy was granted.

Strictly speaking, the low rent test remains but for almost all circumstances (save for excluded tenancies) it is not relevant as a qualifying criterion as the tenant will have the right to enfranchise even if the tenancy is not one at a low rent.

It can still be relevant for determining the basis of valuation. See **7.12** below.

The rules for ascertaining whether the low rent test is fulfilled are complex and have been amended on a number of occasions. It is beyond the scope of this book to set them out in detail. Where they might apply, even though in infrequent circumstances, such as establishing the correct method of valuation, a careful analysis should be undertaken.

7.6 PRELIMINARY INVESTIGATIONS BY THE TENANT

7.6.1 General

Particular care needs to be taken to ensure not only that the qualifying criteria are met, but that any potential issues arising are anticipated and that funding is available for the payment of the estimated price. The following are some primary matters which need to be considered:

- the title of the house and the lease itself must be checked; the existence of supplemental leases, deeds of variation, licences and the like, both of the house and any ancillary premises, should be ascertained and copies obtained;
- the name and address of any landlord and their title and the chain of superior titles;
- the extent of the premises to be included;
- a valuation should be obtained and possibly a survey;
- are there any special classes of landlord, leases of an unusual type, e.g. shared ownership or any other unusual features which require further investigation?
- What rights of way, other rights or covenants does the tenant need to be included?
- How is the price to be funded?

Some of these areas are looked at in more detail below.

7.6.2 Checking the title

Checking the title of the tenant and the period of ownership should be straightforward if the title is registered. It will also be necessary to obtain the lease and other relevant deeds and documents. One would expect that most primary deeds will be with a lender if the house is subject to a mortgage. However, as many lenders no longer retain deeds, these may be held by the tenant or possibly by solicitors who handled the conveyancing. Whilst any deed amending the term of a lease or the extent of a demise should be registered, some relevant documents such as a licence for alterations will not be. It can sometimes be helpful to check the conveyancing file relating to the acquisition of the property.

Check carefully for additional premises demised. It is possible that these could be registered under a separate title number.

Is there a garden, driveway or outbuildings which might be included? These must also be let under a long lease.

The chain of superior titles should also be easy to check if the landlord's title is registered. It is not so easy if it is not registered. As stated above, there is no entitlement to obtain title information from the landlord prior to service of the tenant's notice.

An inspection, probably by the surveyor carrying out the valuation, will be useful. Particular care needs to be taken where the house is not structurally detached. Check for whether and, if so, the extent of any underlapping or overlapping with adjoining premises.

Floor and location plans of the property showing how it relates to any adjoining premises should be considered.

7.6.3 Information about the landlord

It will be necessary to obtain the name and address of the freeholder and other superior landlords. These could be obtained from a number of possible sources such as rent or service charge demands (the landlord being obliged to provide a name and address in England and Wales for service of notices), from a notice under Landlord and Tenant Act 1985, s.1 (see Chapter **12**), office copy entries of the landlord's title where registered, Companies House (where a landlord is a corporate body) or by direct enquiry of a landlord or their agent.

There is no provision for obtaining information from the landlord concerning its title prior to service of the tenant's notice but where the superior titles are registered it will be readily available from the Land Registry.

7.6.4 Obtaining a valuation and funding

Whilst there is no requirement that a professional valuer be instructed in anything other than a very simple case, it will be essential because of the complex formulae for assessing the price to be paid. Also, whilst there is a right to withdraw from the transaction up to one month after a price has been agreed or determined, in view of the costs which will have been incurred and the potential liability for the landlord's costs, it will be prudent to ascertain as far as possible the parameters of the likely price to be paid so that funding arrangements may be established in principle.

For further information on valuation and choosing a valuer, see Chapter **10**.

The price and the fees of the tenant's advisers and those of the landlord will need to be funded. An estimate should be made. Funding is likely to be more critical the shorter the unexpired term of the lease and the higher the value of the house. The exercise is often used as an opportunity to remortgage the house at a lower interest rate.

7.6.5 Rights of way and covenants

As rights may be lost if notice is not given to the landlord of the desire to include them within the relevant time limits, advance planning is required here.

Consideration should be given to what rights and covenants will be required for the house and any ancillary land or premises. The rights granted by the lease are a good starting point. Any rights attaching to the freehold title will, unless personal to the current freeholder, pass on the acquisition of the freehold unless specifically excluded.

7.7 OTHER PREMISES INCLUDED

These need to be appurtenant to or used in conjunction with the house. Key points to note are as follows:

- they must be let with the house but this could be by supplemental lease or deed;
- they must also meet the long tenancy condition.

Types of premises which could be included:

- a garage – but a car space might not be, depending on the nature of the right;
- outbuildings, such as a shed or greenhouse;
- garden and yard;
- other appurtenances, such as a driveway.

The landlord can require the inclusion of premises where it would cause hardship or inconvenience for it to retain them, e.g. if it is left with an isolated piece of land. It can also ask for exclusion of certain additional premises if the landlord has an interest in other premises and hardship or inconvenience might be caused if it did not retain them. There is a two-month time limit from the date of service of the tenant's notice for the landlord to specify such premises. In such cases it is recommended that these matters be included in the notice of reply.

7.8 TENANT'S NOTICE

The enforcement process is triggered by the service of a tenant's notice.
Key points about the tenant's notice are as follows. It must:

- be in the prescribed form or substantially to the same effect and contain the particulars set out in the 1967 Act and the Notices Regulations (it is

not proposed to list these here, reference should be made to s.22, to Sched. 3, para. 6 to the 1967 Act and to the Notices Regulations);
- show that the financial limits are not exceeded where the valuation is on the 'original' basis (see **7.12** below);
- state the name and address of the person on whom it was served and of any other recipient;
- be signed either by the tenant personally or by their agent, similarly if joint tenants, by both or by their agents;
- but there is no need to state a proposed price.

The notice is not invalidated by any inaccuracy in the particulars or by misdescription of the property to which the claim extends. It can be amended by leave of the court. There is an anomaly in the legislation that not all particulars fall within this saving provision. As with the exercise of previous rights, it is better to get the notice right as far as possible rather than rely on this saving provision. Note that it is possible to serve a new notice without prejudice to the first. However, there could be issues as to the price payable, particularly with a short lease, and on costs and also on assignment.

7.8.1 Service of the notice of tenant's claim

Service on the freeholder or even on an intermediate landlord is sufficient but if the tenant knows of other persons who have an interest superior to their own, he must serve copies on them.

7.8.2 Method of service

Under the Landlord and Tenant Act 1927, s.23, the notice can be served in person or at the last known address in England and Wales by registered or recorded post. However, these methods are not mandatory and it may be necessary to consider other methods.

Note the requirement of a landlord of a dwelling under the Landlord and Tenant Act 1987 to include in a rent demand the address in England and Wales for service. Service on a former landlord where notice of change of landlord has not been given is valid service.

If the landlord or other recipient is a company, it could be served at the registered office.

7.8.3 When can it be given?

Notice can be given during the tenancy or its continuance, even if the contractual term has expired and the tenant is holding over. There is an exception where notice to terminate the tenancy has been given by the tenant and in other limited special circumstances.

7.8.4 Effect of tenant's notice

The primary effect of a tenant's notice is:

- a contract is made on the statutory terms; the usual remedies follow for breach of contract which are enforceable in the county court;
- the price is on the basis laid down in the 1967 Act;
- the contract is on the Statutory Conditions of Sale set out in the Enfranchisement Regulations;
- the tenancy automatically continues until three months after the claim has been determined;
- the landlord can only start forfeiture proceedings with the leave of the court;
- any contract that the landlord has entered into for the sale of the freehold to a third party is discharged unless certain conditions are met;
- compulsory purchase: the tenant will benefit from any increase in the value if they have served a valid notice;
- if the process delays the date of any rent increase, then in limited circumstances there may be a liability for the tenant to pay compensation to the landlord.

Key practice points

- As with the exercise of other rights, use a pre-printed form of notice to minimise the risk of missing out key information.
- Consider serving the notice by hand (where possible) or by ordinary post as well as by recorded delivery. It is not unknown for recorded delivery mail to be returned unsigned even where a current address is used. Avoid the potential risk of argument as to whether the notice has been properly served.
- The notice should be registered at the Land Registry or as a land charge if the landlord's title is unregistered.
- Unlike with other enfranchisement rights there is no statutory time by which an application has to be made to the LVT to enforce the right. The Limitation Acts possibly apply. Note that failure to comply with the terms of the statutory contract can ultimately lead to the claim being lost or deemed withdrawn.
- The right is assignable. Assignment must be at the same time as the assignment of tenancy. It is better to include it in the deed of transfer/assignment of the flat.

7.9 LANDLORD'S RESPONSE

The landlord/recipient of the tenant's notice will wish to undertake an investigative process with a view to considering whether the tenant has established a right, if so, to what premises, and other matters necessary to decide how to respond. The landlord's formal response is by service of a notice in reply. See **7.9.3** below.

A non-exhaustive list of matters a landlord may wish to look at is as follows:
- Investigate the tenant's entitlement.
- Consider whether there are any technical objections to the validity of the tenant's notice and if so, whether to raise these.
- Whether to admit or not to admit the tenant's claim.
- Whether to instruct a surveyor and/or a valuer.
- Checking the landlord's title and any others which are superior to the tenant.
- Whether the landlord wishes to reserve any rights or impose any restrictive covenants.
- Whether there is an estate management scheme.
- Whether the landlord's interest is subject to a charge.
- If there are other landlords, who is the reversioner who will have the conduct of proceedings on behalf of all landlords.
- If the tenant's claim requires him to satisfy the residency test, deciding what evidence should be obtained or lines of enquiry undertaken to verify/attack the tenant's assertion.
- If the low rent test is relevant, checking whether it is met.

The landlord would usually require the tenant to deduce title and pay a deposit. This does not prejudice the landlord's right to challenge the claim.

At any time after service of the tenant's notice the landlord may:

- require the tenant to pay a deposit of £25 or three times the annual rent, whichever is the greater; the tenant has 14 days in which to pay;
- require evidence of the tenant's entitlement; this can be done at any time by written notice to deduce title and (where relevant) to provide a statutory declaration regarding the tenant's occupation on which the tenant relies. The tenant has 21 days to comply. If the tenant's property is registered, office copy entries will suffice, otherwise an epitome of title attaching copies of relevant deeds should be supplied.

The landlord should obtain a valuation. The costs of the valuation, assuming they are reasonable, fall to be paid by the tenant. Similar principles apply to choosing and using a valuer as for the tenant. See Chapter **10**.

7.9.1 Landlord's own residence

A resident landlord may oppose a claim where he reasonably requires possession for his own occupation or that of an adult member of his family. However, this right is extremely restricted since in particular it only applies subject to fulfilment of certain conditions, mainly that the landlord's interest must be purchased or created prior to 18 February 1966. If the landlord establishes his right of opposition under this ground, he will be liable to compensate the tenant.

7.9.2 Landlord's obligations

- The landlord must serve copies of the tenant's notice on all other persons with a relevant interest (freeholder or intermediate landlord) not mentioned in the tenant's claim and to inform the tenant if it does so.
- Where the recipient believes itself to be the reversioner or it knows who is the reversioner it must notify the claimant and serve copies of the tenant's notice on all persons known or believed to have a superior interest to that of the tenant.
- If the reversioner or other landlord's interest is subject to a mortgage, the landlord must notify the mortgagee.
- The landlord must provide information and assistance to other landlords. A landlord who is not the reversioner is liable to contribute to the costs of the reversioner not recoverable from the tenants.

Failure to observe these obligations can lead to a liability to compensate the party who suffers as a result of the default.

7.9.3 Landlord's notice in reply

The primary provisions governing service of the landlord's notice in reply are in s.22 and Sched. 3 to the 1967 Act and in the Notices Regulations.

The notice in reply must:

- be in a prescribed form; reference should be made to the Notices Regulations for the detailed requirements as to its content;
- in particular state whether or not the landlord admits the tenant's claim and if not, the grounds for disputing it;
- be served within two months of the date of service of the notice of tenant's claim.

It should be noted that failure to serve a notice in reply does not prevent the landlord dealing with valuation nor challenging the validity of the tenant's claim, although there could be costs consequences for non-service. Any admission made in the notice will be binding unless induced by reckless misrepresentation by the tenant. See *Jassi v. Gallagher* [2006] EWCA Civ 1065.

Other points to note:

- If the landlord does not admit the claim, grounds with full details must be given.

PART III: INDIVIDUAL RIGHTS

- If the landlord wishes premises to be included or excluded from the premises sought to be included in the claim, this must be done within a two-month period of service of the tenant's claim or else the landlord will lose its right in this regard.

> **Key practice points**
> - The landlord's solicitor should request the tenant to deduce title and pay a deposit as soon as possible following service of the tenant's notice. If the validity of the tenant's notice is disputed, the request can be made without prejudice to any right to challenge the notice.
> - Whilst the failure to serve a notice in reply does not of itself have any immediate adverse consequences for the landlord, the right to require the exclusion or inclusion of premises can be lost and it is generally prudent to serve a notice in reply. Even if the landlord disputes the tenant's right it should include reference to these matters.

7.10 PROCEDURE SUBSEQUENT TO LANDLORD'S REPLY

If the tenant's claim is admitted, the subsequent procedure is governed primarily by the Enfranchisement Regulations which set out the statutory conditions of sale. To recap, the service of a valid tenant's notice creates a statutory binding contract for sale.

If the tenant's claim is not admitted, the tenant would need to apply to the court to enforce his claim, assuming he considered that the landlord's basis of objection was ill-founded.

If no notice in reply is served by the landlord, the tenant will need to apply to the court to assert his right. He can do so at any time after two months from the date when the notice in reply should have been served.

Note: the landlord can still challenge the tenant's claim, so unlike with exercise of other rights, there is no deemed admission by the landlord's failure to serve notice in time or at all. However, it may be penalised in costs.

If the tenant's right is admitted:

- The procedural timetable, governed by the Enfranchisement Regulations, usually runs alongside the negotiations as to price.
- The requirement to complete is triggered by agreement as to price. If there is no agreement on price, the tenant should apply to the tribunal for a determination of this issue and of any other point in dispute in relation to, in particular, the rights or covenants to be included in the conveyance or the extent of the house and premises.
- Court or tribunal proceedings will suspend the timetable.
- See also the procedural flowchart at **B7** in Appendix **B**.
- Notices must be in writing but (apart from the tenant's notice and the landlord's notice in reply) there are no prescribed forms. Whilst notice, e.g.

RIGHT OF A TENANT TO ACQUIRE THE FREEHOLD

by letter would suffice, it is recommended that pre-printed forms are used where possible.

7.10.1 Landlord's title

The tenant can require the landlord to deduce title if there is no notice in reply within two months of service of the tenant's notice or at any time after the service of a notice in reply if the landlord admits the claim or if it denies it, but the claim is subsequently established. Note: see also the following paragraphs regulating rights and covenants.

The landlord has four weeks to deduce title.

7.10.2 Rights of way and restrictive covenants

The landlord may, on written notice to the tenant, require the tenant to state which rights the tenant wishes to include in the conveyance. This can be done at the time of or at any time after service of the notice in reply

The tenant can serve a notice to the landlord requiring the landlord to state what rights and restrictive covenants the landlord wishes to include in the conveyance. This must be done at the same time before service of the tenant's notice requiring the landlord to deduce title.

The recipient has four weeks to respond or is deemed not to require any such rights or covenants to be included.

Regardless of these notice provisions, even if the landlord has served no such notice, the tenant will lose the right to require the inclusion of rights and restrictive covenants if he has not communicated details of such to the landlord on or before requiring the landlord to deduce title. Similarly, if the tenant has not served the relevant notice, the landlord must communicate details of the rights and covenants it wishes to include within four weeks of the tenant's request for it to deduce title otherwise it too will lose its right to require such matters to be included in the conveyance.

Key practice points

- The landlord should specify the rights and covenants it wishes to be included in the conveyance when serving its notice in reply.
- The tenant should serve a similar notice no later than his request for the landlord to deduce title.

The statutory contract includes a timetable of service or requisitions on title and objections.

7.10.3 Preparation of the conveyance

The tenant is responsible for preparing the transfer/conveyance although it may in practice be prepared by the landlord, particularly where the house is part of an estate as the landlord is likely to have a standard form.

7.10.4 Contents of the transfer/conveyance

Certain rights are automatically included, such as those of support and similar. It is recommended that these be specified so that they are clearly set out for the purposes of the Land Registry title. Rights of way are those necessary for the reasonable enjoyment of the house and premises.

7.10.5 Common facilities and maintenance

There is no satisfactory mechanism save where there is an estate management scheme for either forcing the landlord to provide such facilities or for the tenant to pay for them. There may be some technical arguments for inclusion of relevant provisions by implication in certain circumstances but in practice it is recommended that the parties try to reach agreement on these issues outside of the statutory framework.

7.10.6 Rights reserved

Certain of these are automatically reserved in a similar way to those that are included. However, from the landlord's perspective it is recommended that there be an express reservation of a right to build on adjoining property, assuming that the landlord holds such a right, with a view to avoiding any argument as to whether such building might infringe any right of air or light of the tenant's premises.

7.10.7 Restrictive covenants

The landlord cannot per se require the inclusion or continuance of covenants in its lease. The exceptions to this are where they are capable of benefiting other property subject to the fulfilment of other conditions, namely:

- the covenant is enforceable by persons other than the landlord;
- if it is enforceable only by the landlord, it will materially enhance the value of other property.

The landlord should have included reference to any estate management scheme in the notice of reply, but this will bind the property in any event. It is usual to refer to the scheme specifically in the transfer/conveyance.

The landlord can also require the inclusion of covenants if they do not interfere with the existing use of the house but materially enhance the value of other property in which the landlord has an interest.

The tenant can require the inclusion of restrictive covenants continued in his lease which affect other premises. However, there can be a difficulty if the landlord is no longer the owner of the other property. In this circumstance, the tenant would need not to merge the lease with the freehold so that the benefit of the covenant would continue. See **7.13** below.

7.10.8 Overriding position on covenants

Neither party can require the inclusion of a covenant which is unreasonable in view of changes since the tenancy was created or of the interests having regard to neighbouring properties which are or were subject to similar tenancies. Reference should be made to s.10 of the 1967 Act.

Key practice points

- The landlord may try to impose/retain onerous covenants. Tenants and their advisers should scrutinise critically any such proposed covenants which may have an adverse effect on the enjoyment of the house or its value, e.g. if there is a covenant against making alterations.
- A copy of any applicable estate management scheme should be obtained and checked and restrictions compared with covenants proposed by the landlord.

7.11 COMPLETION

This must be at least four weeks after the purchase price has been agreed or determined. The timetable for completion begins after such agreement or determination but the completion date itself is triggered by a notice given by either party specifying the first working day after four weeks of the giving of that notice.

There can be an extended time limit for completion in certain circumstances, in particular where there is a subtenant involved or if there are other relevant court or tribunal proceedings pending or on death or incapacity.

There is interest payable for late completion.

7.11.1 Failure to comply with statutory contract terms or completion notice

Either party may give two months' written notice referring to condition 10 and specifying its default and requiring the defaulting party to make good. If the tenant fails to comply, the contract is discharged and the landlord can forfeit the deposit. If the landlord fails to comply, the contract is discharged and the tenant does not have to pay the landlord's costs and his deposit is returned.

Since the tenant almost invariably wishes the contract to be completed, he is unlikely to want to serve a default notice and will more likely seek to use other remedies such as seeking specific performance of the contract.

Service of a default notice is without prejudice to accrued remedies such as damages

7.11.2 Practical matters on completion

The tenant can be required to pay rent and other payments due under the lease up to the date of completion with the date itself apportioned in favour of the landlord.

For mortgages, see **7.18** below. In practice, standard conveyancing procedures will be used to ensure that any charges on superior titles are discharged, e.g. an undertaking from the landlord's solicitor to repay any mortgage and to obtain and provide the discharge form DS1.

Clearly, if there are special circumstances, such as a missing landlord or dealing with a mortgagee in possession, reference should be made to the relevant statutory requirements and/or special care taken to ensure that clear title is obtained.

7.12 VALUATION

7.12.1 Valuation date is the date of service of the notice of tenant's claim

There are three methods of valuation. Establishing which method applies can be very complex – see below. It is rare that a house qualifies under the 'original' qualifying criteria so as to benefit from the first (most advantageous from the tenant's perspective) method known as a s.9(1) valuation. Where it is considered that there is a possibility that a s.9(1) valuation might apply the matter might be discussed initially between the tenant's solicitor and valuer and if there is likely to be sufficient money at stake it is recommended that the advice of specialist counsel be obtained.

The valuation principles are highly technical and these matters are usually referred to specialist valuers, one for the tenant and one for the landlord. The main provisions are in ss.9 and 9A of the 1967 Act. For further details on valuation issues and for an example of a valuation for this type of claim, see Chapter **10**.

RIGHT OF A TENANT TO ACQUIRE THE FREEHOLD

Summary of the valuation position

The three bases of valuation are:

- Where the original qualifying criteria are met as to the low rent test, the rateable value limits and long tenancy provisions, the tenant's claim must not rely on the amendments made to these criteria in the Leasehold Reform, Housing and Urban Development Act 1993, the Housing Act 1996 or the Commonhold and Leasehold Reform Act 2002. Where the tenant can fulfil the 'original' criteria, then the basis of valuation is under s.9(1). The house and premises must also fall within the additional rateable value or other financial limits.
- Where the original criteria are not met then the basis of valuation will be under s.9(1A) or (1C). Section 9(1A) applies where the original qualifying criteria are met but the house exceeds additional rateable value and financial limits. A s.9(1C) valuation is similar to that under s.9(1A) but with modification of some of the valuation assumptions.

The key differences between a valuation under s.9(1) and under s.9(1A) or (1C) are as follows:

- Under s.9(1) there will be no marriage value regardless of the unexpired length of term of the tenant's lease.
- It is based on a site value and modern ground rent whereas the new bases of valuation use market value. A marriage value is payable unless there is more than 80 years unexpired at the date of service of the tenant's notice.
- All methods have various assumptions and disregards applied to them.
- Under s.9(1), the value of improvements made by the tenant can be included; under s.9(1A) or (1C) improvements made by the tenant or his predecessors in title are not taken into account.

In view of the importance of establishing the correct basis of value, particularly where the term of the lease has less than 80 years unexpired at the date of the tenant's notice, careful consideration should be given to the qualifying criteria as to whether the low rent and rateable value and other financial limits are met.

7.13 MERGER

The title of the tenant's lease and of the freehold once acquired will not merge automatically. They cannot merge if the tenant's leasehold interest is subject to a mortgage without the consent of that mortgagee. In most cases the tenant will wish for the interests to be merged. A specific request to the Land Registry in this respect will be made. Further consideration should be given in each case as to whether this is appropriate. See in particular **7.10.7** above regarding the continuance of covenants.

7.14 WITHDRAWAL

The tenant may withdraw one month after the price has been agreed or ascertained by giving written notice to the landlord.

7.14.1 Consequences of withdrawal

- The tenant's claim ceases to have effect.
- The tenant is liable to compensate the landlord for interference with the landlord's right to dispose of/deal with the house or any neighbouring premises.
- The tenant is barred for 10 months from serving another tenant's notice to acquire the freehold.
- The tenant must vacate any notice or land charge registered to protect the tenant's notice.

Key practice point

- If the tenant does not exercise his right to withdraw within the one-month time period he is bound to complete the purchase in accordance with the terms of the statutory contract.

7.15 COSTS

The tenant is due to be liable for the landlord's costs whether or not the matter proceeds to completion. There are some limited exceptions, e.g. where the landlord fails to complete after default notice is given.

7.15.1 Which types of costs are payable?

The following costs are payable:

- costs of investigation of the tenant's right and title;
- valuation fees, but not negotiation costs;
- conveyancing costs;
- the reasonable costs of any other relevant reversioner.

7.15.2 Amount of costs

The costs must be reasonable. In the event of a dispute the LVT can determine as to whether any element of the landlord's costs should be included and, if so, what is a reasonable amount.

Tenants should scrutinise carefully any claim for costs submitted by the landlord, in particular, to make sure that any costs relating to negotiations are not included.

The LVT tends to take a fairly conservative approach to the assessment of costs which is of help to the tenant but not so much help to the landlord.

7.16 POSITION WHERE MORE THAN ONE LANDLORD

There are provisions governing the position where there is more than one landlord and as to the entitlements between landlords.

7.16.1 Intermediate landlords

All are entitled to payment of their reasonable costs. They are entitled to separate representation in circumstances in which their title is in question, which would include the extent to which they should benefit from any rights or covenants.

The tenant will acquire all interests in the property which are above his own.

A price must be agreed or determined for each interest. This is paid to the reversioner on behalf of all landlords, but the other landlords can require payment direct.

The lease of any tenant below the tenant's lease will remain unaffected.

The reversioner is the holder of the intermediate interest who has an interest of at least 30 years after the termination of the claimant's tenancy, the termination date being the later of the term date or the date of service of the notice of tenant's claim.

If there is more than one such intermediate interest then the holder of that which is most immediate to the claimant's tenancy will be the reversioner.

If there is no intermediate landlord holding such an interest (as will often be the case), the freeholder will be the reversioner.

The court can appoint another landlord to be the reversioner or remove the reversioner depending on the circumstances, e.g. if it refuses to act or if it would be more appropriate for another landlord to be the reversioner.

7.17 RENTCHARGES

The property can be transferred free of rentcharges with agreement of the rentcharge owner or compulsorily with an application under the Rentcharges Act 1977. Some rentcharges will be overreached. Sometimes the property can be subject to a rentcharge with the rent adjusted or can be apportioned. See ss.8 and 11 of the 1967 Act.

7.18 MORTGAGES AND DEBENTURES

Mortgages are automatically discharged if the tenant pays the necessary amount to the mortgagee or into court.

The mortgagee can join in the transfer to release the mortgage but in practice will follow the standard conveyancing protocols, e.g. an undertaking from the landlord's solicitor and the provision of a discharge form DS1. See **7.11.2** above.

The strict requirement is to pay as much as necessary to redeem the mortgage, where there are two or more mortgages then according to their priority.

There are mechanisms for dealing with mortgages where evidence of receipt in a conventional way cannot be obtained. Reference should also be made to the Land Registry Practice Guide 27 (November 2006).

7.18.1 Debentures

The primary position is that these would be discharged without payment to the debenture holder. However, this is risky as there are exceptions and arguments which can apply and therefore the tenant's solicitor should take a prudent approach; they should undertake a company search, and ensure that the debenture holder releases its rights and that it provides a certificate of non-crystallisation. If a receiver has been appointed or there is a mortgagee in possession of the landlord's interest, then the tenant's notice can be served on them.

7.18.2 Tenant's mortgage

This is not affected and there can be no merger of the freehold or leasehold interest without the mortgagee's consent. In practice the matter would be dealt with with the consent of the mortgagee and the tenant will often require additional funding which would result in the creation of a new charge over the freehold interest which is to be conveyed to the tenant.

7.19 SPECIAL LANDLORDS

Certain public bodies have a right to oppose the tenant's claim where required for development purposes with a certificate from the Secretary of State. There are also limited exceptions for special types of shared ownership lease. Charities are generally bound by the 1967 Act; the Crown is not. However, the Crown may be willing to sell the freehold by separate negotiation.

There are also special provisions for, e.g. a landlord under a disability and missing landlords. In this latter respect, see **7.22** below.

7.20 FORUM

The county court has jurisdiction over most issues except for those relating to the establishment of the valuation/price which is vested in the LVT. However, the LVT has concurrent jurisdictions in certain matters, in particular relating to the content of the conveyance and apportionment of rent and in practice those matters would be referred to the LVT if not directly then by transfer from the county court

For procedural matters relating to the LVT see Chapter **9**.

7.21 CONTRACTING OUT

As one would expect, there are a number of anti-avoidance provisions intended to prevent contracting out. These catch not only those provisions which are intended to exclude or modify the tenant's rights to enfranchise, but also where they have that effect in practice, or they render the tenant liable to a penalty or a disability if he exercises his right. There are limited exemptions, e.g. the 1967 Act would not invalidate an agreement under which the tenant is entitled to acquire the freehold on different terms (which in any case would not prejudice the tenant's right to proceed under the 1967 Act). A surrender of the relevant lease is possible, but the court can state that there is a bad bargain unless the agreement to the surrender has the court's prior approval. Therefore, to ensure that the tenant is bound, it would normally be necessary to obtain such approval. There is a technical issue as to whether the tenant must first serve a tenant's notice in order to give the court jurisdiction.

7.21.1 Design of houses

It might be possible for a landlord to design houses so there is a significant overlap between them with the intention that they would not be 'houses' for the purposes of the 1967 Act. However, it is then possible that the units concerned would become flats for the purposes of the collective enfranchisement and right to a new lease legislation. Another option would be to exclude key parts of the house from the demise, but whether or not a tenant would pay a capital sum for a long lease in these circumstances might be debatable.

7.22 MISSING LANDLORD

The missing landlord procedure where a landlord cannot be found or its identity ascertained only applies where the tenant wishes to acquire the freehold and not to a claim for a new lease of the house.

If there is more than one landlord, and the identity and address of one is known, then if it is the reversioner it can deal with the claim notwithstanding the absence of the other landlord(s), subject to obtaining directions from the court. If it is not the reversioner, then it can apply to the court to be treated as the reversioner. The reversioner can then negotiate the price and sign the conveyance, etc. The missing landlord's part of the price would be paid into court.

Where there is known or believed to be only one relevant landlord, in other words, the freeholder, so that the previous option is not available, then the tenant can apply to the court for directions. The tenant would need to establish that full and proper steps to trace the landlord had been made and that he is entitled to acquire the freehold under the 1967 Act. The court would then give directions as to how the tenant's notice is to be served, e.g. by way of advertisement, and would then deal with matters such as how the price was to be assessed and the execution of the conveyance. It is, however, a convoluted and expensive procedure.

If a landlord is traced after the tenant has applied to the court, the tenant cannot take further steps in the proceedings but the court can give directions.

It should also be noted that if the identity of the landlord is known but the title has passed to the Crown *bona vacantia*, e.g. because the landlord is a company which has been struck off the register (this could include a foreign corporation which has been dissolved), then the usual and more common procedure would be to contact the Treasury Solicitor. Assuming the Treasury Solicitor is satisfied as to the position, he will usually be willing to negotiate a deal with the tenant without recourse to the statutory procedure.

7.23 DEATH OF THE TENANT

7.23.1 Death after service of a notice of tenant's claim

The benefit of the notice passes to the tenant's personal representatives who can continue the claim on his behalf. See s.7.

7.23.2 Death before service of the notice

If the tenant had the right to acquire the freehold of his house immediately prior to his death, then so long as the personal representatives hold the lease they may exercise the right. They must serve the tenant's notice within two years of the grant of probate or letters of administration (s.6A).

If a member of the tenant's family acquires the tenancy, he is treated as having been the tenant during any period when he was resident in the house as his main residence. The persons who also may fall within the definition of a member of the tenant's family are set out in s.7(7).

CHAPTER 8

Right to a new lease of a house

8.1 OVERVIEW

The right to extend the lease of a house is contained in the Leasehold Reform Act 1967. Because of its more restrictive qualifying criteria, the limited extension which is obtained if successful and the generally more attractive option of acquiring the freehold, it is hardly ever used. Therefore it is not proposed to deal with this right other than very briefly.

8.2 FINDING YOUR WAY AROUND THE LEGISLATION

Reference should be made to the 1967 Act. The relevant statutory instruments are the Leasehold Reform (Enfranchisement and Extension) Regulations 1967, SI 1967/1879; the Leasehold Reform (Notices) Regulations 1997, SI 1997/640 (as amended by SI 2002/1715 (for England) and SI 2003/991 (W.140) (for Wales)) and the Housing Association Shared Ownership Leases (Exclusion from Leasehold Reform Act 1967) Regulations 1987, SI 1987/1940. See Chapter **7**.

8.3 KEY FEATURES

- The qualifying criteria are similar to those for enfranchising a house, save that here the house must fulfil a low rent test and fall within a certain rateable value and other financial limits.
- The right is exercised by the service of a tenant's notice. On service of a valid notice the landlord is bound to grant and the tenant is bound to accept a new lease.
- The new lease is for a term of 50 years from the date of expiry of the existing lease.
- No premium is payable but the tenant pays a ground rent. In most cases this is the same as during the existing term but is reviewed after the expiry

of that term The new ground rent is calculated in accordance with the 1967 Act.
- The tenant is liable for the costs of the landlord investigating the right of the tenant to the grant of the new lease and of any valuation.
- Notwithstanding the exercise of the right, a tenant still has the right to acquire the freehold following the separate procedure under the 1967 Act in that regard but has no further right to extend the lease.

PART IV

Miscellaneous

CHAPTER 9

The Leasehold Valuation Tribunal

9.1 OVERVIEW

The Leasehold Valuation Tribunal (LVT) is a creature of statute and its procedure is primarily governed by the Leasehold Valuation Tribunals (Procedure) (England) Regulations 2003, SI 2003/ 2099. There is another set of similar regulations relating to Wales (SI 2004/681 (W.69)) but here we will deal with those relating to England.

9.2 KEY POINTS OF THE PROCEDURE

- The parties are known as the applicant and respondent.
- There is no prescribed form of application but each application must contain certain prescribed information.
- The particulars to be provided are such as are sufficient for an application to be determined and no prejudice is likely to be caused to another party. It is important to note this should not be seen as giving carte blanche to make fundamental omissions in applications and whilst an inaccuracy is unlikely to be as critical as that in a notice initiating a claim, nevertheless care should be taken to ensure that so far as possible relevant prescribed information and documentation is included/attached.
- A specimen application in relation to collective enfranchisement is included at **A8** in Appendix **A**.
- See **www.rpts.gov.uk** which contains information about the LVT and its procedures. However, at the time of publication this is primarily concerned with disputes and not with collective enfranchisement and similar applications and there are currently no forms to download. However, this is likely to change in the future.
- Generally, the procedures in an LVT are flexible. If its rules are not complied with, the LVT can dispense with or relax those requirements. LVT employees are generally helpful and will give guidance on how to deal with particular issues and directions.

- There may be circumstances where particular issues are referred by the court for determination by the LVT.
- Practitioners should note that revised guidance notes on the implementation of LVT procedures were issued by the LVT, which took effect on 8 January 2007. At the time of writing these relate solely to the London panel. These changes were introduced in an attempt to save costs and streamline the LVT's working practices. A booklet, *Leasehold Enfranchisement*, together with accompanying guidance notes, can be obtained from the LVT. Briefly, the changes affect the way the London panel will deal with the listing of applications and the postponement and dismissal of cases. Other panels are likely to follow suit. One of the key changes relates to requests for postponement/adjournment of hearings. See **9.10** below.

9.3 SERVICE

The LVT serves the application on relevant parties.

9.4 DISMISSAL FOR ABUSE OF PROCESS

The LVT can dismiss an application as an abuse of process. It must give a party 21 days' notice of the opportunity to be heard as to why the application should not be dismissed. This power is often used to hurry along claims which are in limbo or perceived as such. The power is rarely used and the Lands Tribunal has made it clear that an applicant must be given clear and specific notice of the intention to dismiss. See *Campomar and another* v. *Pettiward's Estate Trustees* [2005] EGLR 83.

9.5 PRE-TRIAL REVIEW

A pre-trial review (PTR) can be held either at the request of the parties or at the LVT's own motion. The purpose of the PTR is usually to narrow down and identify the issues in dispute.

9.6 STATEMENTS OF CASE

The LVT would normally require the parties to prepare a statement of case setting out the issues. No expert reports will usually be ordered as part of the directions. There is no formal requirement for the contents of experts' reports to comply with the Civil Procedure Rules, but it is suggested this is good practice. Where there is a dispute of fact, witness statements are recommended.

9.7 INSPECTIONS

The LVT has a power to inspect relevant premises, not only the premises in question but also where there are comparables for valuation purposes.

9.8 HEARINGS

Hearings are in public. There is no requirement that a party be represented by solicitor or counsel. Twenty-one days' notice must usually be given, but this can be abridged in urgent cases. The LVT will expect a bundle of documents to be prepared for the hearing. The LVT will consider whether any application can be determined on the basis of written rather than oral representations. It will take account of the views of the parties before deciding whether this would be appropriate. Applications relating to missing landlords or costs are more likely to be dealt with by written representation.

9.9 USE OF INTERMEDIATE HEARINGS

It is sometimes useful to request an intermediate hearing (although this can lead to additional costs), if there is one particular point in dispute which is preventing the parties from moving on to dealing with the remainder of the claim.

9.10 POSTPONEMENT

It is common practice for parties to apply for postponement of hearings, particularly when more time is required for negotiation of terms, and also where terms have been agreed and the parties would like an additional period to complete. In the past such requests have been granted routinely. There are indications that a tougher approach will be adopted by the LVT. For example, the London panel's guidance notes, which took effect on 8 January 2007, make it clear that requests for postponement will only be granted in exceptional circumstances and that parties should be ready to proceed on the date set for the hearing.

A hearing date will be vacated if the parties confirm that terms have been agreed. However, if terms are agreed, apart from outstanding issues on recoverable costs, the LVT has no continuing jurisdiction. Care should be taken by those advising tenants that, where the material terms are agreed, the matter is completed within the relevant timescale and, if it is not, an application is made to the county court by the appropriate date, which should be diarised.

9.11 COSTS

If the LVT dismisses an application as frivolous or vexatious or an abuse of process, or if a party has acted in such a manner or unreasonably in connection with the proceedings, costs can be awarded against it. In England and Wales these costs are limited to £500 and therefore may not prove much of a deterrent. There are indications that the LVT will be taking a firmer stance against parties who act unreasonably.

9.12 APPEALS TO THE LANDS TRIBUNAL

Appeal from the LVT is to the Lands Tribunal. This can only be made with either permission of the LVT or the Lands Tribunal. Appeal must be made 21 days from the sending of reasons for the decision. If the LVT refuses permission to appeal, an application for permission may be made to the Lands Tribunal within 28 days of the LVT's refusal.

Although in principle the appeal at the Lands Tribunal is by way of rehearing, in practice this is limited by the scope of the permission given. The Lands Tribunal's procedure is governed by the Lands Tribunal Rules 1996 as amended. In England, it has the same limited power of awarding costs up to £500 on the same basis as an LVT (see above) whilst in Wales, the Lands Tribunal still has a discretion to award full costs.

The Lands Tribunal is regarded as a court of law, as such appeal is to the Court of Appeal and is limited to points of law. Permission to appeal must be sought directly from the Court of Appeal.

9.13 LVT DECISIONS

Decisions of the LVT are printed on its website; many are also available on the LEASE website (see Appendix C).

Decisions of the LVT are not binding but they can give a useful indication of its approach to particular issues, and also as to what 'novel' propositions are being made by parties.

CHAPTER 10

The valuer and valuation issues

10.1 INTRODUCTION

The valuer's work can conveniently be divided into three sections. First, a report will be required giving the landlord or the tenant as the case may be an estimate of the price to be paid or received for the freehold or new lease. Such a report may also include advice upon the figure(s) to be inserted in the notice or counter-notice for collective enfranchisements and flat lease extensions. Secondly, the valuer will be required to negotiate with the other party or its valuer. Thirdly, the valuer may be required to give expert evidence to an LVT and, in the case of an appeal, to the Lands Tribunal.

The valuer may be required to provide additional services such as verifying that a property physically qualifies and checking plans. On occasion, a detailed measured survey may be required, for instance to establish qualification (namely, that for collective enfranchisement the non-residential parts of the building comprise 25 per cent or less).

Whilst there will be simple cases where the input of the valuer is straightforward, in many cases the success of the project from the client's perspective will be the result of close co-operation between the solicitor and the valuer.

It is essential that the valuer has a good understanding of the law and it is helpful if the solicitor has an understanding of the valuation principles.

10.2 KEY TERMINOLOGY

There follows a brief explanation of some of the key terms likely to be encountered in leasehold reform valuation matters.

- 'Capitalisation rate': this is the interest rate used to assess the present value of an income stream such as a ground rent.
- 'Deferment rate': this is the interest rate applied to the freehold value to arrive at a present value of that interest.

- 'Development value': this expression refers to the additional value that might attach to a property where there is the potential for development; it would frequently take the form of the potential to extend or to add an additional floor.
- 'Hope value': this expression essentially refers to the value attaching to the hope of a future event occurring. It has been most commonly used in the context of the hope of tenants not participating in a collective enfranchisement subsequently wishing to obtain a lease extension; more recently, the expression has come to represent an added value to the freeholder's interest as a result of the expectation that a tenant will apply to extend the lease or purchase the freehold prior to their lease expiring.
- 'Landlord's interest': the value of the landlord's interest is defined in the legislation; in a simple case it comprises the sum of the capitalised ground rent payable under the terms of the lease and the present value of the freehold interest deferred for the unexpired term of the lease.
- 'Marriage value': an element of value that arises only on the merger or 'marriage' of the landlord's interest with the tenant's interest; it is arrived at by deducting from the freehold value the value of the landlord's interest and also of the tenant's interest.
- 'Relativity': the relationship between the value of a freehold interest and the value of the tenant's interest (see below) is known as the relativity; thus, if the value of the freehold interest is £1,000 and the value of the tenant's interest is £800, the relativity is 80 per cent.
- 'Section 15 rent': this is a matter to be considered only in s.9(1) valuations relating to houses under the Leasehold Reform Act 1967; it is defined in s.15(2) of the 1967 Act.
- 'Tenant's interest': this is the value of the tenant's existing lease, excluding tenant's improvements and excluding that part of the value attaching to the 'right to enfranchise'.
- 'Years purchase': this is a common expression used by valuers to define the multiplier used to calculate the present value of receiving an annual income over a defined period.

10.3 HOW TO SELECT A VALUER

A valuer with specialist knowledge of leasehold reform matters is likely to be a Member or Fellow of the Royal Institution of Chartered Surveyors (MRICS or FRICS).

Whilst personal recommendation is often likely to be the best source of an introduction, there are various published sources:

- The *Estates Gazette* contains a directory on a monthly basis: under 'Specialist Property Services', subheading 'Leasehold Enfranchisement'.

THE VALUER AND VALUATION ISSUES

- The Royal Institution of Chartered Surveyors recommendations service can be useful: see Appendix **C**.
- LEASE, the government sponsored Leasehold Enfranchisement Advisory Service, also maintains a list of valuers: see Appendix **C**.
- Leasehold reform is a specialist area and not all residential valuers would be suitably qualified to assist. The valuer should be asked about his experience in this field.

In areas where there is a good deal of leasehold reform work, particularly in Central London, there may be valuers who work exclusively either for landlords or for tenants although most will regularly act for both.

10.4 HOW TO INSTRUCT A VALUER

The initial approach should preferably be made by telephone so that the case may be discussed in outline and the availability of the valuer established within the timescale required.

Many valuers will have a fairly standard instruction letter and terms and conditions specific to their firm available to be sent on request.

The information required by the valuer is likely to include the following:

- a description of the property and the address of the property;
- full name, address and contact details for the client;
- contact details for access to inspect;
- office copy entries;
- copy lease(s);
- copy headlease(s) where there are intermediate leasehold interests;
- copy licences, particularly relating to tenant's improvements;
- a plan of the property together with a note as to whether this needs to be checked;
- where the valuer is acting for a landlord, a copy of the tenant's initial notice (if served);
- in a collective enfranchisement matter, a specimen standard lease of a flat with details of any variations in leases of specific flats where known, together with a schedule of ground rents, rent review particulars and lease commencement and termination dates.

Also in a collective enfranchisement matter, a briefing note including background information and any likely complications such as the inclusion of a caretaker's flat or development value would be helpful.

Where a block of flats contains a commercial element, the cost of a valuation in respect of that part might be significant. It is not unusual in such circumstances to request in the first instance an illustrative valuation with further advice being sought at a later date if required.

There are two principal aspects to the valuer's expertise in leasehold reform matters:

- the technical ability and up-to-date knowledge of the detailed valuation issues and negotiating points;
- the degree of local knowledge of values.

In Central London, some of the major estates will engage a specialist firm to deal with the technical aspects and a local estate agent or valuer to provide the valuation input. It is rare that a tenant will engage more than one valuer. In selecting an appropriate valuer, therefore, a compromise will on occasion have to be made. In these cases it is usual to appoint a specialist, if needs be from outside the immediate area of the property, although in such circumstances the valuer will have to carry out additional work in order to familiarise himself with local values.

10.5 VALUER'S FEES

There is no set basis for the valuer's remuneration. Most commonly, the valuer will quote for the initial report either a fixed fee (possibly plus disbursements) or a percentage of freehold value.

In the case of a proposed collective acquisition, if the client is a newly formed company, the valuer will wish to have sufficient information to be assured that his fee will be paid.

For the second stage of the work, namely negotiations and liaison, the valuer will most commonly quote a fee based on a time charge, possibly subject to a minimum fee. Where acting for tenants, some valuers will offer a performance-related fee and where acting for landlords, some valuers will propose a fee based on a percentage of the premium. In both of these latter cases there may be a time charge as well or a minimum fee.

Performance-related fees where the valuer is acting on behalf of a tenant are best agreed once the counter-notice has been seen. Some landlords will counter-notice at extraordinarily high figures which if used as the basis for a performance-related fee can lead to a very high fee being incurred.

Where a matter is referred to the LVT or on appeal to the Lands Tribunal, the valuer's fee will normally be calculated on a time basis. Performance-related fees are not permitted in these circumstances.

There may be additional fees for administration of the collective enfranchisement, assistance with the structuring of the transaction, introduction of finance and other services.

Where the valuer is acting for a tenant, it should be borne in mind that the tenant will also be responsible for the reasonable valuation fees of the landlord(s). Where the valuer is acting for a landlord it will usually require to be paid by its client within a reasonable time. The client, however, should bear in mind that it can recover a reasonable fee (not necessarily the full amount) from the tenant in due course.

10.6 KEY PRACTICE POINTS

10.6.1 Generally

- The necessary copy documents should be collated and sent to the valuer prior to his inspection.
- Clear instructions should be given to the valuer together with relevant background information.
- Probably less than one in a hundred cases will be referred to the LVT.
- The tenant's offer figure in the case of a lease extension or a collective enfranchisement needs to be realistic and capable of justification by the valuer, whereas this rule does not currently apply to the landlord's counter-offer. The tenant and his adviser should not generally be unduly concerned when the landlord proposes what appears to be an excessive price.
- Remember that it may be appropriate to approach the landlord to ask if it will consider a 'voluntary' transaction prior to service of a formal notice. This may well save costs. It is rarely worthwhile delaying too long if a swift response is not received.
- Copy notices, counter-notices and other relevant documentation sent or received by the solicitor should be promptly copied to the valuer, where appropriate.

10.6.2 Collective enfranchisement

The valuer should be consulted on the terms of the participation agreement. The valuer may well be able to introduce investors to take up non-participant and other interests.

Consideration should be given as to whether the client, the solicitor or the valuer should manage the process.

The valuer may consider providing a very approximate preliminary indication of likely premium cost in order to assist prospective participants to decide whether or not they may wish to join in a scheme and incur full report fees.

PART IV: MISCELLANEOUS

10.6.3 Flats: lease extensions

It is essential to remember that marriage value becomes payable as soon as there is 80 years or less unexpired at the valuation date. This is relevant to both flat lease extensions and collective enfranchisements. The inclusion of marriage value can vastly increase costs.

A lease extension application can be made only after a flat has been registered in the name of the prospective applicant for a period of at least two years. Where a flat is purchased without taking an assignment of a notice and a lease extension application is intended to be made, the unexpired term therefore needs to be sufficiently in excess of 82 years to allow for the necessary procedures to be completed before marriage value is taken into account.

10.6.4 Houses

The valuer may wish the solicitor to advise on the applicable valuation rule. See Chapter 7.

There is no requirement to state a price in notices under the 1967 Act but a tenant is well advised to obtain a valuation prior to the service of the tenant's notice initiating the claim.

10.7 UNDERSTANDING THE REPORT

There is no standard form of report and so the layout and content will vary from one valuer to another.

A typical report will cover the extent of the valuer's instructions followed by details of the location, description, accommodation, construction, tenure and town planning.

It is important to read through all of these sections. The solicitor will frequently not have seen the property and will gain an understanding of what is involved from the report. The valuer will often request in its report that the tenure and town planning sections in particular be checked by the solicitor acting.

The report will then typically continue with a brief outline of the formal procedure and an explanation as to the valuation methodology followed by the estimated premium. This is often accompanied by detailed calculations. Particularly in cases which are considered highly negotiable, the valuer will sometimes illustrate a range of figures, often referring to the 'landlord's approach' and the 'tenant's approach'.

An appropriate offer or counter-offer figure will often be included. In a proposed collective acquisition, advice will normally be provided (if requested) as to how the overall anticipated price might be equitably shared.

It should be appreciated that the capital figures incorporated in the report will frequently not be the same as 'market values' due to the assumptions required by the relevant legislation, such as the property being treated as being in 'lease condition' and values excluding 'the right'.

Further, it should be appreciated that the report will usually not be as definitive as might be expected in a valuation, e.g. for loan security purposes. It will rather be an estimate of how a future negotiation might be concluded and which is subject to future influences such as additional valuation evidence or LVT or Lands Tribunal decisions that become known during the period of negotiation.

Such factors might well be referred to within the body of the report and on occasion the possible effect of a potential change in a relevant matter such as deferment rate might be illustrated.

10.8 NEGOTIATIONS

The negotiations are conducted by the valuers for the landlord and tenant respectively.

If a voluntary settlement is to be attempted without service of a formal notice, there will be instances where this is best initiated either by the solicitor or the client in the alternative. This issue is best discussed between the solicitor and valuer.

The solicitor serving a counter-notice will commonly notify the applicant of the identity of the landlord's valuer and request the identity of the applicant's valuer. Once received, the respective solicitors should pass this information on promptly to enable the negotiations to commence.

The negotiations are conducted on a technical basis, item by item, commencing with agreement of the basic factual information and then moving on to agreement of capital values, capitalisation and deferment rates and the like.

Where the matter becomes protracted and an agreement is not reached within two months of the counter-notice, the solicitor and valuer for each party should discuss with their respective clients the desirability of making an application to the LVT for a hearing date either at the soonest opportunity, being two months after the counter-notice, or at the latest opportunity, being before six months after the counter-notice, or at some time in between. This application can be made either by the landlord or the tenant but if it is not made by either party, the claim will fall away. These dates are critical.

Most simple claims and many complex or protracted claims are settled prior to additional costs being incurred in the preparation of expert reports for and hearings at the LVT.

Those not settled prior to that stage are sometimes settled 'at the door' of the LVT.

PART IV: MISCELLANEOUS

It is for the solicitor to negotiate the terms of the new lease or transfer. These negotiations may take place in parallel with the valuer's negotiations as to the price or may take place once the price has been agreed.

The valuer and the solicitor should discuss the terms of the new lease or transfer during the course of the negotiations as to the price as the value may be affected by the legal terms.

10.9 LEASEHOLD VALUATION TRIBUNALS

After an application is made for an LVT hearing, the LVT will either notify the respective party's solicitors of a proposed date or will request a list of dates to avoid. It is essential that the solicitor should immediately notify the valuer, particularly where a 14-day period is given during which the unavailability of the valuer will allow an alternative date to be offered.

Changes of hearing date beyond the permitted period can be extremely difficult to achieve.

The LVT will set down a timescale, which is covered in Chapter **9** and discussed in the chapters dealing with each specific right.

The 'applicant' (who can be either the landlord or the tenant) is required to make a statement of case to which the 'respondent' must reply within the given timescale.

The solicitor and valuer should discuss the statement of case or reply as appropriate and decide if one or the other will prepare the relevant document. Very often it will be a joint production.

Whilst it is permissible for the subsequent valuer's expert report to come to a conclusion different from that put forward in a statement of case or reply, this is not desirable unless there is some good reason, such as new evidence having come to light in the intervening period.

The LVT will also direct that the respective parties agree a statement of facts. In a straightforward case this may be entirely dealt with by the valuers. In a more complex case the solicitors will also be involved.

Lastly, the LVT will direct that by a certain date each party's valuer must prepare an expert report.

In a complex case, the expert report might involve a great deal of preparation and not infrequently will incur a greater cost than that of the valuer's time at the LVT.

The RICS recommends that wherever possible the valuer should not act both as expert and as advocate. It is, however, quite common that the valuer will so act in straightforward low-value cases and on occasion in more complex higher-value matters.

Where there is to be a separate advocate, usually counsel, he should ideally be involved prior to the statement of case stage and should also be consulted on the statement of agreed facts and the expert report.

It should be borne in mind that the valuer will need to allow time for liaison with the solicitor and for conferences with counsel.

10.10 COLLECTIVE ENFRANCHISEMENT: STRUCTURING AND FINANCIAL CONSIDERATIONS

The valuer involved in a collective enfranchisement may well have a wealth of experience of previous matters where issues both common and unusual may have been raised.

Such experience should, where appropriate, be harnessed when considering the structuring and financial aspects.

Many leasehold reform valuers will also have experience of property management and will be able to consider in advance the practical issues likely to arise following enfranchisement. They may also be able to introduce suitable accountants, insurance brokers and other professionals necessary for the future running of the building by the lessee group.

Where there are non-participators or other areas of the building requiring financing, such as caretaker's accommodation and commercial units, the valuer may well be able to introduce suitable investors.

10.11 VALUATION PRINCIPLES

10.11.1 Collective enfranchisement

Overall, the method is very broadly similar to the arrangement for flats. The first two elements apply to all flats within the building; 50 per cent of the marriage value is payable in respect of participating tenants' flats where the unexpired terms are 80 years or less. Marriage value does not apply in respect of non-participating tenants' flats.

There will frequently be other heads of claim, such as for a caretaker's flat, car parking not demised with the flats and development value.

Figure 10.1 on p.161 shows a simple valuation calculation.

10.11.2 Flats: lease extension

As with houses, there is now no marriage value payable if the lease has an unexpired term of more than 80 years when the claim is made. As advised in Chapter **6**, tenants and their advisers should be alert to situations where that threshold is looming.

The premium payable to the landlord essentially comprises three or four elements:

PART IV: MISCELLANEOUS

- an amount to compensate the landlord for loss of ground rent during the remainder of the existing term;
- an amount to compensate the landlord for not receiving possession of the flat at the end of the existing term (together these are known as the value of the landlord's interest);
- 50 per cent of the marriage value: the marriage value is arrived at by deducting from the value of the extended lease, the adjusted value of the existing lease and the value of the above-mentioned landlord's interest; the adjustments made primarily relate to condition and the assumption that the tenant does not have the right to extend;
- there may be other compensation due in respect of loss of development value.

Figure 10.2 on p.162 shows a typical simple valuation calculation.

10.11.3 Houses

There are three valuation methods for houses. The correct approach depends upon the individual circumstances, which are covered in Chapter **7**.

In most cases found today where the qualification arises out of the Leasehold Reform, Housing and Urban Development Act 1993, marriage value will be included in the calculation as will any compensation that might be due in respect of loss of development value. Therefore, by far the most common basis of valuation is under s.9(1C) of the 1967 Act.

There is no marriage value payable if the lease has an unexpired term of more than 80 years when the claim is made. It is thus important that tenants with unexpired terms in excess of 80 years should make a claim before that threshold. Claims made even just after this point has passed are likely to be a great deal more costly.

Figure 10.3 on p. 163 shows a typical simple valuation on a s.9(1C) basis.

10.12 RECENT DEVELOPMENTS IN VALUATION

10.12.1 Tenant's offer

In recent years, there have been a number of court decisions on the question of the level of the tenant's offer in individual flat lease extension and collective enfranchisement notices. The current position is that the tenant's offer must be at a level which is capable of being supported by a valuation. This does not necessarily mean that the tenant should offer the amount that it actually expects to pay. An unrealistically low offer at the notice stage may, however, lead to the notice being invalid. The current position relating to landlord's counter-notices is not affected by these cases.

10.12.2 Deferment rate

For some time a number of the major London land-owning estates have been contending that the deferment rate used in the calculations for all classes of property are too high.

A lower deferment rate increases the cost to the tenant and the effect of this is greater the longer the lease.

The first notable success for landlords occurred in the Lands Tribunal in 2004 in *Cadogan Holdings Ltd* v. *Pockney*, EW Lands LRA/27/2003. This concerned a terraced house in a good part of Chelsea where the Tribunal decided that a 5¼ per cent deferment rate was appropriate as opposed to the 6 per cent that would have been commonly agreed prior to this case.

In 2005, the Lands Tribunal in *Arbib* v. *Cadogan* [2005] 3 EGLR 139 OR (which was in fact a group of appeals heard together) decided that the appropriate deferment rate for houses in the best areas of Central London was 4½ per cent and for flats 4¾ per cent.

The decisions in these cases also had the effect of lowering rates being agreed in the rather less good parts of Central London and, to an extent, beyond, than had previously been the case.

In September 2006 the Lands Tribunal decided in another group of appeals heard together, this time with financial experts representing certain of the parties in addition to valuers, that the appropriate deferment rate for houses was 4¾ per cent and for flats 5 per cent.

The appeal is generally referred to as *Cadogan* v. *Sportelli* EWLANDS LRA/50/2005 or '*Sportelli*'.

Whilst it is stated in the decision that the rates will need to be considered in relation to the facts of each individual case, it is elsewhere stated that it is expected that these rates will apply everywhere.

Whilst the effect of this decision in the very best Central London locations is modestly beneficial to tenants, its effect outside these areas varies from moderately disadvantageous to catastrophic.

It had previously been the case that quality of location was reflected not only in open market values but also in the level of the deferment rate applied, and thus in suburban areas where a deferment rate may previously have been taken at perhaps 7 to 8 per cent or more, the effect of this decision is enormous. Individual cases where the cost has increased by a factor of three or more are not uncommon.

It remains to be seen if this decision is appealed in the future.

10.12.3 Hope value

The *Sportelli* decision has altered the position regarding 'hope value'. Previously, in collective enfranchisements, the landlord was on occasion allowed a proportion of the marriage value in respect of non-participating flats as 'hope value'. There was, however, no consistent approach by LVTs.

This Lands Tribunal has, however, decided that in future there should be no hope value in these cases at all.

In the case of lease extensions of flats where hope value has not previously been considered, there is no change.

For houses, again there had not previously been any consideration of hope value. This Lands Tribunal has, however, decided that there should be included in the value of the landlord's interest an element of 'hope value' to reflect the possibility of the tenant wishing to purchase the freehold interest prior to the end of their lease. This is a novel concept and one where the cost to tenants is increased.

At least one subsequent LVT has decided that this concept is incorrect and thus a further appeal might be anticipated.

THE VALUER AND VALUATION ISSUES

Inputs

Number of Flats	6
Length of lease remaining (yrs)[a]	50
Ground rent (per flat per annum fixed)	£100
Virtual Freehold Vacant possession value of each flat[b]	£300,000
Relativity between freehold & long leasehold	99%
Value of each of the existing flat leases[c]	£230,000
Yield: Capitalisation	6.00%
Yield: Deferment	5.00%

A **Diminution in value of Freeholders' Interest**

Capitalised Ground Rents

Initial Total Ground rents per annum;			£600		
Years' purchase for:	50 years at 6.0%	15.7619			
				£9,457	
					£9,457

Reversionary interests

Value of freehold interest with vacant possession			£1,800,000		
Present value of £1 after	50 years at 5.0%	0.0872			
				£156,967	
					£156,967
Value of the Freeholders' Interest excluding Marriage Value					**£166,424**

B **Marriage Calculation**

Value of freehold interest with vacant possession	£1,800,000	
Less		
The value of the Diminution of the Freeholders' Interest (as above)	£166,424	
The value of the lessees' existing leases	£1,380,000	
	£1,546,424	
Total marriage value	£253,576	
Freeholders' share @ 50%		**£126,788**
Total enfranchisement price excluding costs		**£293,212**

(a) The period from the valuation date until the expiry of each of the flat leases.
(b) Excludes tenants Improvements.
(c) Excludes tenants Improvements and that part of the value which is attributable to the right to enfranchise.

Figure 10.1 Typical simple valuation for a collective enfranchisement under the Leasehold Reform, Housing and Urban Development Act 1993, as amended by the Commonhold and Leasehold Reform Act 2002

PART IV: MISCELLANEOUS

Inputs

Length of lease remaining (yrs)[a]	50
Ground rent (per annum fixed)	£100
Virtual Freehold Vacant possession value[b]	£300,000
Relativity between freehold & long leasehold	99%
Value of the extended lease (Existing lease plus 90 years)	£297,000
Value of the existing lease[c]	£230,000
Yield: Capitalisation	6.00%
Yield: Deferment	5.00%

A Diminution in value of Freeholders' Interest

Capitalised Ground Rents

Initial Total Ground rents per annum; £100
Years' purchase for: 50 years at 6.0%   15.7619
                                                          £1,576
                                                                        £1,576

Reversionary interests
Reversion to Freehold before lease extension   £300,000
Present value of £1 after   50 years at 5.0%   0.0872
                                                          £26,161

Less
Reversion to Freehold after lease extension   £300,000
Present value of £1 after   140 years at 5.0%   0.0011
                                                          (£324)
                                                                        £25,837

Value of the Freeholders' Interest excluding Marriage Value   **£27,413**

B Marriage Calculation

Value of the Lessees' extended lease (Existing lease plus 90 years)   £297,000

Less
The value of the Diminution of the Freeholders' Interest (as above)   £27,413
The value of the lessees' existing lease   £230,000

                                                          £257,413

Total marriage value   £39,587

Freeholders' share @ 50%   **£19,793**

Total enfranchisement price excluding costs   **£47,207**

(a) The period from the valuation date until the expiry of the lease.
(b) Excludes tenants Improvements.
(c) Excludes tenants Improvements and that part of the value which is attributable to the right to enfranchise.

Figure 10.2 Typical simple valuation for a flat lease extension under the Leasehold Reform, Housing and Urban Development Act 1993, as amended by the Commonhold and Leasehold Reform Act 2002

THE VALUER AND VALUATION ISSUES

Inputs

Length of lease remaining (yrs)[a]	40
Ground rent (per annum fixed)	£150
Freehold Vacant possession value[b]	£500,000
Relativity between freehold & long leasehold	99%
Value of the existing lease[c]	£350,000
Yield: Capitalisation	5.50%
Yield: Deferment	4.75%

A Diminution in value of Freeholders' Interest

Capitalised Ground Rents

Initial Total Ground rents per annum;			£150	
Years' purchase for:	40 years at 5.5%	16.0461		
			£2,407	
				£2,407

Reversionary interests

Value of freehold interest with vacant possession			£500,000	
Present value of £1 after	40 years at 4.75%	0.1563		
			£78,128	
				£78,128
Value of the Freeholders' Interest excluding Marriage Value				**£80,535**

B Marriage Calculation

Value of freehold interest with vacant possession	£500,000	
Less		
The value of the Diminution of the Freeholders' Interest (as above)	£80,535	
The value of the lessees' existing lease	£350,000	
	£430,535	
Total marriage value	£69,465	
Freeholders' share @ 50%		**£34,732**
Total enfranchisement price excluding costs		**£115,268**

(a) The period from the valuation date until the expiry of the lease.
(b) Excludes tenants Improvements.
(c) Excludes tenants Improvements and that part of the value which is attributable to the right to enfranchise.

Figure 10.3 Typical simple house valuation under Leasehold Reform Act 1967, s.9(1C)

CHAPTER 11

Companies, corporate formalities and taxation

11.1 OVERVIEW

This chapter looks at some of the key considerations from a company and tax law perspective. Clearly, these are potentially complex areas and for the purposes of this book, only general information can be given.

Company law considerations will apply mainly to the exercise of collective rights. Participating tenants and their advisers need to consider the appropriate corporate structure (although in RTM matters this is prescribed) and the rights and obligations of the company and its officers.

There are a number of changes to company law in the Companies Act 2006 which will apply as and when the relevant provisions come into force.

In almost all enfranchisement matters and to a lesser extent in RTM matters, potential tax issues will arise.

11.2 COLLECTIVE ENFRANCHISEMENT STRUCTURES

The structure used to initiate the process of collective enfranchisement should be carefully considered before the process is begun and practitioners should ensure that their clients understand the applicable regulatory and tax issues.

It is important that participating tenants have the appropriate structure in place to move the enfranchisement process forward and that the structure is properly crafted to regulate the relationship between them.

11.2.1 Nominee purchaser

At present the right to collective enfranchisement may be exercised by a group of qualifying tenants acting through a nominee purchaser. 'Nominee purchaser' is not defined and, as such, can in theory be any legally recognised entity. It is rare, however, to see individuals, trusts, partnerships and unincorporated associations acting as nominee purchaser as these arrangements do not usually allow the participating tenants sufficient control over the freehold ownership and management. The use of a Limited Liability Partnership was mooted by Parliament as an option but was rejected. It is therefore not possible to nominate an LLP as LLPs must be trading vehicles with a view to making profit.

The primary options when considering the structure of a nominee purchaser are therefore (1) a company limited by guarantee or (2) a company limited by shares. The two structures have a number of common characteristics:

- limited liability;
- separate legal identity;
- easily transferable membership and management;
- liability to corporate taxation;
- regulated by Memorandum and Articles of Association and (usually) by the Companies Act 1985.

There are advantages and disadvantages to both structures, some of which are set out below.

11.2.2 Company limited by guarantee

The liability of the company's members to contribute to its assets on winding up is limited by the amount specified in its Memorandum of Association. This will usually be £1. A company limited by guarantee has no authorised or issued share capital so additional members can be accepted without reference to a fixed share capital, subject to any provisions of the Articles limiting membership.

Companies limited by guarantee are preferred for charitable and not-for-profit organisations as the intention is that any profits made should be reinvested into the company and there should be no payout to members. It is not impossible for companies limited by guarantee to distribute profits but this is not their primary aim as they are not designed to be companies trading with a view to making profits. This dovetails neatly with the purpose of the enfranchisement legislation which also allows tenants to increase the capital value of their leasehold interest by varying the lease to create a longer term at a peppercorn rent. Without rental income from the participating tenants, the freehold company is unlikely to make any profit.

A practical advantage of a company limited by guarantee is that there are no share certificates to be issued (and potentially lost by tenants!) and there is therefore no need to transfer shares between outgoing and incoming tenants with the attendant formalities.

PART IV: MISCELLANEOUS

The main disadvantage of this type of company is that it makes no provision for unequal contributions made by the tenants. This makes it inappropriate in a great many cases where more flexibility as to contributions and benefits to participators is required.

11.2.3 Company limited by shares

The company issues shares (with or without share certificates) to its members. The members' liability to contribute to the company's assets in the event of the company being would up is limited to the amount unpaid on the members' shares. Where shares are fully paid up, there is no further liability for the member to contribute on a winding up.

The advantage of a company limited by shares is that shares or the rights attaching to them can be issued according to the contributions made by the participating tenants. This is likely to assist where there are some participating tenants who cannot contribute either fully or at all to the purchase price. The participating tenants who contribute more can have proportionately increased rights by either having more shares or shares of a different class and/or with additional rights. There is also greater scope for distributing profits. It should, however, be noted that minority shareholders will qualify for protection in accordance with usual company law principles and that an unequal share structure may increase the administrative burden on the company's officers.

Shares can also be transferred and held on trust and pass by operation of law to personal representatives of a deceased tenant or the trustee in bankruptcy of an insolvent tenant. This can be both an advantage and a disadvantage, particularly as there is a risk that a nominee purchaser can be a simple 'off the shelf' company limited by shares which may not have bespoke Articles.

Key considerations

It is vital that a nominee purchaser, whether a company limited by shares or by guarantee, has appropriate bespoke Articles, e.g. to ensure that membership remains with persons who are owners of flats in the building. Many company formation agents now offer companies limited by guarantee as standard for the purposes of collective enfranchisement.

Some of the issues relating to the structure and operation of the companies may be subject to change when the Companies Act 2006 enters into force. It is currently anticipated that there will be a phased introduction of the Act but that the Act will come fully into force by October 2008. It is not proposed to detail the proposed changes here.

11.3 RTE COMPANY

The Leasehold Reform, Housing and Urban Development Act 1993 will require the right to collective enfranchisement to be exercised by a nominee purchaser which is a company limited by guarantee. This provision is not yet in force. It is proposed that there will be prescribed Memorandum and Articles of Association but these have not yet been published. The rationale behind this is to ensure consistency in the exercise of the right. There is some dispute over how best to create a prescribed company constitution which will be both consistent for all RTE transactions yet flexible enough to provide for the infinite variety of circumstances which may be involved. As mentioned elsewhere in this book, this uncertainty has delayed the introduction of the RTE company to the point where some commentators doubt whether it ever will be introduced. See Chapter **4**.

11.4 RTM COMPANY

Tenants are only permitted to exercise the right to manage through an RTM company which must be formed prior to the service of the claim notice. There is only one permissible structure for the RTM company which is limited by guarantee. The Memorandum and Articles of Association are prescribed and the only permitted amendment is the insertion of the RTM company's name, registered office and property address. See Chapter **5**.

11.5 DIRECTORS' DUTIES

The corporate structures used in enfranchisement and RTE claims do not have any special status. The officers of the company must comply with the usual directors' duties. The key difference in terms of duties is that directors are likely to be volunteers and are therefore highly unlikely to have any contracts of service with the company. Their duties will flow from their position as officeholders and not employees.

Some of the key duties are as follows:
Fiduciary duties:

- to act in good faith in the best interests of the company;
- to act for proper purposes;
- not to make secret profits;
- to avoid conflicts of interest.

Common law duties:

- of skill and care;
- of mutual trust and confidence.

Statutory duties:

- to creditors and employees;
- to disclose interests in contracts;
- to observe restrictions on, *inter alia*, loans to directors and substantial property transactions;
- health and safety matters;
- procedural requirements;
- to ensure that the company does not trade whilst insolvent.

Directors' duties have been codified for the first time ever in the Companies Act 2006. When this comes into force, directors' duties will be regulated by the provisions of the Act and will include for the first time a duty to promote the success of the company.

11.6 VOTING RIGHTS

The usual structure for a nominee purchaser will be that one flat has one vote. Where there are joint holders of a flat, they will be entitled to one share or one membership and their vote will count as one. Aside from RTE and RTM companies it is a matter for the participant tenants to decide on the appropriate voting structure but deviation from the standard system is uncommon.

The number of members required for a quorum for meetings and other procedural matters for board and company meetings should be considered.

The voting rights for RTM companies are governed by statute. See **5.23** above.

11.7 TAX ISSUES

Taxation is a highly complex subject and it is not proposed to go into any detail here but rather to highlight some potential issues. The taxes with which a corporate nominee purchaser, an RTE company and an RTM company will be concerned are corporation tax, Stamp Duty Land Tax (SDLT) and VAT. The members of the company and leaseholders may be concerned with capital gains tax (CGT), income tax and SDLT in both collective enfranchisement and individual enfranchisement processes. In all enfranchisement matters, the landlord will be primarily concerned with CGT.

11.7.1 Corporation tax and VAT

The purchase of a freehold by a nominee purchaser will usually result in the company holding the property as a bare or simple trustee for the participating tenants. In these circumstances the property should not be recorded as an asset of the company as the company is not the beneficial owner. The company will also be regarded as tax transparent so that any tax payable due to income or capital gains from the property will be the responsibility of the participating tenants. This should mean that no corporation tax will be payable in most circumstances.

In the event that the participating tenants have decided to finance the purchase through a company limited by shares using equity finance, it is likely that the company will hold the property absolutely. This means that any profit realised from the property would be taxable on the company and a corporation tax return may be required. It also means that any payment to the shareholders of the company is likely to be a distribution and subject to income tax on the shareholders. The usual rules relating to the mechanics of making distributions will also apply.

VAT will not usually be an issue as the property will usually be residential. It is possible that the former landlord may have elected to waive any VAT exemption and, in these circumstances, VAT will be payable by the nominee purchaser. It would be very rare for a nominee purchaser to be registered for VAT as it would not usually be a trading company and therefore the VAT could not be offset.

An RTM company will need to consider the tax treatment of service charges and, in particular, any sinking fund. Usually, RTM companies will be treated as mutual companies and will only be subject to corporation tax on investment income.

There is a possibility that investment income earned on service charges may be treated as trust income. RTM and management companies should seek specific tax advice on the effect that this may have.

11.7.2 CGT: tenant's perspective

Many participating tenants will not have to be overly concerned about CGT as it is a charge on the disposal of the property. The key consideration is that the enfranchisement process will usually add value to the property, thus increasing the potential liability to CGT.

The disposal of the property (either the leasehold with the share of the freehold, the extended leasehold or the freehold purchased under the 1967 Act) would usually qualify for principal private residence relief and therefore be exempt from charge. If, however, the tenant does not qualify for such relief, CGT will be chargeable on the gain subject to any relevant allowance.

For collective enfranchisement matters, this may be of concern to the original participating tenants who have contributed to the costs of setting up the nominee purchaser and purchase price where applicable. Such tenants will want to ensure that their contribution to the costs and purchase price can be offset against the gain since it is arguably an improvement to the property.

It should be noted that there is a specific provision denying the availability of principal private residence relief to those participating tenants who have exercised the right to enfranchise with a view to making a profit. Although this provision is little used in practice, tenants seeking to exercise their rights in order to maximise their gain from the property should seek specific advice.

According to Revenue guidance, the leasehold and freehold titles remain separate for the purposes of calculating any CGT payable on disposal. This could lead to some quite substantial tax liabilities if a sale is effected soon after the freehold is purchased and relief is not available.

In cases of individual enfranchisement, this should be less of a problem as the two interests (the original interest and either the freehold of a house or the extension of the lease) will merge. Any expenditure should therefore be deductible.

11.7.3 CGT: landlord's perspective

Where tenants exercise their right to collective or individual enfranchisement by purchasing the freehold or obtaining a lease extension, the landlord will be making a chargeable disposal for CGT purposes.

Because the enfranchisement process is deemed to be compulsory acquisition, the landlord may qualify for roll-over relief provided that:

- the land is disposed of to an authority (in this case the nominee purchaser) having compulsory powers;
- the landowner did not take any steps to advertise his willingness to dispose of the property or make it known to the tenants that he would be willing to dispose of the property;
- the whole of the consideration realised is applied in acquiring other land;
- the acquisition of the new land takes place or an unconditional contract is entered into in the period beginning 12 months before and ending three years after the disposal of the old land (note that the Revenue has discretion to allow a longer period by notice);
- the landowner makes a claim.

This effectively allows the landowner to defer the payment of any CGT until the disposal of the new land. It should be noted that purchasing a property which will have the benefit of the principal private residence exemption will not be classed as new land for the purposes of claiming roll-over relief.

Landlords wishing to take advantage of roll-over relief should insist that any sale takes place in the context of a statutory claim, i.e. that a notice initiating a claim is served. Care should be taken that the notice is not served as a contrivance between the landlord and the tenant purely for the purpose of the landlord claiming roll-over relief as this might be susceptible to challenge by the Revenue.

11.7.4 SDLT

There will be no SDLT implications on the exercise of the RTM as it is not an interest in land and is therefore outside the scope of SDLT.

For the extension of an individual lease under the 1993 Act, the extension operates as a surrender of the existing lease and a regrant of the extended lease as a matter of law. SDLT will be potentially chargeable on the consideration paid for the grant of the extended lease depending on whether the consideration exceeds the threshold.

The purchase of the freehold either individually or collectively will be within the scope of SDLT and is currently chargeable as an ordinary purchase of property in the usual way. In cases of collective enfranchisement, the nominee purchaser will usually be regarded as a bare trustee so that the SDLT liability falls on the participating tenants, as bare trustees are tax transparent. SDLT is calculated on the price and reference should be made to the usual SDLT scale for residential purposes.

When and if RTE companies are introduced, special provisions will apply which will require the following calculation to be undertaken:

- divide the freehold price by the number of participating tenants;
- use the resulting figure to establish the rate of tax applicable to the transaction;
- multiply the total consideration by the rate of tax to reach the figure chargeable.

Example calculation

Five participating tenants purchase their freehold through an RTE company at a price of £300,000.

$$\frac{300,000}{5} = 60,000$$

Applicable rate of tax = 0%

SDLT payable = 0 × 300,000 = £0

The transaction will be notifiable but there are likely to be few freehold purchases by an RTE company which would be of sufficient value to bring them within the chargeable regime, as each participating tenant would be required to contribute over £125,000 towards the purchase price at current rates.

CHAPTER 12

The Commonhold and Leasehold Reform Act 2002 and other relevant rights

12.1 OVERVIEW

When considering the possible exercise of enfranchisement or RTM rights it is useful to have an awareness of other rights which benefit tenants of long leases. These might be used as an alternative or in addition. If tenants are collectively taking over the management of their building, the nominee purchaser or RTM company will have to observe statutory landlord obligations such as following the consultation procedures for major works, the cost of which is to be collected through a service charge.

This chapter contains a note of the main reforms of the Commonhold and Leasehold Reform Act 2002 and summarises the rights applicable to tenants of long leases which have not been covered so far in this book. A number of these rights have been amended by the 2002 Act.

For information on the progress of the bringing into force of these rights, enquiry should be made of Communities and Local Government, see Appendix C. A search on its website using the keyword 'commonhold' should find the correct page.

As only a brief outline of each right is given readers are advised to refer to the primary legislation for more detailed guidance. The relevant statutory provisions for each right are given.

12.2 COMMONHOLD AND LEASEHOLD REFORM ACT 2002

The 2002 Act is a significant piece of legislation affecting landlords and tenants. It introduces a new scheme for the ownership of land called commonhold and reforms the law applying to residential leasehold property. Its primary provisions can be summarised as follows.

Part 1:

- defines the nature of commonhold;
- defines the commonhold unit and the common parts;
- defines the constitution and operation of the commonhold association.

The introduction of commonhold creating a new type of flat ownership more akin to freehold, whilst potentially significant, has been less so in practice as there has been very little take up of it.

Part 2:

- gives tenants a new right to manage their block of flats;
- amends the law for collective enfranchisement under the Leasehold Reform, Housing and Urban Development Act 1993; in particular, further simplifies the qualifying criteria;
- introduces the concept of an RTE company through which a collective enfranchisement claim must be exercised (when these provisions are in force);
- amends the law for the right to a new lease of a flat under the 1993 Act;
- amends the law for the right of tenants of houses to buy the freehold or extend their lease under the Leasehold Reform Act 1967;
- strengthens the protection of tenants against the demanding of unfair charges;
- amends the existing consultation requirements relating to service charges and introduces further safeguards for service charge monies;
- extends the jurisdiction of the LVT.

As stated above, some of the provisions for strengthening the rights of tenants are not yet in force.

12.3 OBTAINING INFORMATION FROM THE LANDLORD

Tenants of flats have a right to serve a notice on the landlord or any person receiving rent on behalf of the landlord requiring the name and address of the person who owns the freehold interest in the flat and details of the tenant's immediate landlord.

This right is provided by s.41 of the 1993 Act. It, e.g. allows tenants to obtain details of any intermediate leases.

The recipients of the notices are required to respond within 28 days.

Under s.1 of the Landlord and Tenant Act 1985, a tenant may make a written request for details of the landlord's name and address to any person who demands rent payable under the lease or acts as agent for the landlord.

The information must be provided within 21 days and failure to do so constitutes an offence.

12.4 RIGHT OF FIRST REFUSAL

If the landlord of a building comprising solely or partly of flats wishes to dispose of its reversionary interest it must first offer it to the qualifying tenants on the same terms.

The right is provided in Part I of the Landlord and Tenant Act 1987 and there are supplementary provisions in the Tenants' Rights of First Refusal (Amendment) Regulations 1996, SI 1996/2371.

In order for the right to apply:

- the premises must be such as specified in the 1987 Act;
- the landlord must not be an exempt landlord;
- the tenants must be qualifying tenants; and
- there must be a proposed 'relevant disposal'.

The number of flats (which must be two or more) held by qualifying tenants must exceed 50 per cent of the total number of flats and the internal floor area of any non-residential parts of the premises must not exceed 50 per cent of the internal floor area of the whole of the premises.

Examples of exempt landlords are local authorities, the Housing Corporation and private sector resident landlords.

A tenant is a qualifying tenant unless his tenancy is:

- a protected shorthold tenancy;
- a business tenancy under Part II of the Landlord and Tenant Act 1954;
- a tenancy terminable on cessation of employment; or
- an assured tenancy under the Housing Act 1988.

Most transfers of a freehold or leasehold reversion will constitute relevant disposals for the purposes of the 1987 Act. The landlord is obliged to serve a notice in a required form. The form of the notice depends on the notice of the disposal, e.g. there is a different notice if there is a proposed sale by auction than if there is a sale by private treaty. It is a criminal offence for the landlord, and possibly for the landlord's advisers, not to serve the offer notice.

In order to exercise the right more than half of the qualifying tenants have to agree to accept the offer. This must be done within two months of service of the landlord's offer.

It should be noted that acceptance by the tenants does not constitute a binding obligation on the landlord to sell, or the tenants to buy. If the tenants serve their acceptance notice, there follows a procedural timetable leading to an exchange of contracts or withdrawal. Failure to follow the statutory timetable would lead to the tenants losing the right of first refusal in respect of that offer.

Where the landlord fails to offer its reversionary interest to the tenants or sells to a third party at a lower price than that offered to the tenants, the tenants can compel the new owner to sell the freehold back to them at the price it paid for it.

12.5 NOTICE OF ASSIGNMENT OF THE FREEHOLD

If a landlord assigns his freehold interest the new landlord must give notice in writing of the assignment and of its name and address to any tenant under s.3 of the Landlord and Tenant Act 1985.

Notice must be given not later than the next day on which rent is payable under the lease or, if that is within two months of the assignment, the end of that period of two months. Failure to give notice constitutes an offence.

Under s.3A of the Landlord and Tenant Act 1985, on assignment of the freehold the new landlord must also give notice to the tenant informing him about his rights under Part I of the Landlord and Tenant Act 1987. If it fails to give notice within the time allowed it will commit an offence.

12.6 SERVICE CHARGES

As is well known, a great many disputes relating to the administration of blocks of flats relate to service charges, their imposition and collection. The following is a checklist of some of the principal considerations when dealing with a service charge dispute.

When looking at whether or not an item of service charge is recoverable:

- Does it fall within the ambit of the service charge provisions of the relevant lease? Have the contractual formalities within the lease been observed, e.g. as to the timing of demands, certification of accounts, etc.?
- If there is a request for payment to a reserve or sinking fund, does the lease permit this?
- Have the legal formalities for a demand, e.g. the name and address of the landlord, been observed?
- What is the limitation period applicable and has it expired? Also, is the item stale in the sense that it was incurred more than 18 months prior to the demand?
- Have the statutory consultation procedures for major works or long-term agreements been followed?
- Have the statutory accounting formalities been observed (once these provisions are in force)?
- Is the charge reasonable? Is there any set off which might be applied?

12.6.1 Service charges: general provisions

Section 19 of the Landlord and Tenant Act 1985 provides that any service charge must be reasonable.

Both landlords and tenants have a right to ask the LVT to decide whether a charge, or a proposed charge, is reasonable.

The 1985 Act sets out the basic rules for service charges, defining what is considered a service charge and setting out requirements for reasonableness.

Section 42 of the Landlord and Tenant Act 1987 requires the landlord to hold any service charge monies on trust in order to pay for the services for which the service charges were levied and subject to that on trust for the tenants.

Once in force, s.42A of the 1987 Act will require the landlord to hold any service charge monies in a designated trust account. A tenant or a recognised tenants' association will be entitled, on written request, to inspect documents relating to that account.

Failure by the landlord to comply with s.42A of the 1987 Act will entitle tenants to withhold payment of service charges and will constitute a criminal offence.

12.6.2 Demands for service charges

In most cases the lease will provide for estimated service charges to be demanded in advance. However, if demands are issued after completion of any works or provision of any service a statutory time limit applies.

Under s.20B of the 1985 Act, the landlord must issue the demand within 18 months of incurring the cost. If the demand is provided later than this the landlord cannot recover the costs at all, unless a notice was served during the 18-month period stating that costs have been incurred and that the tenant will be required to contribute to them by payment of a service charge.

Under s.47 of the 1987 Act, any demand for service charges must state the name and address of the landlord. Where a demand does not contain such information the amount demanded is treated as not being due from the tenant before such information is provided.

Once in force s.21B of the 1985 Act will require that any demand for service charges must be accompanied by a summary of the rights and obligations of tenants in relation to service charges.

12.6.3 Statement of account

Tenants have a statutory right to seek a summary of the service charge account from the landlord under s.21 of the 1985 Act.

The request must be in writing and can be sent direct to the landlord or to the managing agent.

THE COMMONHOLD AND LEASEHOLD REFORM ACT 2002

Where a landlord has received such a demand it must provide the summary within one month (or within six months of the end of the 12-month accounting period, whichever is later).

Failure to comply with s.21 constitutes an offence.

A new s.21 of the 1985 Act was introduced by the 2002 Act but is not yet in force. Under the new section, the landlord will be required to issue an annual summary of account to each tenant without the need for a request being made.

If the landlord fails to provide the summary the tenant will have a statutory right to withhold service charges under s.21A of the 1985 Act.

12.6.4 Right to further information

As well as receiving the summary of the service charge account, a tenant has the right to inspect documents supporting the summary.

Section 22 of the 1985 Act provides that the right must be exercised within a period of six months from receipt of the summary of the service charge account.

There are further rights of investigation of service charges and management provided by the right to a management audit under s.76 of the 1993 Act and the right to appoint a surveyor to advise on service charges under s.84 of and Sched. 4 to the Housing Act 1996.

Unless there are no more than two flats in a building, the right to a management audit is exercisable by not less than two-thirds of the tenants acting together. The right to appoint a surveyor is not available to individual tenants but to a recognised tenants' association only.

12.7 ADMINISTRATION CHARGES

The main provisions in respect of administration charges can be found in s.158 of and Sched. 11 to the 2002 Act.

Administration charges are defined as an amount payable by a tenant as part of or in addition to rent, which is payable directly or indirectly for:

- the grant of approvals under the lease or applications for such approvals;
- the provision of information or documents by or on behalf of the landlord;
- costs arising from non-payment of a sum due to the landlord;
- costs arising in connection with a breach (or alleged breach) of the lease.

Any administration charge levied by the landlord must be reasonable in order for it to recover the charge. As with service charges, a tenant may make an application to the LVT for a determination of reasonableness.

12.8 INSURANCE

12.8.1 Obtaining information from the landlord

If the lease provides for the landlord to arrange the insurance of the building, a tenant or the secretary of a recognised tenants' association can ask the landlord for a written summary or for a copy of the building insurance policy.

The relevant provisions are in the Schedule to the Landlord and Tenant Act 1985.

The landlord must comply within 21 days of receiving the request and failure to do so constitutes an offence.

As the insurance constitutes a service charge, the reasonableness of the costs of the insurance may be challenged before the LVT.

12.8.2 Insurance through the tenant's own insurer

If the tenant of a house is required under the lease to insure the property with an insurer nominated by the landlord, the tenant has a statutory right to effect the insurance with an insurer of his own choice, so long as he gives notice to the landlord and certain requirements relating to the insurance cover are satisfied.

The right is set out in s.164 of the 2002 Act and in the Leasehold Houses (Notice of Insurance Cover) (England) Regulations 2004, SI 2004/3097, as amended by SI 2005/177, and the Leasehold Houses (Notice of Insurance Cover) (Wales) Regulations 2005, SI 2005/1354 (W.102).

The insurance arranged by the tenant must:

- be with an insurer operating within the requirements of the Financial Services and Markets Act 2000;
- cover the interests of both the landlord and the tenant;
- cover all the risks which the lease requires to be included in the insurance; and
- provide cover to a sum not less than the amount required under the lease.

The tenant must serve a notice of cover in the prescribed form on the landlord no later than 14 days after having placed the insurance or within 14 days of any request by the landlord.

12.9 GROUND RENT

A tenant is not liable to pay any ground rent unless the landlord has demanded it by notice. The notice must be in the prescribed form and must specify:

- the landlord's name and address;
- the amount of ground rent due; and
- the date on which the tenant is liable to pay it.

This is set out in s.166 of the 2002 Act, in the Landlord and Tenant (Notice of Rent) (England) Regulations 2004, SI 2004/3096 and the Landlord and Tenant (Notice of Rent) (Wales) Regulations 2005, SI 2005/1355 (W.103).

The notice of demand must include a summary of the tenant's legal rights and obligations. The date specified for payment must not be less than 30 days or more than 60 days after date of service of the notice.

12.10 ESTATE CHARGES UNDER ESTATE MANAGEMENT SCHEMES

Estate management schemes (EMS) under the 1967 Act or the 1993 Act create obligations on tenants and landlords within the scheme area to contribute towards the costs of the scheme. These will usually be for works to amenity areas, gardens and roads and will be directed towards ensuring that the appearance and quality of the area as a whole is adequately maintained.

According to s.159 of the 2002 Act, any EMS charge which is not specified in the scheme must be reasonable and any person liable to pay such a charge may apply to the LVT for a determination of the reasonableness of the charge.

12.11 CONSULTATION ON MAJOR WORKS

Where a landlord proposes to carry out works of repair, maintenance or improvement which would amount to a service charge of more than £250 per tenant, it must formally consult all tenants before proceeding by giving notice of its intentions and seeking their views on the proposed works.

The relevant provisions are in s.20 of the Landlord and Tenant Act 1985, in the Service Charges (Consultation Requirements) (England) Regulations 2003, SI 2003/1987, as amended by SI 2004/2939 and the Service Charges (Consultation Requirements) (Wales) Regulations 2004, SI 2004/684 (W.72), as amended by SI 2005/1357 (W.105).

The landlord must serve a notice on each tenant (and on the secretary of a recognised tenants' association) describing the proposed works and identifying the persons the landlord intends to ask for an estimate of costs. The tenant (and any tenants' association) then has a period of 30 days in which to send any comments to the landlord and to nominate an alternative contractor.

Thereafter, the landlord must serve a second notice, the notice of proposals, which sets out the proposed works in more detail and the likely costs by quoting two estimates for the works. One of the estimates must be from a contractor wholly unconnected with the landlord. Where the tenants or the association have nominated a contractor, the landlord must try to obtain an estimate from that contractor.

Again, it must invite observations and allow 30 days for them to be made.

The landlord must have regard to the observations it has received. It is not obliged to follow or act on the comments but, if challenged later at the LVT on the reasonableness of the costs, it will need to show that it paid regard to observations or provide justification of why it did not.

In cases where the works are considered urgent, the landlord may apply to the LVT for an order to dispense with the consultation procedure.

If the landlord fails to comply with the consultation requirements and has not obtained a dispensation from the LVT, it will be unable to recover the cost of the works from the tenants beyond the statutory limit of £250 per tenant.

12.12 CONSULTATION ON LONG-TERM AGREEMENTS

Where a landlord proposes to enter a contract for the provision of services for a period of more than 12 months and the apportioned cost would amount to £100 a year or more per tenant, it must formally consult all tenants before proceeding.

The relevant provisions are in s.20 of the Landlord and Tenant Act 1985, in the Service Charges (Consultation Requirements) (England) Regulations 2003, SI 2003/1987, as amended by SI 2004/2939 and the Service Charges (Consultation Requirements) (Wales) Regulations 2004, SI 2004/684 (W.72), as amended by SI 2005/1357 (W.105).

The process and timescale are similar to those for major works.

The landlord must serve a notice of intention on each tenant (and on the secretary of any recognised tenants' association) describing the proposed agreement and identifying the proposed contractor, if already known at this stage. The tenant (and any tenants' association) has a period of 30 days in which to make any observations and to nominate an alternative contractor.

If a tenant or the association nominates an alternative contractor the landlord must try to obtain an estimate from that contractor.

It must then serve a further notice on the tenants or the association quoting two estimates for the works and including a statement identifying any connection between the contractor and the landlord.

Again, the landlord must allow observations for a minimum period of 30 days. As with major works, the landlord must have regard to the observations and give its reasons in writing for awarding the contract.

The landlord will not be able to recover charges beyond the statutory amount of £100 per tenant per annum if it fails to comply with the consultation procedure.

12.13 WORKS UNDER LONG-TERM AGREEMENTS

If the landlord has already entered into a long-term agreement for maintenance, repair and improvement works, the consultation procedure for further major works is less burdensome.

The requirements are set out in Sched. 3 to the Service Charges (Consultation Requirements) (England) Regulations 2003, SI 2003/1987 and in Sched. 3 to the Service Charges (Consultation Requirements) (Wales) Regulations 2004, SI 2004/684 (W.72).

The consultation takes place on the initial award of the long-term agreement with the contractor which is subject to the requirements described above.

For any subsequent proposals for major works, the landlord must still serve the major works consultation notice but will not invite the nomination of an alternative contractor as one has already been appointed. The landlord must have regard to any observations received before proceeding.

12.14 APPOINTMENT OF A MANAGER

If the management of a property by the landlord is considered unsatisfactory the tenants may exercise their right to manage under the 2002 Act. See Chapter 5.

If the RTM cannot be exercised the tenants may apply to the LVT for the appointment of a manager. This is a fault-based right and is often difficult and protracted to obtain.

The right is set out in Part II of the Landlord and Tenant Act 1987.

In certain cases, the right to appoint a manager is not available, e.g. where the landlord is a local authority, a registered housing association or a charitable housing trust. It is also not available where the landlord is resident on the premises and less than half of the flats contained in the premises are held on long leases.

12.15 VARIATION OF LEASES

In order to vary a lease, the consent of every party to the lease is required. However, the terms of a lease may also be varied by an order of the LVT.

12.15.1 Variation of a single lease (flat)

Any party to a long lease of a flat may make an application to the LVT for the lease to be varied. The grounds for the application are that the lease fails to make satisfactory provision in respect of certain matters which are listed in s.35(2) of the Landlord and Tenant Act 1987.

Where an application is made by an individual tenant in respect of his flat, any other party to the lease may apply to the LVT seeking that the variation should also apply to one or more other leases under s.36 of the 1987 Act.

12.15.2 Variation of two or more leases (flats)

Under s.37 of the 1987 Act, an application may also be made for an order to vary two or more leases.

A variation of two or more leases can be sought if the object of the variation cannot be satisfactorily achieved unless all the leases are varied to the same effect. The landlord or any tenant or an RTM company can apply for the variation.

Where the application is in respect of less than nine leases, all (or all but one) of the parties concerned must consent to it. Where the application is in respect of more than eight leases, it must not be opposed by more than 10 per cent of the parties concerned and at least 75 per cent of them must consent to it. For these purposes the landlord constitutes one of the parties concerned.

The LVT may make an order to vary the leases in accordance with the application or as it considers appropriate. It may also order a party to pay compensation to another if that party is likely to be disadvantaged by the variation of the leases. However, it cannot order a variation that would cause a disadvantage to another tenant which could not be remedied by payment of compensation.

The Leasehold Valuation Tribunals (Procedure) (England) Regulations 2003, SI 2003/2099, as amended by SI 2004/3098 and the Leasehold Valuation Tribunals (Procedure) (Wales) Regulations 2004, SI 2004/681 (W.69), as amended by SI 2005/1356 (W.104) apply.

Notice of the application must be served on anyone likely to be affected by the proposed variation and failure to do so will allow the affected parties to apply to the LVT for cancellation or modification of the variation or, in some cases, to bring an action for damages.

12.15.3 Variation of leases (houses)

An application for the variation of a lease of a house can only be made on the ground that the lease fails to make satisfactory provision for the insurance of the property, including the recovery of the costs of such insurance.

This right can be found in s.40 of the Landlord and Tenant Act 1987.

12.16 FORFEITURE AND POSSESSION

12.16.1 Breach of a covenant or condition in the lease

Forfeiture or re-entry is the final sanction available for a landlord if a tenant is in breach of the lease. If the tenant is in breach of a covenant or condition in the lease the process is commenced by the service of a notice under s.146 of the Law of Property Act 1925.

However, s.168 of the 2002 Act restricts the landlord's right to serve such a notice.

The tenant must have admitted the breach or the occurrence of the breach must have been determined by a court, an arbitration tribunal or the LVT. The landlord may make an application to the LVT for such a determination.

The s.146 notice may not be served by the landlord until 14 days after admission or the final determination of the breach. This enables the tenant to remedy the breach in the meantime.

12.16.2 Failure to pay service charges or administration charges

The same applies if the tenant fails to pay service or administration charges.

The landlord may not serve a s.146 notice unless the tenant has admitted the failure to pay or the matter has been determined by a court, an arbitration tribunal or the LVT.

The tenant has 14 days after the determination in which he may pay the outstanding service or administration charges.

This is set out in s.81 of the Housing Act 1996, as amended by s.170 of the 2002 Act.

12.16.3 Failure to pay small amounts for short time

There are also controls on the use of forfeiture and re-entry for the tenant's failure to pay a small amount of rent, service charges or administration charges (or a combination of them) for a short time.

These provisions can be found in s.167 of the 2002 Act, in the Rights of Re-entry and Forfeiture (Prescribed Sum and Period) (England) Regulations 2004, SI 2004/3086 and the Rights of Re-entry and Forfeiture (Prescribed Sum and Period) (Wales) Regulations 2005, SI 2005/1352 (W.100).

APPENDIX A

Precedents

Collective enfranchisement

A1
Letter of intent

Proposed acquisition of freehold of [*property*]

This letter of intent relates to the possible acquisition by the owners of flats in [*property*] of the freehold of that building using the statutory rights given to tenants of blocks of flats under the Leasehold Reform, Housing and Urban Development Act 1993 as amended by the Commonhold and Leasehold Reform Act 2002.
 I/We understand and agree that:

1. I/We am/are interested in participating in the possible acquisition of the freehold of [*property*] ('the property').
2. This letter represents my/our agreement with the other lessees who are also interested in participating in the proposed acquisition ('participating lessees') as to the general principles on which the possible acquisition of the freehold is to proceed.
3. The Lessees' Committee presently consists of [*name*] (of Flat . . .) and [*name*] (of Flat . . .). [*name*] will be the nominated point of contact to co-ordinate the exercise on behalf of participating lessees and to liaise with and give instructions to the solicitors and the surveyors. The other members of the Lessees' Committee will be the secondary points of contact should [*name*] not be available. It is agreed that no member of the Lessees' Committee will incur any liability as a result of so acting, it being recognised that they are simply acting in a voluntary capacity.
4. I/We will act in good faith towards the other participating lessees and will disclose at the earliest date any information I/we may have which may be material to the proposed acquisition.
5. I/We will contribute [equally *or set at any other basis*] together with the other participating lessees towards the costs and disbursements incurred in the initial investigation, including obtaining a valuation of the property; investigating the freehold and other relevant titles; checking that the qualifying criteria are met; and obtaining legal advice. The costs involved will be in the region of those set out in the letter to [*name*] dated [*date*]. Should the Lessees' Committee believe that it is desirable to incur costs in excess of those estimated I/we will be given a choice as to whether I/we wish to contribute further.
6. I/We understand that if I/we participate in the exercise of the right, then I/we will be required to contribute in [equal proportions *or set at any other basis proposed*] to the purchase price of the freehold interest in the property. I/We further understand that presently the likely price is unknown and that no professional valuation of the property has been undertaken, although this is recommended by the nominated solicitors.
7. The participating lessees' contributions to cost will be held by the nominated solicitors namely [*name and address of solicitors*] who are instructed to use such funds only for matters relating and incidental to the proposed acquisition.

LETTER OF INTENT

8. On completion of the initial investigation, the Lessees' Committee will provide me/us with details of the findings and if appropriate I/we will be invited to participate in the collective enfranchisement should there be sufficient participating lessees interested in proceeding.
9. I/We am/are the lessee under a long lease of a flat in [*property*]. I/We do not own more than two flats in the building.
10. I/We should take my/our own independent legal advice if I/we wish on our legal rights and obligations.

....
Signed

....
[*Print name of lessee*]

....
Signed

....
[*Print name of second lessee*]

Flat no.: ....

Tel no.: ....

Email address (if you are happy to be contacted by email):

....

Dated: ....

I attach a cheque for £... made payable to [*name*] Solicitors being a contribution towards the costs.

A2

Participation agreement

THIS AGREEMENT is made on [*date*]

BETWEEN each of the Tenants named in the Schedule hereto, each of whom is hereinafter referred to as a 'Tenant' and all of whom are hereinafter referred to collectively as 'the Tenants'.

1. **Definitions and interpretations**
   1.1 In this Agreement:
      1.1.1 'claim' means the claim to exercise the right to enfranchise the property;
      1.1.2 'enfranchisement' means the acquisition of such interests together with the grant of such rights as are specified in sections 1 and 2 of the legislation;
      1.1.3 'exercising the right to enfranchise' or such similar expression as may be appropriate means compliance with the procedure laid down by the legislation and the Regulations within the prescribed time limits;
      1.1.4 'legislation' means the Leasehold Reform, Housing and Urban Development Act 1993 (as amended by the Commonhold and Leasehold Reform Act 2002) together with the Schedules thereto;
      1.1.5 'participating flat' in relation to each Tenant means the flat specified in the Schedule hereto as being a flat in respect of which he is participating in the claim;
      1.1.6 'his proportion' in relation to each Tenant means the portion specified as his proportion in the Schedule hereto;
      1.1.7 'property' means the freehold property known as [*property*] registered at the [*district*] district land registry under title number [*title number*];
      1.1.8 'Regulations' means the Leasehold Reform (Collective Enfranchisement and Lease Renewal) Regulations 1993, SI 1993/2407.
   1.2 The following terms have the meanings conferred on them by the legislation and the Regulations: qualifying Tenant, reversioner, relevant landlord and Initial Notice:
      1.2.1 where the context so requires words importing the masculine gender include the feminine gender and vice versa;
      1.2.2 where the context so requires words importing the singular include the plural;
      1.2.3 where a Tenant consists of two or more persons, any covenant made hereunder by a Tenant shall be deemed to be made by such persons jointly and severally.

PARTICIPATION AGREEMENT

2. Background

2.1 This Agreement relates to the proposed acquisition by the Tenants of participating flats at the property of the freehold interest in the property using the statutory rights given to Tenants of blocks of flats under the legislation.

2.2 [The Tenants have attempted to negotiate a private deal for the purchase of the freehold from the reversioner, however these negotiations have been unsuccessful and the Tenants now wish to exercise their rights under the legislation.]
[delete as appropriate]

2.3 This Agreement represents the agreements, warranties and covenants of the Tenants to each other and to the process.

2.4 The Tenants agree that in order to purchase the freehold interest in the property from the reversioner a company ought to be formed to act as the nominee ('the Nominee Company'). The Nominee Company will initiate the process by serving the Initial Notice, dealing with matters arising out of the Initial Notice and ultimately becoming the freeholder of the property.

2.5 Prior to the formation of the Nominee Company the conduct of this matter is to be dealt with by the Lessees' Committee presently consisting of *[name and address]* and *[name and address]*. *[name]* has agreed to be the nominated point of contact to co-ordinate the exercise on behalf of the Tenants until the matter is taken over by the Nominee Company and to liaise with and give instructions to the solicitors and surveyors. The other members of the Lessees' Committee will be the secondary points of contact should *[name]* not be available.

3. It is hereby agreed as follows:

3.1 Each and every Tenant warrants to every other party hereto:

    3.1.1 that he is and shall, on the date on which the Initial Notice is to be served pursuant hereto, be:

        (i) a qualifying Tenant of the participating flat; and
        (ii) entitled to participate in the claim in respect of the participating flat and he is not aware of any reason why he may be prohibited from so participating;

    3.1.2 pursuant to the agreements contained in subparagraph 3.3 of this Agreement he has or will have the funds to provide his proportion of the costs referred to in that sub-paragraph, when required and demanded.

3.2 Each and every Tenant agrees with every other party hereto as follows:

    3.2.1 He will act in good faith towards the other Tenants, the Nominee Company and the Lessees' Committee.

    3.2.2 He will become a member of the Nominee Company, once formed.

    3.2.3 He will not cause or permit to be done any act or thing which will or may result in his being prohibited from participating in the claim in respect of the participating flat or which will or may result in the Initial Notice to be served pursuant hereto being or becoming invalid or which will or may prevent enfranchisement pursuant to the claim, including but without prejudice to the generality of the foregoing, he will not sign, prior to the service of the Initial Notice any other initial notice in respect of the whole or part of the property.

    3.2.4 He will provide to the Lessees' Committee or the Nominee Company, once formed, or their duly appointed agents within seven days of any

APPENDIX A2

        demand by the same any documents necessary to deduce his title to the participating flat.

3.2.5 He will comply with the obligations imposed on him by the legislation and the Regulations in relation to the claim to the extent that he is aware of the obligations.

3.2.6 He will not direct any enquiries in relation to the claim, the exercise of the right to enfranchise or compliance with any of the obligations contained herein to any of the advisers at any time instructed by the Lessees' Committee or the Nominee Company, once formed, in circumstances in which he is or should be aware of a potential conflict of interest arising for the adviser or advisers.

3.2.7 The Tenant will use his best endeavours prior to an assignment of his flat during the course of the claim to obtain:

    (i) a direct covenant by the assignee thereof with the Tenants for the time being participating in the claim to be bound on the said assignment by the Tenant's covenants contained herein in place of the Tenant;

    (ii) the binding agreement of the assignee thereof to notify the Lessees' Committee or the Nominee Company, as the case may be, within 14 days of such assignment that such assignment has taken place and that he is electing to participate in the claim; and

    (iii) the binding agreement of the assignee thereof to become a member of the Nominee Company.

3.3 Each and every Tenant further agrees with the Tenants as follows:

3.3.1 He has received information from the Lessees' Committee in respect of the costs involved in exercising the right to enfranchise, including the purchase price of the freehold interest in the property; legal costs of both the Tenants'/nominee company's solicitors and the reversioner's solicitors; other potential professional fees which may be incurred by the Tenants'/Nominee Company's solicitors and the reversioner's solicitors; and disbursements, including the costs of setting up the Nominee Company but understands that the final costs may vary depending on the circumstances of the acquisition and for example, whether there are any complications or delays.

3.3.2 In the event that enfranchisement pursuant to the claim is to be by completion following the making of a binding contract between the Nominee Company and the reversioner:

    (i) He will pay to the Nominee Company or its duly appointed agent his proportion of the deposit payable by the Nominee Company on, or prior to, exchange of contracts between the Nominee Company and the reversioner pursuant to the exercise of the right to enfranchise, such sum to be paid within seven days of receiving a written request from the Nominee Company or its duly appointed agent (or earlier in the case of urgency).

    (ii) He will pay to the Nominee Company or its duly appointed agent (after deduction of the amount paid by him under the last preceding subclause):

        (a) all outstanding rent and service charge arrears and any other sums due under or in respect of the lease or leases of the participating flat (or any agreements collateral thereto) in respect of which a vendor's lien would otherwise exist following enfranchisement, such sum to be paid within seven days of receiving a written request from the Nominee Company or its duly appointed agent (or earlier in the case of urgency);

(b) His proportion of all other sums for which the Nominee Company is or may be liable by virtue of the legislation or the Regulations in relation to the claim and of all sums in respect of which a vendor's lien would otherwise exist following enfranchisement, such sum to be paid within seven days of receiving a written request from the Nominee Company or its duly appointed agent (or earlier in the case of urgency).

(iii) He will pay to the Nominee Company or its duly appointed agent on demand by the same his proportion of all other sums which the Nominee Company reasonably has incurred or will incur in relation to the claim including, but without prejudice to the generality of the foregoing, legal and valuation fees.

(iv) He will pay the initial sum of £. . . towards the costs of the exercise which will be held by the solicitors for the Nominee Company and used for the purposes of the proposed acquisition and matters incidental thereto.

3.3.3 In the event that enfranchisement pursuant to the claim is to be by virtue of a vesting order from the court he will pay to the Nominee Company or to its duly appointed agent such sums as are specified in subparagraphs 3.3.2(ii) and (iii) hereof, within seven days of receiving a written request from the Nominee Company or its duly appointed agent (or earlier in the case of urgency).

3.3.4 Regardless as to how completion of the enfranchisement takes place, he will contribute his proportion of the purchase price within 7 days of receiving a written request from the Nominee Company or its duly appointed agent (or earlier in the case of urgency).

3.3.5 In the event that enfranchisement pursuant to the claim cannot be achieved in circumstances where there is no default by the Nominee Company in complying with its obligations hereunder or under the legislation or Regulations but due to an act or omission by any Tenant or Tenants who has or have participated or are for the time being participating in the claim or any default by the same in complying with obligations under the legislation or the Regulations or hereunder, he will pay to the Nominee Company or its duly appointed agent such sums as are specified in subparagraphs 3.3.2(ii)(b) and (iii) hereof, within seven days of receiving a written request from the Nominee Company or its duly appointed agent (or earlier in the case of urgency).

3.3.6 In the event that the Initial Notice served pursuant hereto is withdrawn (whether deemed or otherwise) in circumstances where a joint and several liability for cost is incurred by the reversioner or by any other relevant landlord in relation to the claim imposed by the legislation or by the Regulations on the members of the Nominee Company, he will pay his proportion of such costs to the reversioner or other relevant landlord in accordance with such obligation.

3.3.7 He will take his own independent legal advice if he requires advice on his legal rights and obligations whether under the terms of this Agreement or otherwise.

APPENDIX A2

4. Not a partnership agreement

This Agreement does not constitute a partnership agreement.

....
Signed

....
[*Print name of Tenant*]

....
Signed

....
[*Print name of second Tenant*]

Flat no.: . . ..

I attach a cheque for £. . . made payable to [*name*] Solicitors.

SCHEDULE

Flat	Tenant	Proportion

A3

Breakdown of costs

Proposed Acquisition of Freehold under the Leasehold Reform, Housing and Urban Development Act 1993 (as amended by the Commonhold and Leasehold Reform Act 2002)

[address of the property]

Estimated costs

Step	Estimated legal costs (£)
Initial discussions and correspondence; detailed investigations of matters affecting the property including consideration of historical correspondence; preliminary review of legal structure and qualifying criteria and advising; drafting circular letters and Letter of Intent/Participation Agreement between Tenants	
Involvement in setting up of limited company to acquire freehold; obtaining details relevant to the formation of the company; drafting and finalising Memorandum and Articles of Association and liaising with company formation agent; registering change of name; and dealing with company law compliance procedures including the first minutes of a meeting of the Board and membership to the company.	
Drafting and serving of preliminary notices and the notice of claim; dealing with any counter-notice received; and associated continuing correspondence and consideration of matters arising.	
Dealing with procedural formalities; continuing correspondence/negotiations with freeholder; liaising with surveyor, reviewing position and further advising on law and tactics.	
Conveyancing work including checking of title, draft contract, searches, enquiries, and checking details of all leases. Corresponding with landlord's solicitors. Completion of purchase and registration of title.	
Conclusion of matters, reporting to tenants and service of notice of change of freeholder on all tenants and	

APPENDIX A3

incidental correspondence, dealing with general enquiries, co-ordinating tenant's funds and final accounting.

- The above assumes a negotiated settlement without the matter being referred to the Leasehold Valuation Tribunal (LVT). A reference to the LVT will add considerably to the costs.
- There are optional matters depending on to what extent tenants or their co-ordinator wish to deal with administration matters themselves.
- The fees are exclusive of VAT and disbursements.
- The main disbursements are:

Stamp duty land tax	On a sliding scale based on the purchase price:
	Nil up to £125,000
	1% on £125,000 to £250,000
	3% on £250,001 to £500,000
	4% on £500,001 and above
Land Registry fees	Also on a sliding scale starting at £40
	Up to £700 depending on the purchase price
Local authority search	On average £180 up to £300 in some London Boroughs
Other searches	Around £40
Company Formation Agent	£350 to £400
Valuer	[Varies widely, insert information as appropriate]

- These figures are a rough guide only and will differ in each case depending on the particular circumstances.
- It is recommended that at some stage the advice of an accountant be obtained on matters relating to the nominee company, e.g. on the treatment of participating tenants' contributions.

There is a liability to pay for the landlord's costs of making reasonable investigations, providing requested information to the tenants and costs for having the property valued and legal costs in respect of dealing with notices and general procedure under the right to enfranchise legislation, including a conveyance of the freehold.

A4
Specimen spreadsheet of basic information

Tenant name	Flat number	Lease date, start date and term	Ground rent	Dates of rent review	Participating (P) or non-participating (NP)	Participation agreement returned signed	Contributions paid: amounts and dates	Contact details

A5

Specimen Articles of Association

The Companies Acts 1985 to 1989
A private company limited by shares
ARTICLES OF ASSOCIATION OF

[*name of company and company registration number*]

1. Preliminary

The regulations contained in Table A in the Schedule to the Companies (Tables A to F) Regulations 1985, SI 1985/805 as amended by the Companies (Tables A to F) (Amendment) Regulations 1985, SI 1985/1052 and as further amended by the Companies Act 1985 (Electronic Communications) Order 2000, SI 2000/3373 (such Table being hereinafter called 'Table A') shall apply to the company save in so far as they are excluded or varied hereby and such regulations (save as so excluded or varied) and the Articles hereinafter contained shall be the Articles of Association of the Company.

2. Interpretation

2.1 In these Articles:

'acquisition of the property' means the acquisition of the freehold interest and any superior interest to a Lease in the property by the Company;

'the Act' means the Companies Act 1985, but so that any reference in these Articles to any provision of the Act shall be deemed to include a reference to any statutory modification or re-enactment of that provision for the time being in force;

'Lease' [give details];

'Unit' means any residential unit forming part of the property and which is the subject of a Lease;

'Unitholder' means the person or persons to whom a Lease of a Unit has been granted or assigned and so that whenever two or more persons are for the time being Unitholders of a Unit they shall for all purposes of these Articles be deemed to constitute one Unitholder;

'property' means the land and buildings known as [*address of the property*];

'participating Unitholder' means a Unitholder who contributes to the purchase price, disbursements and any other applicable fees for the acquisition of the property;

['non-participating Unit' means a Unit which is owned by a Unitholder who is not a Participating Unitholder;]

['Reversionary Value' means the value which may be realised from a Non-Participating Unit by either (a) the grant of a New Lease; or (b) the grant of an Overriding Lease; or (c) the grant of a share in the Company to the owner of a non-participating Unit, which includes the right to a New Lease by private treaty;]

['reversionary event' means an event specified in the preceding definition of 'Reversionary Value';]

['new lease' means a new lease granted pursuant to the rights contained in the Leasehold Reform, Housing and Urban Development Act 1993 (as amended) or pursuant to a private treaty, on substantially similar terms to the Leases of Units in [*property*] with appropriate modifications, such as those relating to the rent and term and those reasonably required further to changes in legislation. A New Lease granted pursuant to a private treaty shall be one which is for a minimum term or minimum extended term of 90 years; and]

['overriding lease' means a lease of the non-participating Unit granted out of the freehold interest and being interposed between the freehold and the Lease of the non-participating Unit. The Overriding Lease shall be for a minimum term of 90 years.]

3. Members

3.1 The Company is a private company and accordingly no offer or invitation shall be made to the public (whether for cash or otherwise) to subscribe for any shares in or debentures of the Company, nor shall the Company allot, or agree to allot (whether for cash or otherwise) any shares in or debentures of the Company with a view to all or any of those shares or debentures being offered for sale to the public.

3.2 At the date of adoption of these Articles the share capital of the Company is £... divided into [... 'A' Ordinary Share(s) of £1] and ...Ordinary Shares of £1 each.

3.3 The subscribers to the Memorandum of Association shall be members of the Company. Save as otherwise provided for in these Articles, no person shall be admitted as member of the Company other than a Unitholder. The Company must accept as a member every person who is or who shall have become entitled to be admitted as a member pursuant to these Articles.

3.4 The lien conferred by regulation 8 Table A shall attach also to the fully paid up shares, and the Company shall also have a first and paramount lien on all shares, whether fully paid or not, standing registered in the name of any person indebted or under liability to the Company, whether he shall be the sole registered holder thereof or shall be one of two or more joint holders, for all monies presently payable by him or his estate to the Company. Regulation 8 in Table A shall be modified accordingly.

3.5 The directors are generally and unconditionally authorised for the purpose of section 80 of the Act to exercise any power of the Company to allot and grant rights to subscribe for or convert securities into shares of the Company at any time or times during the period of five years from the date of adoption of these Articles and the directors may, after that period, allot any shares or grant any such right under this authority in pursuance of an offer or agreement so to do made by the Company within that period. The authority hereby given may at any time (subject to Section 80) be renewed, revoked or varied by ordinary resolution.

APPENDIX A5

3.6 In accordance with section 91(1) of the Act sections 89(1) and 90(1) to (6) (inclusive) of the Act shall not apply to the Company.

3.7 The provisions of section 352 of the Act shall be observed by the Company and every member of the Company other than the subscribers to the Memorandum of Association shall either sign a written consent to become a member or sign the register of members on becoming a member. If two or more persons are together a Unitholder each shall so comply, they shall together constitute one member and the person whose name first appears in the register of members shall exercise the voting powers vested in such member.

[3.8

3.8.1 The 'A' Ordinary Share shall be issued to a Unitholder whose contribution to the price for the acquisition of the property shall include a sum attributable to a non-participating Unit and not being paid by the other Unitholders ('Contributing Member').

3.8.2 Save as provided for elsewhere in this Article 3.8, the 'A' Ordinary Share shall not carry any right to receive notice of and attend and vote at any meeting of the members.

3.8.3 If a Contributing Member ceases to become the holder of an Ordinary Share, from the moment he ceases to become such a holder, the 'A' Ordinary Share shall carry with it the right to attend general meetings and to receive notice of the same, but only to the extent that the purpose or one of the purposes of such meetings is to discuss matters relating to the non-participating Unit. The right to vote at such meetings shall only apply to decisions or resolutions which affect or in any way relate to the non-participating Unit. Where, pursuant to these Articles, a Contributing Member does have a right to receive notices and attend and vote at general meetings, such rights shall apply to and be exercisable by a Contributing Member in the same way as these rights apply to and are exercisable by the holder of an Ordinary Share.

3.8.4 The 'A' Ordinary Share shall remain vested in a Contributing Member only for the period it takes the Contributing Member to realise the Reversionary Value in a non-participating Unit and have that value distributed to him or (if at the time the Contributing Member is the holder of any Ordinary Share) when the Reversionary Value is put towards the costs for carrying out repairs and/or improvements to the Contributing Member's Unit and any remaining sum is distributed to the Contributing Member. In order for the Reversionary Value to be realised, distributed to the Contributing Member and/or incurred in carrying out repairs and/or improvements to the Contributing Member's Unit, the members of the Company shall procure that all necessary resolutions are passed.

3.8.5 Once the Reversionary Value is dealt with in accordance with Article 3.8.4 an 'A' Ordinary Share shall automatically be reclassified as an Ordinary Share which shall carry no rights whatsoever and shall be bought back by the Company at its nominal value, provided that the Company satisfies all relevant requirements in respect of the same or transferred to a third person or body nominated by the Company.

3.8.6 Save as otherwise permitted by this Article 3.8, the 'A' Ordinary Share shall not be transferable.]

3.9 After the acquisition of the property no shares shall be issued to the Unitholder of a part of the property, the freehold interest of which no longer remains within the ownership of the Company.

4. Transfer of shares

4.1 An Ordinary Share may only be and shall be transferred simultaneously with the disposal by the holder of such Ordinary Share of the Lease to which the Ordinary Share relates and then only to the person or persons who acquire that Lease. Where a member's interest in a Lease determines for any reason other than the disposal of the Lease or bankruptcy or death of the member, a transfer of that member's Ordinary Share shall take place in a manner and to such person or body as the Company shall direct.

4.2 Each subscriber to the Memorandum of Association and any other member who is not a Participating Unitholder shall cease to be the holder of Ordinary Shares on the acquisition of the property and at that point forwards only Participating Unitholders and the successors to their units (of whole or of part) and their legal personal representative or representatives or their trustee in bankruptcy (as applicable) shall be entitled to be holders of Ordinary Shares of the Company. Any cessation of membership pursuant to this Article shall take place in a manner which the Company shall direct. This restriction shall not apply to the Ordinary Shares issued once the acquisition of the property takes place.

4.3 The price to be paid on the transfer of each share shall be the nominal value thereof.

4.4 If the holder of an Ordinary Share refuses or neglects to transfer it in accordance with these Articles, the Chairman for the time being of the directors, or failing him, one of the directors duly nominated by a resolution of the Board for that purpose, shall forthwith be deemed to be the duly appointed attorney of that holder with full power in his name and on his behalf to execute, complete and deliver a transfer of his share to the person to whom it should be transferred under the provisions of these Articles and the Company may receive and give a good discharge for the purchase money and enter the name of the transferee in the register of members as the holder by transfer of the said shares.

4.5 (a) If the holder of an Ordinary Share shall die or be adjudged bankrupt his legal personal representative or representatives or the trustee in his bankruptcy shall be entitled to be registered as the holder of the Ordinary Share provided that he or they shall for the time being be a Unitholder of the Unit formerly held by the deceased or bankrupt member or entitled to the legal estate as though he was or they were a Unitholder provided that any registration of a member is in accordance with these Articles and in particular so that after the acquisition of the property only the legal personal representative or representatives or the trustee in bankruptcy of a Participating Unitholder shall be entitled to be registered as a member.

(b) If the holder of an Ordinary Share shall die or be adjudged bankrupt and his share at the date of such death or bankruptcy is not transferred to the person becoming entitled in consequence of such death or bankruptcy to the Lease in respect of which such Ordinary Share is held, the directors may give notice in writing to the personal representative or the trustees in bankruptcy or other person or persons who have the right to transfer such share requiring him or them to transfer such share and if such notice shall not be complied with within one month thereof, the provisions of Article 4.4 hereof shall apply thereto in like manner as if the holder of the said share had neglected to transfer the same in accordance with the said Article.

APPENDIX A5

4.6 If two or more persons are jointly entitled to the Lease such persons shall jointly hold the share allotted or assigned in respect of the Lease but they shall have only one vote in respect of such share and such vote shall be cast by the holder whose name first appears in the register of members or in the event of the death of such holder then the said vote shall be cast by the holder whose name next appears in the register of members in respect of the relevant share. For all purposes of the Company such joint holders shall be deemed to be one person.

4.7 The instrument of transfer of any share shall be executed by or on behalf of the transferor who shall be deemed to remain a holder of the share until the name of the transferee is entered in the register of members in respect thereof.

4.8 The transferee of any share shall pay and indemnify the Company against all reasonable administrative fees incurred by the Company in respect of the transfer of the share.

4.9 The directors shall not register any transfer of an Ordinary Share save pursuant to these Articles.

4.10 The directors shall be bound to register transfers made in accordance with these Articles but no other transfers shall be registrable.

5. General meetings and resolutions

5.1 An annual general meeting and an extraordinary general meeting called for the passing of a special resolution or a resolution appointing a member as a director shall be called by at least 21 clear days' notice. All other extraordinary general meetings shall be called by at least 14 clear days' notice but a general meeting may be called by shorter notice if it is so agreed:

(a) in the case of an annual general meeting, by all the members entitled to attend and vote thereat; and

(b) in the case of any other general meeting, by a majority in number of the members having a right to attend and vote, being a majority together holding (subject to the provisions of any elective resolution of the Company for the time being in force) not less than 95% of the total voting rights at the meeting of all the members.

5.2 The notice shall specify the time and place of the meeting and, in the case of an annual general meeting, shall specify the meeting as such.

5.3 The notice shall be given to all the members and to the directors and any auditors and to every legal personal representative or trustee in bankruptcy of a member where the member, but for his death or bankruptcy, would be entitled to receive notice of the meeting.

5.4 Regulation 38 in Table A shall not apply to the Company.

5.5 No business shall be transacted at any general meeting unless a quorum is present. Subject to Article 5.6 below, two persons entitled to vote upon the business to be transacted, each being a member or a proxy for a member or a duly authorised representative of a corporation, shall be a quorum.

5.6 If and for so long as the Company has only one member, that member present in person or by proxy or (if that member is a corporation) by a duly authorised representative shall be a quorum.

5.7 If a quorum is not present within half an hour from the time appointed for a general meeting the general meeting shall stand adjourned to the same day in the next week at the same time and place or to such other day and at such other time and place as the directors may determine; and if at the adjourned general meeting a quorum is not present within half an hour from the time appointed therefor such adjourned general meeting shall be dissolved.

5.8 Regulations 40 and 41 in Table A shall not apply to the Company.

5.9 If and for so long as the Company has only one member and that member takes any decision which is required to be taken in general meeting or by means of a written resolution, that decision shall be as valid and effectual as if agreed by the Company in general meeting, subject as provided in Article 5.11 below.

5.10 Any decision taken by a sole member pursuant to Article 5.9 above shall be recorded in writing and delivered by that member to the Company for entry in the Company's minute book.

5.11 Resolutions under section 303 of the Act for the removal of a director before the expiration of his period of office and under section 391 of the Act for the removal of an auditor before the expiration of his period of office shall only be considered by the Company in general meeting.

5.12 Unless resolved by ordinary resolution that regulation 62 in Table A shall apply without modification, the appointment of a proxy and any authority under which the proxy is appointed or a copy of such authority certified notarially or in some other way approved by the directors may be deposited or received at the place specified in regulation 62 in Table A up to the commencement of the meeting or (in any case where a poll is taken otherwise than at the meeting) of the taking of the poll or may be handed to the chairman of the meeting prior to the commencement of the business of the meeting.

5.13 Any member of the Company entitled to attend and vote at a general meeting shall be entitled to appoint another person (whether a member or not) as his proxy to attend and vote instead of him and any proxy so appointed shall have the same right as the member to speak at the meeting.

5.14 Every member present at a meeting by proxy shall be entitled to speak at the meeting and shall be entitled to one vote on a show of hands. In any case where the same person is appointed proxy for more than one member he shall have as many votes as the number of members for whom he is proxy. Regulation 54 in Table A shall be modified accordingly.

6. Appointment of directors

6.1 Regulation 64 in Table A shall not apply to the Company.

6.2 Save for the persons who are deemed to have been appointed as the first directors of the Company on incorporation pursuant to section 13(5) of the Act and as provided for in Article 6.8, no person who is not a member of the Company shall in any circumstances be eligible to hold office as a director.

6.3 The maximum number and minimum number respectively of the directors may be determined from time to time by ordinary resolution in general meeting of the Company. Subject to and in default of any such determination there shall be no maximum number of directors and the minimum number of directors shall be one.

6.4 The directors shall not be required to retire by rotation and regulations 73 to 80 (inclusive) in Table A shall not apply to the Company.

6.5 No member shall be appointed a director at any general meeting unless either:

(a) he is recommended by the directors; or
(b) not less than 14 nor more than 35 clear days before the date appointed for the general meeting, notice signed by a member qualified to vote at the general meeting has been given to the Company of the intention to propose that member for appointment, together with notice signed by that member of his willingness to be appointed.

APPENDIX A5

6.6 Subject to Article 6.5 above, the Company may by ordinary resolution in general meeting appoint any member who is willing to act to be a director, either to fill a vacancy or as an additional director.

6.7 The directors may appoint a member who is willing to act to be a director, either to fill a vacancy or as an additional director, provided that the appointment does not cause the number of directors to exceed any number determined in accordance with Article 6.3 above as the maximum number of directors and for the time being in force.

6.8 In any case where as the result of death or deaths the Company has no members and no directors the personal representatives of the last member to have died shall have the right by notice in writing to appoint a person to be a director of the Company and such appointment shall be as effective as if made by the Company in general meeting pursuant to Article 6.7 above. For the purpose of this Article, where two or more members die in circumstances rendering it uncertain which of them survived the other or others, the members shall be deemed to have died in order of seniority, and accordingly the younger shall be deemed to have survived the elder.

7. Borrowing powers

The directors may exercise all the powers of the Company to borrow money without limit as to amount and upon such terms and in such manner as they think fit, and to grant any mortgage, charge or standard security over its undertaking and property or any part thereof, and to issue debentures, whether outright or as security for any debt, liability or obligation of the Company or of any third party.

8. Alternate directors

8.1 No person who is not a member of the Company shall be capable of being appointed an alternate director. Regulation 65 in Table A shall be modified accordingly.

8.2 Unless otherwise determined by the Company in general meeting by ordinary resolution an alternate director shall not be entitled as such to receive any remuneration from the Company, save that he may be paid by the Company such part (if any) of the remuneration otherwise payable to his appointor as such appointor may by notice in writing to the Company from time to time direct, and the first sentence of regulation 66 in Table A shall be modified accordingly.

8.3 A director, or any other member appointed by resolution of the directors and willing to act, may act as an alternate director to represent more than one director, and an alternate director shall be entitled at any meeting of the directors or of any committee of the directors to one vote for every director whom he represents in addition to his own vote (if any) as a director, but he shall count as only one for the purpose of determining whether a quorum is present.

9. Disqualification of directors

Save for the persons who are deemed to have been appointed as the first directors of the Company on incorporation pursuant to section 13(5) of the Act, the office of a director shall be vacated if he ceases to be a member of the Company and regulation 81 in Table A shall be modified accordingly.

SPECIMEN ARTICLES OF ASSOCIATION

10. Gratuities and pensions

10.1 The directors may exercise the powers of the Company conferred by its Memorandum of Association in relation to the payment of pensions, gratuities and other benefits and shall be entitled to retain any benefits received by them or any of them by reason of the exercise of any such powers.

10.2 Regulation 87 in Table A shall not apply to the Company.

11. Proceedings of directors

11.1 A director may vote, at any meeting of the directors or of any committee of the directors, on any resolution, notwithstanding that it in any way concerns or relates to a matter in which he has, directly or indirectly, any kind of interest whatsoever, and if he shall vote on any such resolution as aforesaid his vote shall be counted; and in relation to any such resolution as aforesaid he shall (whether or not he shall vote on the same) be taken into account in calculating the quorum present at the meeting.

11.2 Each director shall comply with his obligations to disclose his interest in contracts under section 317 of the Act.

11.3 Regulations 94 to 97 (inclusive) in Table A shall not apply to the Company.

12. The seal

If the Company has a seal it shall only be used with the authority of the directors or of a committee of directors. The directors may determine who shall sign any instrument to which the seal is affixed and unless otherwise so determined it shall be signed by a director and by the secretary or second director. Regulation 101 in Table A shall not apply to the Company.

13. Indemnity

13.1 For the purposes of these Articles a 'Liability' is a liability incurred by any person in connection with any negligence, default, breach of duty or breach of trust by him in relation to the Company or otherwise in connection with his duties, powers or office and 'Associated Company' shall bear the meaning referred to in section 309A(6) of the Act. Subject to the provisions of the Act and without prejudice to any protection from liability which may otherwise apply:

    13.1.1 the directors shall have power to purchase and maintain for any director of the Company, any director of an Associated Company, any auditor of the Company and any officer of the Company (not being a director or auditor of the Company), insurance against any Liability;

    13.1.2 every director or auditor of the Company and every officer of the Company (not being a director or auditor of the Company) shall be indemnified out of the assets of the Company against any loss or liability incurred by him in defending any proceedings in which judgment is given in his favour or in which he is acquitted or in connection with any application in which relief is granted to him by the court for any Liability.

13.2 Regulation 118 in Table A shall not apply to the Company.

APPENDIX A5

14. Rules or byelaws

14.1 The directors may from time to time make such rules or byelaws as they may deem necessary or expedient or convenient for the proper conduct and management of the Company and for the purposes of prescribing the classes of and conditions of membership, and in particular but without prejudice to the generality of the foregoing, they shall by such rules or byelaws regulate:

    (a) the admission and classification of members of the Company, and the rights and privileges of such members, and the conditions of membership and the terms on which members may resign or have their membership terminated and the entrance fees, subscriptions and other fees, charges, contributions or payments to be made by members;

    (b) the conduct of members of the Company in relation to one another, and to the Company and to the Company's servants or agents;

    (c) the setting aside of the whole or any part or parts of any property held, managed or administered by the Company at any particular time or times or for a particular purpose or purposes;

    (d) the procedure at general meetings and meetings of the directors and committees of the directors of the Company in so far as such procedure is not regulated by these Articles;

    (e) and, generally, all such matters as are commonly the subject matter of company rules or rules or regulations appropriate to the Company.

14.2 The Company in general meeting shall have power to alter or repeal the rules or byelaws and to make additions thereto and the directors shall adopt such means as they deem sufficient to bring to the notice of members of the Company all such rules or byelaws, which so long as they shall be in force, shall be binding on all members of the Company. Provided, nevertheless, that no rule or byelaw shall be inconsistent with, or shall affect or repeal anything contained in, the Memorandum or Articles of Association of the Company.

A6

Initial notice

© 2002 Oyez
This Form is copyright
and must not be reproduced

LEASEHOLD REFORM, HOUSING AND URBAN DEVELOPMENT ACT 1993

Section 13

Initial Notice by Tenant
(Note 1)

(1) Insert full name and address of recipient (Note 2).

To(1):

(2) Insert full names and addresses of the qualifying tenants giving this notice (Note 3).

From(2):

(3) The specified premises are those in which the flats are contained.

(4) "Coloured pink" or "edged red" or as the case may be.

(5) A plan must accompany this notice.

(6) Insert a brief description.

1. THE SPECIFIED PREMISES (3)

The premises of which the freehold is proposed to be acquired by virtue of section 1(1) of the Act are shown(4) on the accompanying plan(5) and known as (6):

[P.T.O.

HUD 6/1

APPENDIX A6

(7) Note 4.

2. ADDITIONAL FREEHOLDS(7)

The property of which the freehold is proposed to be acquired by virtue of section 1(2)(a) of the Act are shown (8) on the accompanying plan and known as (9)

(8) Distinguish from the specified premises by different colouring(s).

(9) Insert a brief description.

(10) Note 5.

3. RIGHTS TO BE ACQUIRED

The rights which it is proposed should be granted under section 13(3)(a)(iii) of the Act are (10):

HUD 6/2

INITIAL NOTICE

(11) The grounds must apply on the date this notice is given.

(12) Note 6.

4. GROUNDS OF CLAIM (11)

The grounds upon which it is claimed that the specified premises are premises to which Part I Chapter I if the Act applies are (12) :

(13) Note 7.

(14) Specify them.

5. OTHER LEASEHOLDS (13)

The leasehold interest(s) proposed to be acquired under or by virtue of section 2(1)(a) or (b) of the Act [is] [are] (14):

[P.T.O

HUD 6/3

APPENDIX A6

(15) Note 8.

(16) Specify them.

6. MANDATORY LEASEBACK (15)

The flats or other units contained in the specified premises in relation to which it is considered that requirements in Part II of Schedule 9 apply are (16):

7. PRICE

The proposed purchase price is:

(17) Insert the figure. Note 9.

(17) £   for the freehold interest in [the specified premises].

(17) £   for the property within paragraph 2 of this notice.

For the leasehold interest(s) within paragraph 5 of this notice:

(18) Specify different sums for different interests (if any).

(18) £

HUD 6/4

INITIAL NOTICE

(19) Note 3.

8. QUALIFYING TENANTS (19)

The full names of all the qualifying tenants of flats in the specified premises, with the addresses of their flats and the particulars required by the Act, are set out on the accompanying tenant information sheets (20).

(20) Note 10.

(21) Note 11.

9. NOMINEE PURCHASER (21)

The full name(s) of the person(s) appointed to act as the nominee purchaser for the purposes of section 15 of the Act [is][are] (22):

(22) Insert name(s) and address(es).

10. ADDRESS FOR NOTICES

The address in England and Wales at which notices may be given to the nominee purchaser under Part I Chapter I of the Act is (23):

(23) Insert the address.

11. RESPONSE DATE

The date by which you must respond to this notice by giving a counter-notice under section 21 is (24):

(24) Specify a date at least two months after this notice is given.

[P.T.O.

HUD 6/5

211

APPENDIX A6

(25) Note 12. **12. OTHER RELEVANT LANDLORD(S)** (25)

(26) Insert name(s) and address(es), or indicate 'NONE'.

Copies of this notice are being given to (26):

Dated

Signed

(27) All must sign. Qualifying tenants (27)

HUD 6/6

INITIAL NOTICE

NOTES

1. Part I Chapter I of the Act gives tenants of flats a collective right to acquire the freehold of their premises. This notice is the initial notice from qualifying tenants claiming to exercise that right.

2. This notice is properly given to the reversioner of the premises. The reversioner is normally the freeholder: see section 9 and Schedule 1 Part I (one freeholder) and Part IA (multiple freeholders). Where the entire freehold is not held by the same person, the recipient may be one of the freeholders. Where no freeholder can be found or ascertained, this notice may be served on a relevant landlord within section 9.

3. This notice must be given by qualifying tenants in the premises at the date this notice is given, comprising at least half the total number of flats in the premises. A qualifying tenant is defined by section 5 of the Act. Where the lease is vested in trustees, section 6 (4) and (5) apply.

4. This notice must specify any appurtenant property (such as a garage or yard) which it is proposed to acquire, as well as any property used in common which is to be included.

5. Specify them with care, using the accompanying plan and distinctive colours. For example:

   'a vehicular right of way at all times over the road coloured brown on the accompanying plan'

   'a free right of foul drainage through the pipe, the line of which is shown green on the accompanying plan'

6. Set out the grounds by reference to section 3. The right to enfranchise applies to premises

   (a) they consist of a self-contained building or part of a building;

   (b) they contain at least two flats held by qualifying tenants; and

   (c) the total number of flats held by qualified tenants is at least two-thirds of the total number of flats in the premises.

Premises excluded from the right are set out in section 4.

7. Section 2 gives qualifying tenants the right to acquire intermediate leasehold interests and (where necessary) the interests of tenants in common parts and in the additional property referred to in paragraph 2 of this notice.

8. By virtue of section 36 and Schedule 9, Part II, the nominee purchaser is obliged to grant leases back where any flat is let under a secure tenancy, or where a housing association is the freeholder.

9. Where the freehold of the whole premises is not owned by the same person, the proposed price for each of the freehold interests should be given, specifying the relevant part.

10. Separate information sheets should be completed for each tenant. Information sheets are available on the Oyez Form HUD 7.

11. Section 15 provides that a nominee purchaser is to conduct on behalf of the participating tenants all proceedings arising out of this notice, with a view to acquisition by the nominee purchaser on their behalf of the freehold and other interests which fall to be acquired.

12. A copy of this notice must be given to every other person known or believed to be a relevant landlord: see Schedule 3 Part II. Normally this means intermediate lessees.

© 2002 Oyez 7 Spa Road, London SE16 3QQ.
[All rights reserved]

HUD 6

8.2002
5044653
HUD 6/7

A7

Counter-notice

© 2003 Oyez
This Form is copyright and must not be reproduced

LEASEHOLD REFORM, HOUSING AND URBAN DEVELOPMENT ACT 1993

Section 21

Counter-Notice by Reversioner

(Note 1)

(1) Insert full name and address (Note 2 and Note 13).

To(^{1}):

(2) Insert full name and address (Note 3).

From(^{2}):

(3) Note 4.

(^{3}) The reversioner admits that on the date the initial notice was given, the participating tenants were entitled to exercise the right to collective enfranchisement in relation to the specified premises.

(4) Insert item.

The reversioner accepts the following proposals contained in the initial notice(^{4}):

[P.T.O.

HUD 8/1

COUNTER-NOTICE

The reversioner does not accept the following proposals contained in the initial notice (4):

The reversioner makes the following counter-proposal to each of the proposals which are not accepted (4):

(5) Note 5.   The reversioner makes the following additional leaseback proposals (5):

(6) Note 6.   The following rights are intended to be granted under section 1(4) of the Act (6):

The freehold property to be disposed of under section 1(4) of the Act is (6):

HUD 8/2

APPENDIX A7

(7) Note 7.   The nominee purchaser is required to acquire the following interests under section 21(4)(^{7}):

(8) Note 8.   [The freeholder] desires to retain the following rights(^{8}):

[P.T.O.
HUD 8/3

COUNTER-NOTICE

(9) Note 9.

The provisions which the reversioner considers should be included in any conveyance to the nominee purchaser in accordance with section 34 and Schedule 7 are [set out on the accompanying schedule](^{9}):

OR

(10) Note 4.

(11) Specify them.

(^{10}) The reversioner does not admit that on the date the initial notice was given that the participating tenants were entitled to exercise the right to collective enfranchisement in relation to the specified premises, for the following reasons(^{11}):

HUD 8/4

APPENDIX A7

(12) Note 10.

[An application for an order under section 23(1) of the Act is to be made by on the grounds that he or she intends to redevelop the whole or a substantial part of the specified premises.] (^{12}):

(13) Insert the address in England and Wales.

The address in England and Wales at which notices may be given to the reversioner under Part I Chapter I is(^{13}):

[P.T.O.

HUD 8/5

COUNTER-NOTICE

(14) Note 11. [The following copy notices received or given under sections 42 or 45 accompany this counter-notice](14):

(15) Note 12. The specified premises [are] [are not] (15) within the area of a scheme approved as an estate management scheme under section 70 of the Act.

Dated

Signed

Reversioner

(16) Insert full name and address. [Reversioner's agent](16)

HUD 8/6

APPENDIX A7

NOTES

1. Where qualifying tenants have given initial notice of their claim to exercise the right to collective enfranchisement, the reversioner must serve a counter-notice by the date specified in the initial notice.

2. This notice must be given to the nominee purchaser named in the initial notice.

3. This notice is properly given by the reversioner. Normally, the reversioner is the freeholder: see section 9 and Schedule 1, Part I (one freeholder) and Part IA (multiple freeholders).

4. Delete one of these alternatives. This notice signifies that either the reversioner does admit or that he or she does not admit that the participating tenants are entitled to exercise their right to collective enfranchisement.

5. The reversioner may specify leaseback proposals relating to secure tenancies, lettings by a housing association, units let to a person who is not a qualifying tenant, or where there is a resident landlord: section 21(3).

6. Where the initial notice proposes the acquisition of property used in common by a qualifying tenant and occupiers of other premises, the freeholder may instead grant rights equivalent to those formerly enjoyed by the flat, or substitute other property over which equivalent rights may be granted: section 1(4).

7. By section 21(4), any relevant landlord whose interest is being acquired may require the nominee purchaser to acquire also his or her interest in any property which would cease to be of use to him or her, or would not be capable of being reasonably managed or maintained.

8. Where rights are necessary for the management or maintenance of property in which he or she is to retain an interest, any relevant landlord may state what rights he or she desires to retain over any property to be acquired by the nominee purchaser.

9. If the provisions are brief, they can be set out here. But if (as seems likely) they are detailed, a separate schedule attached to this notice is often the easiest way to describe them.

10. Where it is applicable, this paragraph should be included and completed whether or not the reversioner admits the claim.

11. Where notices have been given under Part I Chapter II (individual rights of flat tenants to acquire new lease) copies should either accompany this counter-notice or follow as soon as possible.

12. Delete one of the alternatives "are/are not".

13. If more space is required for further names and addresses, use Oyez continuation sheet HUD 20a.

HUD 8/7

A8

Specimen Leasehold Valuation Tribunal application

In the Leasehold Valuation Tribunal
BETWEEN:

[*name of applicant*] **Applicant**

and

[*name of respondent*] **Respondent**

APPLICATION UNDER SECTION 24 OF THE LEASEHOLD REFORM, HOUSING AND URBAN DEVELOPMENT ACT 1993

1. The Applicant is [*name*] a company registered in England and Wales under Company No. [*number*] whose registered office address is at [*address*]. The Applicant's representatives are [*name and address of solicitors*].
2. The Applicant is the nominee purchaser for the tenants whose names and addresses appear in Annex 1.
3. The Respondent is [*name and address*]. All notices to be given to the Respondent can be sent to [*name and address of respondent's solicitors*].
4. The Respondent is the freehold proprietor of the premises described in paragraph 5 below.
5. This Application relates to the premises known as [*address of property*] ('the property').
6. This Application is made under section 24 of the Leasehold Reform, Housing and Urban Development Act 1993 ('the Act') as amended by the Commonhold and Leasehold Reform Act 2002.
7. There is a charge over the Respondent's interest believed to exist in favour of [*name and address*].
8. [The intermediate landlord is [*name*] of [*address*]. The intermediate landlord's address for service is c/o [*name*] of [*address*].] [There is no intermediate landlord].
9. The tenants served a notice in accordance with section 13 of the Act dated [*date*] ('the Initial Notice'). The Initial Notice identifies that the Applicant proposes to acquire the freehold interest in the property ('the Specified Premises').
10. The Respondent served its counter-notice in accordance with section 21 of the Act dated [*date*] ('the Counter-Notice').
11. The terms in dispute between the Applicant and the Respondent are as follows:
    (a) the price of the Specified Premises; and
    (b) [*give details*].

APPENDIX A8

12. The Applicant believes that an appropriate value for the freehold interest in the Specified Premises is £. . ..
13. [*give details of other issues*].
14. The following documents are attached to and form part of this Application:
    (a) names and addresses of tenants (Annex 1);
    (b) Initial Notice (Annex 2);
    (c) Counter-Notice (Annex 3);
    (d) Land Registry entries for the freehold title [and intermediate/superior leasehold title(s)] (Annex 4);
    (e) a copy of a specimen long lease of a flat in the Specified Premises;
    (f) [a copy of the superior/intermediate lease(s)].
15. The Applicant is not a party to and not aware of any other application to a court or tribunal or of any order relating to the Specified Premises.

The Applicant believes that the facts stated in this Application are true.

. . . .

Signed for and on behalf of the Applicant by [*name and address of solicitors*]

Dated: . . . .

Right to manage

A9

Letter of intent (right to manage)

Proposed exercise of right to manage of [*property*]

This Letter of Intent relates to the proposed exercise of the Right to Manage (RTM) by the owners of flats in [*property*] using the statutory rights given to tenants of blocks of flats under the Commonhold and Leasehold Reform Act 2002 ('the Act').

I/We understand and agree that:

1. I am/We are interested in principle in participating in the possible exercise of the RTM of [*property*]
2. This letter represents my/our agreement with the other lessees who are also interested in participating in the proposed exercise of the RTM ('participating lessees') as to the general principles on which the matter is to proceed and on the sharing of costs.
3. I/We will become a member of a newly formed company which will be used to acquire the RTM. The RTM company will be one limited by guarantee as is required by the Act so there will be no shares issued and membership will be on the basis of one per flat. The RTM company will comply with the requirements of the Act.
4. Assuming that there are sufficient participating lessees for the purpose and the Board of the RTM company having taken appropriate advice considers it appropriate to do so the RTM company will take the necessary steps to exercise the Right to Manage which will include, for example, service of statutory notices on non-participating lessees and subsequently on the landlord.
5. The proposed initial Board of the RTM company will be [*names and flat numbers*]. As a member of the RTM company I/we will be able to put myself/ourselves forward to be elected as officers of the RTM company should we so wish. [*name*] will be the nominated point of contact to co-ordinate the exercise on behalf of the participating lessees and to liaise with and give instructions to the RTM company's solicitors and the proposed new managing agents. The other members of the Board will be the secondary points of contact should [*name*] not be available. It is agreed that no member of the Board will incur any liability as a result of so acting, it being recognised they are simply doing so in a voluntary capacity.
6. The RTM company may wish to employ the services of professional managing agents to manage [*property*]. The costs of employing a managing agent will be dealt with through the service charges in the same way as the charges of the current managing agents.
7. I/We will contribute equally together with the other participating lessees towards the costs and disbursements incurred in connection with the obtaining of legal advice in connection with the proposed exercise of the Right to Manage and of

LETTER OF INTENT (RIGHT TO MANAGE)

the formation of the RTM company and of the legal and other professional costs incurred in exercising the right itself.

8. I/We understand that the RTM company will be obliged to pay the freeholder's/landlord's reasonable professional costs that they have incurred in the process as is required by the Act whether or not the RTM company completes the exercise of the RTM. I/We will contribute equally together with the other participating lessees towards the amount required by the RTM company for this purpose.

9. The participating lessees' contributions to the costs will be held by the nominated solicitors namely [*name of solicitors*] who are instructed to use such funds only for matters relating and incidental to the proposed exercise of the RTM.

10. I am/We are the lessee(s) under a long lease of a flat in [*property*] (i.e. the Lease I/we hold was originally for a term of more than 21 years).

11. I/We should take my/our own independent legal advice if we wish on our legal rights and obligations.

....

Signed

....

[*Print name of lessee*]

....

Signed

....

[*Print name of second lessee*]

Flat no.: . . . .

Tel no.: . . . .

Email address (if you are happy to be contacted by email):

....

Dated: . . . .

*I attach a cheque for £. . . made payable to [*name*] Solicitors being a contribution towards the costs.

*I have already provided a cheque for £. . . made payable to [*name*] being a contribution towards the costs.

A10

Breakdown of costs

Proposed Right to Manage under the Commonhold and Leasehold Reform Act 2002

[*property*]

Estimated Costs

Step	Estimated Legal Costs (£)
Initial discussions and correspondence; preliminary review of legal structure and qualifying criteria and advising; drafting circular letters and Letter of Intent/Participation Agreement between tenants	
Involvement in setting up of an RTM company limited by guarantee to take over the management. Drafting and finalising Memorandum and Articles of Association, Subscription Agreement and liaising with company formation agent.	
Drafting and service of preliminary notices (e.g. information notice) and Notice of Claim.	
Review of landlord's response (if any) and dealing with procedural formalities, continuing correspondence/negotiations with freeholder, reviewing position and further advising on law and tactics.	
Conclusion of matters, reporting to tenants, dealing with general enquiries, co-ordinating tenant's funds and final accounting.	

- The above assumes a conclusion of the RTM procedure without the matter being referred to the Leasehold Valuation Tribunal (LVT). Please note that reference to the LVT will add considerably to the costs.
- The fees may depend on to what extent tenants or their co-ordinator wish to deal with administrative matters themselves, e.g. dealing with the appointment of members to the RTM company.
- The fees are exclusive of VAT and disbursements.
- The main disbursements are the costs of a company formation agent which should be somewhere in the region of £300 to £400.
- These figures are a rough guide only and will differ in each case depending on the particular circumstances.

- It is recommended that at some stage the advice of an accountant be obtained on matters relating to the limited company, e.g. the likely costs involved in managing the property.
- There is a liability to pay for the landlord's costs of dealing with the notices and general procedure under the right to manage regulations and any accounting or auditing costs.
- The parties are normally responsible for meeting their own costs of an application to the LVT (unless one party has behaved unreasonably and an application is made for costs to be paid accordingly).

A11

Participation agreement

THIS AGREEMENT is made on [date]

BETWEEN:

1. [name of company] whose registered office address is at [registered address] (company registration number [number]) ('the RTM company'), and
2. The Tenants named in the Schedule hereto, each of whom is hereinafter referred to as a 'Tenant' and all of whom are hereinafter referred to collectively as 'the Tenants'.

1. Definitions and interpretations

In this agreement:

1.1 'Claim' means the claim to acquire the Right to Manage the property.
1.2 'Claim Notice' means the service of a notice pursuant to section 79 of the legislation, giving the relevant parties notice of the Tenants' claim. Relevant parties for these purposes means the landlord under a lease of the whole or part of the property, party to such a lease other than the landlord or the Tenant, or a manager appointed under Part 2 of the Landlord and Tenant Act 1987.
1.3 'Right to Manage' means the right given to qualifying Tenants of blocks of flats to collectively take over the management of their block and exercise ancillary rights specified in the legislation.
1.4 'Acquiring the right to manage' or such similar expression as may be appropriate means compliance with the procedure laid down by the legislation.
1.5 'Legislation' means Part 2 of the Commonhold and Leasehold Reform Act 2002 together with any regulations, orders, byelaws or other subordinate legislation made under the aforementioned Act of Parliament from time to time.
1.6 'Participating flat' in relation to each Tenant means the flat specified in the Schedule hereto as being the flat in respect of which he is participating in the claim.
1.7 'His proportion' in relation to each Tenant means the proportion specified as his proportion in the Schedule hereto.
1.8 'Property' means the property known as [give details].
1.9 The following terms have the meanings conferred on them by the legislation: qualifying Tenant and landlord.
1.10 Where the context so requires words importing the masculine gender include the feminine gender and vice versa.
1.11 Where the context so requires words importing the singular include the plural.

PARTICIPATION AGREEMENT

1.12 Where a Tenant consists of two or more persons, any covenant made hereunder by a Tenant shall be deemed to be made by such persons jointly and severally.

2. Background

2.1 This agreement relates to the proposed acquisition by the Tenants of participating flats at the property of the Right to Manage the property using the statutory rights given to Tenants of blocks of flats under the legislation.

2.2 The Tenants have been dissatisfied with the management of the property and wish to exercise their rights under the legislation.

2.3 In order to exercise the Right to Manage, the Tenants formed the RTM company. The RTM company will initiate the process by serving the Claim Notice, dealing with matters arising out of the Claim Notice and ultimately acquiring the Right to Manage the property.

2.4 The directors of the RTM company are [name] and [name] and the RTM company Secretary is [name]. The company registration number of the RTM company is [number] and its registered office address is [address].

2.5 Pursuant to the obligations contained in the legislation the RTM company served participation notices on qualifying Tenants who, at the time the notices were sent, had not elected to become members of the RTM company. The participation notices were sent on [date].

2.6 The RTM company is now considering the service of the Claim Notice. Before a Claim Notice is served it is agreed that an agreement is required representing the agreements, warranties and covenants of the Tenants and RTM company to each other and to the process.

3. It is hereby agreed as follows

3.1 Each and every Tenant warrants to every other party hereto:

  3.1.1 that he is and shall, on the date on which the Claim Notice is to be served pursuant hereto, be:
   (i) a qualifying Tenant of the participating flat; and
   (ii) entitled to participate in the claim in respect of the participating flat and he is not aware of any reason why he may be prohibited from so participating.

  3.1.2 pursuant to the agreements contained in subparagraph 3.3 of this agreement he has or will have the funds to provide his proportion of the costs referred to in that subparagraph, when required and demanded.

3.2 Each and every Tenant agrees with every other party hereto as follows:

  3.2.1 he will act in good faith towards the other Tenants and the RTM company;

  3.2.2 if he has not already done so, he will become a member of the RTM company as soon as reasonably practicable;

  3.2.3 he will not cause or permit to be done any act or thing which will or may result in his being prohibited from participating in the claim in respect of the participating flat or which will or may result in the Claim Notice to be served pursuant hereto being or becoming invalid or which will or may prevent the Right to Manage being exercised pursuant to the claim.

3.2.4   he will provide to the RTM company or their duly appointed agents within seven days of any demand by the same any documents or information necessary to enable the RTM company to acquire the Right to Manage and comply with legal obligations, whether statutory or otherwise, including in respect of serving the Claim Notice, dealing with any counter-notice received, dealing with obtaining all relevant information prior to the acquisition of the Right to Manage and taking over and managing the property;

3.2.5   should he become aware of any information which may in any way affect the claim, he will notify the RTM company of such information immediately and in any event within five days of becoming aware of the information;

3.2.6   he will comply with the obligations imposed on him by the legislation in relation to the claim to the extent that he is aware of the obligations including the landlord's right to access his flat where this is reasonable in connection with matters arising out of the Claim Notice;

3.2.7   he will not direct any enquiries in relation to the claim, the acquisition of the Right to Manage or compliance with any of the obligations contained herein to any of the advisers at any time instructed by the RTM company in circumstances in which he is or should be aware of a potential conflict of interest arising for the adviser or advisers;

3.2.8   the Tenant will use his best endeavours prior to an assignment of his flat during the course of the claim to obtain:

(i)   a direct covenant by the assignee thereof with the Tenants for the time being participating in the claim to be bound on the said assignment by the Tenant's covenants contained herein in place of the Tenant;

(ii) the binding agreement of the assignee thereof to notify the RTM company within 14 days of such assignment that such assignment has taken place and that he is electing to participate in the claim; and

(iii) the binding agreement of the assignee thereof to become a member of the RTM company.

3.3   Each and every Tenant further agrees with every other party hereto as follows:

3.3.1   He has received information in respect of the costs involved in exercising the Right to Manage; legal costs of both the RTM company's solicitors and the landlord's solicitors; other potential professional fees which may be incurred by the RTM company; and disbursements, including the costs of setting up the RTM company but understands that the final costs may vary depending on the circumstances in which the Right to Manage is acquired and for example, whether there are any complications or delays.

3.3.2   Regardless as to how the RTM company takes over the Right to Manage the property:

(i)   he will pay to the RTM company or its duly appointed agent his proportion of all sums for which the RTM company is or may be liable by virtue of the legislation in relation to the claim such sums to be paid within seven days of receiving a written request from the RTM company or its duly appointed agent (or earlier in the case of urgency);

PARTICIPATION AGREEMENT

(ii) he will pay to the RTM company or its duly appointed agent on demand by the same his proportion of all other sums which the RTM company reasonably has incurred or will incur in relation to the claim including, but without prejudice to the generality of the foregoing, legal and accounting fees;
(iii) he has paid or will pay the initial sum of £... towards the costs of the exercise which will be held by the solicitors for the RTM company and used for the purposes of the proposed acquisition and matters incidental thereto.

3.3.3 In the event that acquisition of the Right to Manage pursuant to the claim cannot be achieved in circumstances where there is no default by the RTM company in complying with its obligations hereunder or under the legislation but due to an act or omission by any Tenant or Tenants who has or have participated or are for the time being participating in the claim or any default by the same in complying with obligations under the legislation, he will pay to the RTM company or its duly appointed agent such sums as are specified in subparagraphs 3.3.2(i) and (ii) hereof, within seven days of receiving a written request from the RTM company or its duly appointed agent (or earlier in the case of urgency).

3.3.4 In the event that the Claim Notice served pursuant hereto is withdrawn (whether deemed or otherwise) in circumstances where there is a joint and several liability for costs incurred by the landlord in relation to the claim imposed by the legislation on the members of the RTM company, he will pay his proportion of such costs to the landlord in accordance with such obligation.

3.3.5 He will take his own independent legal advice if he requires advice on his legal rights and obligations whether under the terms of this agreement or otherwise.

4. The RTM company agrees with every other party hereto (and with each member of the RTM company) as follows:

4.1 To prepare and serve the Claim Notice on each person who on the relevant date is:

4.1.1 landlord under a lease of the whole or part of the property;
4.1.2 party to such a lease otherwise than the landlord or Tenant; or
4.1.3 a manager appointed under Part 2 of the Landlord and Tenant Act 1987 to act in relation to the property or any premises contained in the property.

4.2 To comply with all obligations imposed by the legislation on the RTM company and to undertake the procedures in relation to the claim with due diligence in order to successfully acquire the Right to Manage.

4.3 It has instructed [*name of solicitors*] to advise the RTM company upon and provide all necessary assistance in relation to the claim and in relation to compliance by the RTM company with its obligations hereunder.

4.4 To ensure that each Tenant for the time being participating in the claim is kept reasonably informed of all matters relevant to the claim.

4.5 Where the circumstances so require, to take all reasonable steps to negotiate with the persons served with the Claim Notice and where appropriate reach a settlement in relation to the claim.

APPENDIX A11

4.6 To act in accordance with the decision of the majority of the participating qualifying Tenants as to whether orders or determinations of the court or the Leasehold Valuation Tribunal or any other relevant forum made in connection with the claim should be appealed or whether any appeal in respect of the same should be resisted.

4.7 To comply with each of its aforesaid obligations in such a manner so as to minimise so far as is reasonably possible the amounts payable by each of the participating qualifying Tenants and the amounts payable by each of the Tenant members of the RTM company.

5. **Not a partnership agreement**

This agreement does not constitute a partnership agreement.

I/We agree to the above and acknowledge that I/we have been recommended to obtain independent legal advice should I/we have any doubts as to the meaning or effect of any obligation under this agreement.

....
Signed

....
[*Print name of Tenant*]

....
Signed

....
[*Print name of Tenant*]

Flat no.: ....

Dated: ....

[I/We attach a cheque for £. . . made payable to [*name*] Solicitors].

Note: This agreement must be signed by ALL qualifying Tenants of the flat concerned i.e. by all those whose names are shown on the Land Registry title as registered proprietors (owners) of the flat.

SCHEDULE

Flat	Tenant	Proportion

A12

Information notice

Commonhold and Leasehold Reform Act 2002
Section 93

COMMONHOLD AND LEASEHOLD REFORM ACT 2002
INFORMATION NOTICE

TO [name and address]

1. [*name of company*] whose registered office address is at [*address*] (company registration number [*number*]) ('the RTM company'), in accordance with Chapter 1 of Part 2 of the Commonhold and Leasehold Reform Act 2002 ('the 2002 Act') hereby gives notice to you requesting information and inspection of documents pursuant to the rights contained in section 93 of the 2002 Act in connection with its exercise of the Right to Manage the property known as [*address of property*] ('the property').
2. Full particulars of the information required are set out in Part 1 of the Schedule below.
3. Full particulars of the documents of which inspection is sought are set out in Part 2 of the Schedule below.
4. Your replies and documents should be sent to [*name and address of firm of solicitors*] (Ref: [*solicitors' reference*]).

SCHEDULE

Part 1   Information

Tenant and property information

(1) How many flats are there at the property?
(2) Please list the full names and addresses of the tenants of those flats?
(3) How many floors are there in the building at the property?
(4) What areas of the property, including the building thereon, are used in common by all or some of the tenants at the property (e.g. stairways, entrances and halls).
(5) Do any services provided at the property or does the service charge structure currently maintained in any way whatsoever, incorporate any neighbouring properties. If so, how?
(6) Who is responsible for maintaining the basement at the property?
(7) Are any parts of the property the shared responsibility of the flat owners and any other person or party?

APPENDIX A12

Service charges

(8) What are the service charge percentages attributable to each flat? If the service charge percentage attributable to one or more of the flats differs to that detailed in the relevant lease, please explain why?

(9) In respect of which flats are there arrears of service charge as at the date of reply to this notice?

(10) With respect to those flats where there are arrears of service charge:

  (a) How much are the arrears?
  (b) To which service charge period do the arrears relate? If the arrears relate to more than one service charge period, please apportion the total sum payable to the relevant periods in your reply to this question.
  (c) Have demands for payment been made? If so, how many have been made and when?
  (d) Have any of the tenants been threatened with legal action. If so, please provide answers to questions 30 to 32 below (Disputes).

(11) With respect to any reserve/sinking fund maintained by you or a third party please provide the following information in respect of the three years immediately before the date of reply to this notice:

  (a) the flats which have contributed to the reserve/sinking fund;
  (b) the contributions made by each of those flats;
  (c) the date when the contributions were made;

(12) In respect of any expenditure incurred and met from the reserve/sinking fund, in the three years immediately before the date of reply to this notice, please list:

  (a) the individual items of expenditure;
  (b) the date the expenditure was incurred;
  (c) the amount of expenditure on each occasion.

(13) (a) Please advise the amount of unspent service charge monies and reserve fund held by you or any managing agents whether or not held directly or in a trust account.
  (b) Please confirm whether the monies referred to in part (a) of this question are likely to be spent at any time before the Right to Manage is acquired by the RTM company. If any monies are to be spent, please provide full particulars.

Services provided

(14) Please list all the works which have taken place over the last three years or, if no works have taken place over the last three years, all the works which last took place at the property, including, but not by way of limitation, works of:

  (a) repair;
  (b) maintenance;
  (c) improvement; and
  (d) decoration.

In respect of each such work listed, please answer the following:

  (a) When did the work take place?
  (b) How much did the work cost?
  (c) Were all relevant consents obtained prior to the work taking place, including, but not by way of limitation, planning permission and building regulations consent?

(d) Are there any guarantees, warranties, bonds or indemnities in place in respect of the work carried out?
(15) Please provide full particulars of all outstanding work orders, both written and verbal, together with details of all works proposed (including major works).
(16) Please list all the works that are due to take place at the property prior to the Right to Manage being acquired by the RTM company?
(17) Please provide a list of all inspections that have taken place in respect of the services received by the tenants at the property, including, but not by way of limitation, the alarm, fire safety, electricity and heating systems and lift maintenance. In respect of each such inspection, please provide the following additional information:
   (a) time of the inspection;
   (b) date of the inspection;
   (c) identity of the inspecting party;
   (d) areas of the property to which access was required;
   (e) outcome of the inspection;
   (f) date of the next proposed inspection.
(18) With respect to any services that have been or are being provided at the property, whether long-term or short-term, pursuant to contracts entered into with third parties (e.g. contracts with gardeners, lift engineers and cleaners), please answer the following:
   (a) What was/is the subject matter of the service contract?
   (b) What is the name of the contractor?
   (c) What is the address of the contractor?
   (d) What are the main terms of the contract, including the length of the contract, reviews and sums payable?
   (e) Were/are there breaches of any of the terms of the contract? If so, please give details.
(19) Are there any outstanding or unpaid invoices payable by you or any managing agents in respect of the services provided at the property? If so, please provide full particulars including reasons for non-payment?
(20) Which boundaries, walls, fences and/or hedges are maintained by you or any third party on your behalf?
(21) What outgoings are paid by you, or any third party on your behalf, at the property including rates, assessments, charges and any other relevant impositions?
(22) Are you aware of any current/future proposals for the development of the area neighbouring the property and how this would impact on the provision/performance of management services, including access to the property? If so, please give particulars.

Employees

Please give the following details in respect of any employee employed by you or any third party in pursuance of your lease obligations or otherwise in respect of services undertaken at the property:

(23) name and date of birth;
(24) date of commencement of employment;
(25) employment title;

APPENDIX A12

(26) role and responsibilities;
(27) salary and benefits in kind;
(28) particulars of other employment terms;
(29) further particulars of those employees living at the property, including the address of the flat at which the employee resides and telephone contact details.

Disputes

(30) Have any of the tenants complained of breaches of your lease obligations? If so, what was the purported breach complained of and what was the outcome of the complaint?
(31) Have the terms of any of the leases or any dispute between you and any of the tenants been the subject of any proceedings by any court, tribunal or arbitration or are any such proceedings pending?
(32) If the answer to the last question is 'yes', then please give the following further particulars:

  (a) When and where did the dispute take place?
  (b) What was the dispute regarding?
  (c) What was the outcome of the dispute?
  (d) Are there any sums which remain payable by one or more of the tenants pursuant to any such disputes?

State of the property

(33) Are you aware of any of the following issues which may affect the property:

  (a) structural defects;
  (b) drainage defects;
  (c) defective foundations;
  (d) rising damp, dry or wet rot;
  (e) infestation by wood boring insects.

(34) Has the property been the subject of flooding, landslip, subsidence or heave?
(35) Have the tenants complained of any of the matters referred to in questions 33 and 34 of this part of the Notice? If so, please give particulars.
(36) Are you aware of any dangerous or polluting substances at the property or the land surrounding the property? If so, please give particulars.

Insurance

(37) Please give details of any insurance cover relating to the property, including the name and address of the insurer, the policy number, risks covered, the amount of cover, premium, the date to which the property is insured and details of any early exit penalty clause, including (if appropriate) the basis upon which the penalty is calculated.
(38) Please provide particulars in respect of any outstanding insurance claim, including the nature of the claim, the sums involved and the stage the claim has reached.

Easements and rights

(39) Is the property the subject of any easements, licences or rights of access (for any reason whatsoever) of a formal or informal nature the existence of which may have an adverse impact on the provision of management services at the property by the RTM company? If so, please give further particulars.

INFORMATION NOTICE

(40) Does the property have the benefit of any easements, licences or rights of access of a formal or informal nature, which would assist in the RTM company's provision of management services? If so, please provide further particulars.

Equipment

(41) Please provide a schedule of the plant, machinery and equipment kept at the property to facilitate the provision of management services, which is intended to remain at the property on the Right to Manage being acquired by the RTM company.
(42) Have you obtained estimates in respect of proposed works at the property? If so, please provide copies of those estimates.

Licences and consents

(43) In the year prior to the date of this notice, have you received any requests for consents and licences from any tenants at the property? If so, please provide the following details:
  (a) To which flat does the request relate?
  (b) When was the request made?
  (c) What was the nature of the request?
  (d) What was the outcome of the request?

Subletting

(44) Are you aware of any subletting of all or part of any flat at the property?
(45) Please give the full names and addresses of all the subtenants you are aware of.
(46) Has any subtenant entered into a covenant with you to observe and perform the covenants, restrictions and obligations on the part of the tenant contained in the relevant lease?

Orders and Notices

(47) Are you aware of any orders, notices or undertakings in place of whatsoever nature (whether made by a court, tribunal, local authority or any other body) in respect of the property, which would affect the use of the property, particularly in respect of the provision of management services by the RTM company? If so, please provide further particulars.
(48) Have you or any third party served a notice pursuant to section 20 of the Landlord and Tenant Act 1985? If so:
  (a) When?
  (b) What work was the notice served in respect of?
  (c) What was the outcome of the consultation?

Part 2   Documents

Please provide copies of the following documents:

(1) leases and documents evidencing all of the terms of the lettings and any variation;
(2) all drawings and floor plans relating to the property;

APPENDIX A12

(3) all contracts and documents detailed in your answer to questions 17 and 18 in Part 1 of the Schedule to this Notice;
(4) audited accounts to the last service charge accounting year end and for the three management periods before that and a copy of the current year's estimated expenditure;
(5) all receipts and invoices relating to the periods detailed in question 4 of this part of the Schedule to this Notice, including outstanding invoices;
(6) insurance policies and schedules and copy correspondence relating to any insurance claims;
(7) bank statements for any accounts maintained in respect of the service charges for the last two years;
(8) outstanding and unpaid invoices;
(9) any subleases;
(10) all estimates in respect of works carried out at the property;
(11) any contracts of employment referred to in your replies to questions 23 to 29 and related documents;
(12) any other documents referred to in your replies to the other questions in Part 1 of the Schedule to this Notice;
(13) all documents relating to health and safety issues, including water testing, gas and electricity testing, together with PM7 certificates and insurance reports for lifts and boilers;
(14) all outstanding correspondence in respect of the management of the property (the originals to be provided on the RTM company taking over the management of the property);
(15) all other documents relating to information requested in Part 1 of the Schedule to this Notice the provision of which the RTM company might reasonably require for the purposes of effectively taking over the management of the property.

....

Director duly authorised on behalf of the RTM company

Served [*date*] by [*name*] Solicitors of [*address*].

A13

Claim notice

Commonhold and Leasehold Reform Act 2002

TO [*name and address*][1]

1. [*name of RTM company*] ('the company'), of [*address of registered office*], and of which the registered number is [*number under Companies Act 1985*] in accordance with Chapter 1 of Part 2 of the Commonhold and Leasehold Reform Act 2002 ('the 2002 Act') claims to acquire the right to manage [*name of premises to which notice relates*] ('the premises').
2. The company claims that the premises are ones to which Chapter 1 of the 2002 Act applies on the grounds that [*state grounds*].[2]
3. The full names of each person who is both:

    (a) the qualifying tenant of a flat contained in the premises; and
    (b) a member of the company;

    and the address of his flat are set out in Part 1 of the Schedule below.
4. There are set out, in Part 2 of the Schedule, in relation to each person named in Part 1 of the Schedule:

    (a) the date on which his lease was entered into;
    (b) the term for which it was granted;
    (c) the date of commencement of the term;
    [(d) such other particulars of his lease as are necessary to identify it [*may be ignored if no other particulars need to be given*].]

5. If you are:

    (a) landlord under a lease of the whole or any part of the premises;
    (b) party to such a lease otherwise than as landlord or tenant; or
    (c) a manager appointed under Part 2 of the Landlord and Tenant Act 1987 to act in relation to the premises, or any premises containing or contained in the premises;

    you may respond to this Claim Notice by giving a counter-notice under section 84 of the 2002 Act. A counter-notice must be in the form set out in Schedule 3 to the Right to Manage (Prescribed Particulars and Forms) (England) Regulations 2003. It must be given to the company, at the address in paragraph 1, not later than [*specify date not earlier than one month after the date on which the claim notice is given*]. If you do not fully understand the purpose or implications of this Notice you are advised to seek professional help.
6. The company intends to acquire the right to manage the premises on [*specify date, being at least three months after that specified in paragraph 5*].

APPENDIX A13

7. If you are a person to whom paragraph 5 applies and:
    (a) you do not dispute the company's entitlement to acquire the right to manage; and
    (b) you are the manager party under a management contract subsisting immediately before the date specified in this Notice;

    you must, in accordance with section 92 (duties to give notice of contracts) of the 2002 Act, give a notice in relation to the contract to the person who is the contractor party in relation to the contract and to the company.[3]
8. From the date on which the company acquires the right to manage the premises, landlords under leases of the whole or any part of the premises are entitled to be members of the company.[4]
9. This Notice is not invalidated by any inaccuracy in any of the particulars required by section 80(2) to (7) of the 2002 Act or regulation 4 of the Right to Manage (Prescribed Particulars and Forms) (England) Regulations 2003. If you are of the opinion that any of the particulars contained in the Claim Notice are inaccurate you may notify the company of the particulars in question, indicating the respects in which you think that they are inaccurate.

SCHEDULE

Part 1   Full names and addresses of persons who are both qualifying tenants and members of the company

[*set out here the particulars required by paragraph 3 above*]

Part 2   Particulars of leases of persons named in Part 1

[*set out here the particulars required by paragraph 4 above*]

....

Signed by authority of the company [*signature of authorised member or officer*]

Dated: ....

NOTES

1   A Claim Notice (a notice in the form set out in Schedule 2 to the Right to Manage (Prescribed Particulars and Forms) (England) Regulations 2003 of a claim to exercise the right to manage specified premises) must be given to each person who, on the date on which the notice is given, is:
    (a) landlord under a lease of the whole or any part of the premises to which the notice relates;
    (b) party to such a lease otherwise than as landlord or tenant; or
    (c) a manager appointed under Part 2 of the Landlord and Tenant Act 1987 to act in relation to the property, or any premises containing or contained in the property.

    But notice need not be given to such a person if he cannot be found, or if his identity cannot be ascertained. If that means that there is no one to whom the notice must be given, the company may apply to a Leasehold Valuation Tribunal for an order that the company is to acquire the right to manage the property. In that case, the procedures specified in section 85 of the 2002 Act (landlords, etc., not traceable) will apply.

2   The relevant provisions are contained in section 72 of the 2002 Act (premises to which Chapter 1 applies). The company is advised to consider, in particular, Schedule 6 to the 2002 Act (premises excepted from Chapter 1).
3   The terms 'management contract', 'manager party' and 'contractor party' are defined in section 91(2) of the 2002 Act (notices relating to management contracts).
4   Landlords under leases of the whole or any part of the premises are entitled to be members of the company, but only once the right to manage has been acquired by the company. An application for membership may be made in accordance with the company's Articles of Association, which may be inspected at the company's registered office, free of charge, at any reasonable time.

© Crown copyright. This is a prescribed form contained in Schedule 2 of the Right to Manage (Prescribed Particulars and Forms) (England) Regulations 2003 (SI 2003/1988).

A14

Counter-notice

Commonhold and Leasehold Reform Act 2002

TO [*name and address*]¹

1. [I admit that, on [*date on which claim notice was given*], [*name of company by which claim notice was given*] ('the company') was entitled to acquire the right to manage the premises specified in the Claim Notice *or* I allege that, by reason of [*specify provision of Chapter 1 of Part 2 of the Commonhold and Leasehold Reform Act 2002 relied on*], on [*date on which claim notice was given*], [*name of company*] ('the company') was not entitled to acquire the right to manage the premises specified in the Claim Notice [*delete one of these statements, as the circumstances require*].]
2. If the company has been given one or more counter-notices containing such a statement as is mentioned in paragraph (b) of subsection (2) of section 84 of the Commonhold and Leasehold Reform Act 2002, the company may apply to a leasehold valuation tribunal for a determination that, on the date on which notice of the claim was given, the company was entitled to acquire the right to manage the premises specified in the claim notice.²
3. If the company has been given one or more counter-notices containing such a statement as is mentioned in paragraph (b) of subsection (2) of section 84 of the Commonhold and Leasehold Reform Act 2002, the company does not acquire the right to manage those premises unless:
   (a) on an application to a leasehold valuation tribunal, it is finally determined that the company was entitled to acquire the right to manage the premises; or
   (b) the person by whom the counter-notice was given agrees, or the persons by whom the counter-notices were given agree, in writing that the company was so entitled.³

....

Signed [*signature of person on whom claim notice served, or of agent of such person; where an agent signs, insert also* Duly authorised agent of [*name of person on whom claim notice served*]]

Address: ....

            ....

Dated: ....

COUNTER-NOTICE

OR

....

Signed by authority of the company on whose behalf this notice is given [*signature of authorised member or officer and statement of position in company*]

Address: ....

....

Dated: ....

NOTES

1 The counter-notice is to be given to the company that gave the claim notice (a notice in the form set out in Schedule 2 to the Right to Manage (Prescribed Particulars and Forms) (England) Regulations 2003 of a claim to exercise the right to manage specified premises). The company's name and address are given in that notice.
2 An application to a leasehold valuation tribunal must be made within the period of two months beginning with the day on which the counter-notice (or, where more than one, the last of the counter-notices) was given.
3 For the time at which an application is finally determined, see section 84(7) and (8) of the Commonhold and Leasehold Reform Act 2002.

© Crown copyright. This is a prescribed form contained in Schedule 3 of the Right to Manage (Prescribed Particulars and Forms) (England) Regulations 2003 (SI 2003/1988).

A15

Notice of invitation to participate

Commonhold and Leasehold Reform Act 2002

NOTICE OF INVITATION TO PARTICIPATE IN RIGHT TO MANAGE

TO [*name and address*][1]

1. [*name of RTM company*] ('the company'), a private company limited by guarantee, of [*address of registered office*], and of which the registered number is [*number under Companies Act 1985*], is authorised by its Memorandum of Association to acquire and exercise the right to manage [*name of premises to which notice relates*] ('the premises'). The company intends to acquire the right to manage the premises.
2. [The company's Memorandum of Association, together with its Articles of Association, accompanies this notice *or* The company's Memorandum of Association, together with its Articles of Association, may be inspected at [*address for inspection*] between [*specify times*][2] *or* At any time within the period of seven days beginning with the day after this notice is given, a copy of the Memorandum of Association and Articles of Association may be ordered from [*specify address*] on payment of [*specify fee*][3] [*delete one of these statements as the circumstances require*].]
3. The names of –

    (a) the members of the company;
    (b) the company's directors; and
    (c) the company's secretary

    are set out in the Schedule below.
4. The names of the landlord and of the person (if any) who is party to a lease of the whole or any part of the premises otherwise than as landlord or tenant are [*names*].
5. Subject to the exclusions mentioned in paragraph 7, if the right to manage is acquired by the company, the company will be responsible for:

    (a) the discharge of the landlord's duties under the lease; and
    (b) the exercise of his powers under the lease;

    with respect to services, repairs, maintenance, improvements, insurance and management.
6. Subject to the exclusion mentioned in paragraph 7(b), if the right to manage is acquired by the company, the company may enforce untransferred tenant covenants.[4]

7. If the right to manage is acquired by the company, the company will not be responsible for the discharge of the landlord's duties or the exercise of his powers under the lease –
    (a) with respect to a matter concerning only a part of the premises consisting of a flat or other unit not subject to a lease held by a qualifying tenant; or
    (b) relating to re-entry or forfeiture.
8. If the right to manage is acquired by the company, the company will have functions under the statutory provisions referred to in Schedule 7 to the Commonhold and Leasehold Reform Act 2002.[5]
9. [The company intends to appoint a managing agent within the meaning of section 30B(8) of the Landlord and Tenant Act 1985 [*if known, give the name and address of the proposed managing agent here; if that person is the current managing agent, that fact must also be stated here*] or The company does not intend to appoint a managing agent within the meaning of section 30B(8) of the Landlord and Tenant Act 1985 [*delete one of these statements, as the circumstances require*].]
   [*If any existing member of the company has qualifications or experience in relation to the management of residential property, give details in the Schedule below.*]
10. If the company gives notice of its claim to acquire the right to manage the premises (a 'Claim Notice'), a person who is or has been a member of the company may be liable for costs incurred by the landlord and others in consequence of the Claim Notice.[6]
11. You are invited to become a member of the company.[7]
12. If you do not fully understand the purpose or implications of this notice you are advised to seek professional help.

SCHEDULE

The names of the members of the company are: [*names*].

The names of the company's directors are: [*names*].

The name of the company's secretary is: [*name*].

[*If applicable; see the second alternative in paragraph 9*]. The following member[s] of the company has/have qualifications or experience in relation to the management of residential property: [*give details*].

....

Signed by authority of the company [*signature of authorised member or officer*]

Dated: ....

NOTES

1 The notice inviting participation must be sent to each person who is at the time the notice is given a qualifying tenant of a flat in the premises but who is not already, and has not agreed to become, a member of the company. A qualifying tenant is defined in section 75 of the Commonhold and Leasehold Reform Act 2002 ('the 2002 Act').
2 The specified times must be periods of at least two hours on each of at least three days (including a Saturday or Sunday or both) within the seven days beginning with the day following that on which the notice is given.

APPENDIX A15

3. The ordering facility must be available throughout the seven-day period referred to in note 2. The fee must not exceed the reasonable cost of providing the ordered copy.
4. An untransferred tenant covenant is a covenant in a tenant's lease that he must comply with, but which can be enforced by the company only by virtue of section 100 of the 2002 Act.
5. The functions relate to matters such as repairing obligations, administration and service charges, and information to be furnished to tenants. Details may be obtained from the RTM company.
6. If the Claim Notice is at any time withdrawn, deemed to be withdrawn or otherwise ceases to have effect, each person who is or has been a member of the company is liable (except in the circumstances mentioned at the end of this note) for reasonable costs incurred by –
   (a) the landlord;
   (b) any person who is party to a lease of the whole or any part of the premises otherwise than as landlord or tenant; or
   (c) a manager appointed under Part 2 of the Landlord and Tenant Act 1987 to act in relation to the premises to which this notice relates, or any premises containing or contained in the premises to which this notice relates, in consequence of the Claim Notice. A current or former member of the company is liable both jointly with the company and every other person who is or has been a member of the company and individually. However, a former member is not liable if he has assigned the lease by virtue of which he was a qualifying tenant to another person and that other person has become a member of the company.
7. All qualifying tenants of flats contained in the premises are entitled to be members. Landlords under leases of the whole or any part of the premises are also entitled to be members, but only once the right to manage has been acquired by the company. An application for membership may be made in accordance with the company's Articles of Association which, if they do not accompany this notice, may be inspected as mentioned in paragraph 2 of the notice.
8. If the right to manage is acquired by the company, the company must report to any person who is landlord under a lease of the whole or any part of the premises any failure to comply with any tenant covenant of the lease unless, within the period of three months beginning with the day on which the failure to comply comes to the attention of the company –
   (a) the failure has been remedied;
   (b) reasonable compensation has been paid in respect of the failure; or
   (c) the landlord has notified the company that it need not report to him failures of the description of the failure concerned.
9. If the right to manage is acquired by the company, management functions of a person who is party to a lease of the whole or any part of the premises otherwise than as landlord or tenant will become functions of the company. The company will be responsible for the discharge of that person's duties under the lease and the exercise of his powers under the lease, with respect to services, repairs, maintenance, improvements, insurance and management. However, the company will not be responsible for matters concerning only a part of the premises consisting of a flat or other unit not subject to a lease held by a qualifying tenant, or relating to re-entry or forfeiture.
10. If the right to manage is acquired by the company, the company will be responsible for the exercise of the powers relating to the grant of approvals to a tenant under the lease, but will not be responsible for the exercise of those powers in relation to an approval concerning only a part of the premises consisting of a flat or other unit not subject to a lease held by a qualifying tenant.

© Crown copyright. This is a prescribed form contained in Schedule 1 of the Right to Manage (Prescribed Particulars and Forms) (England) Regulations 2003 (SI 2003/1988).

Lease extension

A16

Section 42 notice of claim

© 2002 Oyez
This Form is copyright
and must not be reproduced

LEASEHOLD REFORM, HOUSING AND URBAN DEVELOPMENT ACT 1993

Section 42

Notice of Claim to Exercise Right

(Note 1)

(1) Note 2.   To (1):

(2) Insert full name and address of the applicant (Note 3).   From (2):

(3) Note 4.   The address of the flat in respect of which [I] [we] claim a new lease is (3):

(4) Note 5.   Particulars of [my] [our] lease are as follows (4).

Date:

Parties:

Term:

Date of commencement of term:

[P.T.O.]

HUD 1/1

SECTION 42 NOTICE OF CLAIM

(5) Insert amount.

The premium which [I] [we] propose to pay for the grant of a new lease is (5): £

(6) Note 6.

The other amount(s) which [I] [we] propose to pay in accordance with Schedule 13 of the Act are as follows (6):

(7) Note 7.

The terms which [I] [we] propose should be contained in the new lease are (7):

[P.T.O.

HUD 1/2

APPENDIX A16

(8) Insert full name of person appointed, if any.	The person appointed by [me] [us] to act for [me] [us] in connection with this claim is (8):
(9) Insert the address in England and Wales.	whose address in England and Wales at which notices may be given under Part I Chapter II of the Act is (9):
(10) Note 8.	The date by which you must respond to this notice by giving a counter-notice under section 45 is (10):

Dated

(11) Note 9.	Signed (11)
(12) Note 10.	Copies of this notice are being given to (12):

[P.T.O.

HUD 1/3

NOTES

1. Where a tenant or a personal representative claims to exercise his or her right to acquire a new lease of the flat, he or she must give a notice in this form.

2. This notice must be given both to the landlord as defined in section 40 and to any third party to the tenant's lease.

3. This notice may be given either by the person who has been a qualifying tenant for the last two years, or by the personal representatives of that person. A qualifying tenant is defined in section 5 of the Act with the omission of subsections (5) and (6). Personal representatives have two years from the grant to apply.

4. Insert the full address of the flat, with sufficient particulars to identify the property to which the claim extends.

5. Include such particulars of the tenant's lease as are sufficient to identify it, including the details indicated here.

6. Schedule 13 Part III specifies how the amounts payable to owners of intermediate leasehold interests are to be calculated.

7. Specify the proposed terms, or set them out in a schedule to be attached and refer to that schedule here.

8. This date must be at least two months after the date this notice is given.

9. This notice must be signed by the applicant, or by each of them where joint applicants are making the claim.

10. A copy of this notice must be given to all landlords : Schedule 11, paragraph 2.

A17

Section 45 counter-notice

© 2002 Oyez

LEASEHOLD REFORM, HOUSING AND URBAN DEVELOPMENT ACT 1993

Section 45

Landlord's Counter-Notice

(Note 1)

(1) Insert full name and address of the applicant.

To(^{1}):

(2) Insert full name and address of the landlord.

From(^{2}):

(3) Note 2.

(^{3})The landlord admits that the applicant had on the relevant date the right to acquire a new lease of the flat and:

(a) the landlord accepts the following proposals in the applicant's notice

(4) Note 3

(^{4}):

(5) Note 4.

(b) the landlord does not accept the following proposals in the applicant's notice

(^{5}):

[P.T.O.

HUD 2/1

SECTION 45 COUNTER-NOTICE

(6) Insert counter-proposal(s).

(c) the landlord's counter-proposal to each proposal which is not accepted is (^{6}):

(7) Give reasons.

(^{3}) The landlord does not admit that the applicant had on the relevant date the right to acquire a new lease of the flat for the following reasons (^{7}):

HUD 2/2

APPENDIX A17

(8) Note 2.   (⁸) [The landlord intends to make an application for an order under section 47(1) of the Act on the grounds that he or she intends to redevelop premises in which the flat is contained]
(9) Note 5.   (⁹).

                The address in England and Wales at which the landlord may be given notices under Part I Chapter II of the Act is:

                Date

                Signed

(10) Name and   [Landlord's agent] (¹⁰)
address.

[P.T.O.

HUD 2/3

SECTION 45 COUNTER-NOTICE

NOTES

1. The landlord must give a counter-notice to the notice of claim to a new lease. The counter-notice must be given by the date specified in the notice.

2. Delete whichever does not apply.

3. State which (if any) of the proposals contained in the notice are accepted by the landlord.

4. State which (if any) of the proposals contained in the notice are not accepted by the landlord.

5. Where the landlord either admits or denies the right to a new lease, this paragraph should be included where the landlord intends to apply under section 47(1).

Acquisition of freehold or extended lease (house)

A18

Notice of tenant's claim to acquire the freehold or an extended lease

Leasehold Reform Act 1967

NOTICE OF TENANT'S CLAIM TO ACQUIRE THE FREEHOLD OR AN EXTENDED LEASE

TO: [*name and address of person on whom this notice is served*][1]

[*and* TO: [*name and address of any recipient of a copy of the notice; delete if paragraphs 5–10 are deleted*][1] **Your attention is drawn to paragraphs 8 to 10 of this notice.**]

1. I am the tenant of the house and premises of which particulars are given in the Schedule to this notice.
2. In exercise of my rights under Part I of the Leasehold Reform Act 1967, I give you notice of my desire: [to have the freehold of the house and premises *or* to have an extended lease of the house and premises [*delete whichever is inapplicable*].]
3. The particulars on which I rely are set out in the Schedule to this notice.
4. If you are both my immediate landlord and the freeholder, you must give me, within two months of the service of this notice, a notice in reply in Form 3 set out in the Schedule to the Leasehold Reform (Notices) Regulations 1997 (or in a form substantially to the same effect), stating whether or not you admit my right [to have the freehold of the house and premises *or* to have an extended lease of the house and premises [*delete whichever is inapplicable*] subject to any question as to the correctness of the particulars of the house and premises) and, if you do not admit my right, stating the grounds on which you do not admit it.[2]

   [*The remaining paragraphs of this form should be deleted where the claimant's immediate landlord is known to be the freeholder of the house and premises.*]

5. If you are not my immediate landlord, or if you are my immediate landlord but not the freeholder, you must comply with the requirements of paragraphs 7 and 8, but you need only give me the notice mentioned in paragraph 4 if you are the person designated as 'the reversioner' in accordance with paragraph 2 of Schedule 1 to the Act. If you are the reversioner, you must give the notice mentioned in paragraph 4 within two months of the first service of this notice on any landlord.[3]
6. I have served a copy of this notice on the following person(s) whom I know or believe to have an interest in the house and premises superior to my tenancy: [*insert name and address of each person on whom a copy of the notice has been served*].
7. You must now serve a copy of this notice on any other person whom you know or believe to have an interest in the house and premises superior to my tenancy, and you must record on that copy the date on which you received this notice. If

NOTICE OF TENANT'S CLAIM TO ACQUIRE FREEHOLD OR EXTENDED LEASE

you serve a copy on any person you must add his name and, if you know it, his address to the list at the end of paragraph 6, and give me written notice of the name, and address (if known).
8. If you know who is, or believe yourself or another person to be, the reversioner, you must give me written notice stating the name and address (if known) of the person who you think is the reversioner, and serve copies of it on every person whom you know or believe to have an interest superior to my tenancy, stating on each copy the date on which you received this notice.
9. Anyone who receives a copy of this notice must, without delay, serve a further copy of it on any person whom he knows or believes to have an interest in the house and premises superior to my tenancy but who is not named in the notice, unless he knows that that person has already received a copy of it, and he must also record on each further copy the date on which he received this notice. For each further copy served, you must add the name of the person served and, if you know it, his address to the list at the end of paragraph 6, and give me written notice of the name and (if known) the address of that person.
10. Anyone who receives a copy of this notice and who knows who is, or believes himself to be, the reversioner, must notify me in writing of the name and (if known) the address of the person known or believed by him to be the reversioner, and serve a copy of this notification on every person whom he knows or believes to have an interest superior to my tenancy.

Dated: ....

....

Signed [tenant]

Of [address]: ....
....

[The name and address of my solicitor or agent, to whom further communications may be sent is [name and address] [delete if inapplicable].]

SCHEDULE

Particulars supporting tenant's claim

1. The address of the house.
2. Particulars of the house and premises sufficient to identify the property to which your claim extends.[4]
3. Particulars of the tenancy of the house and premises sufficient to identify the instrument creating the tenancy and to show that the tenancy is and has at the material times been a long tenancy or treated as a long tenancy.[5]
4. Particulars sufficient to show the date on which you acquired the tenancy.[6]
5. (a) Particulars of the tenancy of the house and premises sufficient to show that the tenancy is and has at the material times been a tenancy at a low rent or treated as a tenancy at a low rent.[7]

    OR

    (b) If your claim is based on section 1AA (additional right to enfranchisement only in case of houses whose rent exceeds applicable limit under section 4), particulars of the tenancy sufficient to show that the tenancy is one in

APPENDIX A18

relation to which section 1AA has effect to confer a right to acquire the freehold of the house and premises.[8]

6. Particulars of any other long tenancy of the house or a flat forming part of the house held by any tenant.[9]
7. Where either

   (a) a flat forming part of the house is let to a person who is a qualifying tenant of a flat for the purposes of Chapter 1 or 2 of Part I of the Leasehold Reform, Housing and Urban Development Act 1993; or
   (b) your tenancy is a business tenancy,

   the following particulars:

   (i) the periods for which in the last ten years, and since acquiring the tenancy, you have and have not occupied the house as your residence; and
   (ii) during those periods what parts (if any) of the house have not been in your own occupation and for what periods; and
   (iii) what other residence (if any) you have had and for what periods, and which was your main residence.[10]

8. Additional particulars sufficient to show that the value of the house and premises does not exceed the applicable financial limit specified in section 1(1)(a)(i) or (ii), (5) or (6) of the Act. (These are not required where the right to have the freehold is claimed in reliance on any one or more of the provisions in sections 1A, 1AA or 1B of the Act, or where the tenancy of the house and premises has been extended under section 14 and the notice under section 8(1) was given (whether by a tenant or a subtenant) after the original term date of the tenancy).[11]
9. Additional particulars sufficient to show whether the house and premises are to be valued in accordance with section 9(1) or section 9(1A) of the Act. (These are not required where the right to have the freehold is claimed in reliance on any one or more of the provisions in section 1A, 1AA or 1B of the Act, or where the tenancy of the house and premises has been extended under section 14 and the notice under section 8(1) was given (whether by a tenant or a subtenant) after the original term date of the tenancy).
10. Additional particulars where you rely on section 6 (rights of trustees), 6A (rights of personal representatives) or 7 (rights of members of family succeeding to tenancy on death) of the Act.[12]

NOTES

1 (a) Where the tenant's immediate landlord is not the freeholder, the claim may, in accordance with the Leasehold Reform Act 1967, as amended, be served on him or any superior landlord, and copies of the notice must be served by the tenant on anyone else known or believed by him to have an interest superior to his own (Schedule 3, paragraph 8(1)).
   (b) Where the landlord's interest is subject to a mortgage or other charge and the mortgagee or person entitled to the benefit of the charge is in possession of that interest, or a receiver appointed by him or by the court is in receipt of the rents and profits, the notice may be served either on the landlord or on the person in possession or the receiver (Schedule 3, paragraph 9(1)).
   (c) Any landlord whose interest is subject to a mortgage or other charge (not being a rentcharge) to secure the payment of money must (subject to special provisions applicable to debenture-holders' charges) on receipt of the claim inform the mortgagee or person entitled to the benefit of the charge (Schedule 3, paragraph 9(2)).

NOTICE OF TENANT'S CLAIM TO ACQUIRE FREEHOLD OR EXTENDED LEASE

2 The landlord must (unless note 3 applies) serve a notice in reply in Form 3 set out in the Schedule to the Leasehold Reform (Notices) Regulations 1997 (or in substantially the same form) within two months of the service on him of this notice. If he does not admit the tenant's right to have the freehold or an extended lease, the notice in reply must state the grounds on which the right is not admitted. If the landlord intends to apply to the court for possession of the house and premises in order to redevelop it (section 17) or to occupy it (section 18), his notice must say so. If he does not so intend, but he objects under subsection (4) or (5) of section 2 to the inclusion in the claim of a part of the house and premises which projects into other property, or to the exclusion from the claim of property let with the house and premises but not occupied with and used for the purposes of the house by any occupant of it, he must give notice of his objection with or before his notice in reply; unless in his notice in reply he reserves the right to give it later, in which case it must still be given within two months of the service on him of the tenant's notice. If the landlord admits the claim, the admission is binding on him, unless he shows that he was misled by misrepresentation or concealment of material facts, but it does not conclude any question of the correctness of the particulars of the house and premises as set out in the claim (Schedule 3, paragraph 7).

3 Where the tenant's immediate landlord is not the freeholder, any proceedings arising out of the tenant's notice, whether for resisting or for giving effect to the claim, must be conducted by the person who is designated as 'the reversioner' in accordance with paragraph 2 of Schedule 1 to the Act and he must give the notice in reply. The reversioner is the landlord whose tenancy carries an expectation of possession of the house and premises of 30 years or more after the expiration of all inferior tenancies and, if there is more than one such landlord, it means the landlord whose tenancy is nearest to that of the tenant; if there is no such landlord, it means the owner of the freehold. The tenant will be informed in the notice in reply if it is given by a landlord acting as the reversioner.

4 'Premises' to be included with the house in the claim are any garage, outhouse, garden, yard and appurtenances which at the time of the notice are let to the tenant with the house.

5 In respect of a house, 'long tenancy' has the meaning given by section 3 of the Act. (Special provisions apply in relation to business tenancies, see section 1(1ZC) of the Act inserted by section 140 of the Commonhold and Leasehold Reform Act 2002.) Where there have been successive tenancies, particulars should be given of each tenancy. In the case of a lease already extended under the Act, the date of the extension and the original term date should be given. In addition to section 3 of the Act, section 174(a) of the Housing Act 1985 provides for certain tenancies granted pursuant to the right to buy to be treated as long tenancies. Section 1B of the Act also provides for certain tenancies terminable on death or marriage to be long tenancies for the limited right described in note 11. Under Schedule 4A to the Act, certain shared ownership leases granted by public authorities, housing associations and registered social landlords carry neither the right to enfranchise nor the right to obtain an extended lease.

6 The claimant must have owned the lease for two years prior to the date of the application for enfranchisement or lease extension (section 1(1)(b) of the Act, as amended by sections 138 and 139 of the Commonhold and Leasehold Reform Act 2002).

7 In addition to the provision of section 4 of the Act (meaning of 'low rent'), section 1A(2) of the Act provides for tenancies falling within section 4A(1) of the Act to be treated as tenancies at a low rent for the limited right described in note 11.

8 Section 1AA confers a limited right to enfranchisement (described in note 11) in the case of leases which would qualify but for the fact that the tenancy is not a tenancy at a low rent, with two exceptions. The first is where the lease is excluded from the right under section 1AA(3): i.e. where the house is in an area designated as a rural area, the freehold of the house is owned together with adjoining land which is not occupied for residential purposes, and the tenancy was either granted on or before 1 April 1997 or was granted after that date but before the coming into force of section 141 of the Commonhold and Leasehold Reform Act 2002, for a term of 35 years or less. Information as to the location of designated rural areas is held at the offices of leasehold valuation tribunals. The second exception applies to any shared ownership lease (as defined by section 622 of the Housing Act 1985) originally granted by a housing association or a registered social landlord.

9 Section 1(1ZA) of the Act (inserted by section 138(2) of the Commonhold and Leasehold Reform Act 2002) provides that head lessees do not have rights to enfranchise or a lease

APPENDIX A18

extension where there exist inferior tenancies which confer on the tenant the right to enfranchise and a lease extension under the Act. Under section 1(1ZB) of the Act, where there exists an inferior long tenancy (as defined under section 7 of the Leasehold Reform, Housing and Urban Development Act 1993) of a flat which confers on the tenant the right to enfranchise or a new lease under that Act the head lessee only has the right to enfranchise or a lease extension under the Act where he meets the residence requirement (see note 10). It is therefore necessary to provide details of any other long tenancies.

10 Particulars of residence and occupation are required in relation to those cases specified in paragraph 7 of the Schedule to this notice (see section 1(1ZB) and (1B) of the Act as inserted, respectively, by sections 138 and 139 of the Commonhold and Leasehold Reform Act 2002). The residence requirement in these specified cases is that the tenant has lived in the property as his only or main residence for the last two years or for periods amounting to two years in the last ten years.

11 A claimant who relies on any one or more of the provisions in sections 1A, 1AA or 1B of the Act (or where the tenancy of the house and premises has been extended under section 14 and the notice under section 8(1) was given (whether by a tenant or a subtenant) after the original term date of the tenancy), has the right to have the freehold at a price determined in accordance with section 9(1C) of the Act, but not the right to have an extended lease. Section 1A(1) applies to a tenancy of a house and premises the value of which exceeds the applicable financial limit. Sections 1A(2) and 1B are described in notes 7 and 5 respectively. Section 1AA (described in note 8) applies to certain cases where the long lease fails the low rent test.

12 (a) Where the claimant is giving the notice by virtue of sections 6, 6A or 7 he is required (Schedule 3, paragraph 6(2)) to adapt the notice and show under paragraphs 4 and 7 of the Schedule to the notice the particulars that bring the claim within section 6, 6A or, as the case may be, section 7.

(b) Where the tenancy is or was vested in trustees the claimant should, for the purposes of a claim made in reliance on section 6, state the date when the tenancy was acquired by the trustees, and, where the case falls within paragraphs 7(a) or (b) of the Schedule to the notice, the date when the beneficiary occupied the house by virtue of his interest under the trust, and the particulars of any period of occupation by the beneficiary which are relied upon as bringing the case within section 6.

(c) Section 6A of the Act (inserted by section 142 of the Commonhold and Leasehold Reform Act 2002) provides that where a tenant dies and immediately before his death he qualified for the right to enfranchise or a lease extension, those rights can be exercised (up to two years after the date of probate or letters of administration) by his personal representatives. Where the tenancy is vested in personal representatives, they should, for the purposes of making a claim under section 6A, provide evidence that the deceased tenant qualified for the relevant right immediately before his death, state the date when the tenancy became vested in them, and provide evidence to show that probate or letters of administration have been granted no more than two years before the date of the claim for extension of the lease or enfranchisement.

(d) Where the claimant was a member of the previous tenant's family and became the tenant on the latter's death, for the purposes of a claim made in reliance upon section 7, the claimant should state the date on which the previous tenant acquired the tenancy, particulars of his relationship to the previous tenant and his succession to the tenancy, and particulars in respect of any period of occupation by himself on which the claimant relies as bringing the case within section 7.

© Crown copyright. Form 1 of the Schedule to the Leasehold Reform (Notices) (Amendment) (England) Regulations 2002 (SI 2002/1715)

A19

Notice in reply to a tenant's claim

Leasehold Reform Act 1967

NOTICE IN REPLY TO TENANT'S CLAIM

TO: [*name and address of claimant*]

1. I have received [a copy of] your notice dated [*date*] claiming the right to have [the freehold *or* an extended lease] of the house and premises described in your notice.[1]
2. [I admit your right (subject to any question as to the correctness of the particulars given in your notice of the house and premises).][2]
3. [I do not admit your right, on the following grounds: [*state grounds on which the tenant's right is not admitted*].
4. [The house and premises are within an area of a scheme approved under [section 19 of the Act *or* section 70 of the Leasehold Reform, Housing and Urban Development Act 1993].[3] [*Delete as appropriate or delete entire paragraph if paragraph 2 has been deleted.*]
5. [In my opinion the house should be valued in accordance with section [9(1) *or* 9(1A) *or* 9(1C)] of the Act.][4] [*Delete as appropriate or delete the entire paragraph if paragraph 2 has been deleted.*]
6. [I intend *or* [*name*] intends] to apply to the court for possession of the house and premises under [section 17 *or* section 18] of the Act.][5] [*Delete the entire paragraph, if inapplicable, or delete whichever of the first alternative does not apply and the reference to section 17 or section 18 as the circumstances require.*]
7. [I reserve the right to give notice under section 2 of the Act of my objection to the exclusion from the house and premises claimed by you of property let to you with the house and premises but not at present occupied by you, or to the continued inclusion in the house and premises of parts lying above or below other premises in which I have an interest.][6] [*Delete the entire paragraph if inapplicable.*]
8. [This notice is given by me as the person designated by paragraph 2 of Schedule 1 to the Act as the reversioner of the house and premises.][7] [*Delete the entire paragraph if you are the claimant's immediate landlord and also the freeholder.*]

....

Signed

[The name and address of my solicitor or agent, to whom further communications may be sent is *name and address*]. [*Delete if inapplicable.*]

Dated: ....

APPENDIX A19

NOTES

(References in this Form and these Notes to 'the Act' are references to the Leasehold Reform Act 1967.)

1. This notice must be given within two months of the service of the notice of the tenant's claim. Where there is a chain of landlords, the time limit runs from the date of the first service of the claimant's notice on any landlord (Schedule 3, paragraphs 7(1) and 8(1)(a) to the Act).
2. If the landlord admits the claim he will not later be able to dispute the claimant's right to have the freehold or an extended lease, unless he shows that he was misled by misrepresentation or concealment of material facts, but the admission does not conclude any question as to the correctness of the particulars of the house and premises as set out in the claim (Schedule 3, paragraph 7(4) to the Act).
3. Schemes approved under section 19 of the Act (retention of management powers for general benefit of neighbourhood) and section 70 of the Leasehold Reform, Housing and Urban Development Act 1993 (approval by leasehold valuation tribunal of estate management scheme) provide that within a specified area the landlord will retain powers of management and rights against leasehold houses and premises in the event of the tenants acquiring the freehold.
4. Where section 9(1) of the Act applies, the purchase price and cost of enfranchisement is determined on the basis of the value of the land and there is no element of marriage value.
   Where section 9(1A) of the Act applies, the purchase price and cost of enfranchisement is determined on the basis of the land and the house including 50% of any marriage value (see section 9(1D) of the Act inserted by section 145 of the Commonhold and Leasehold Reform Act 2002). No marriage value is payable if the unexpired term of the lease exceeds 80 years (see section 9(1E) of the Act inserted by section 146 of the Commonhold and Leasehold Reform Act 2002). The fact that the tenant has security of tenure will be taken into account in determining the price.
   Where section 9(1C) of the Act applies, the purchase price and cost of enfranchisement is determined on the same basis as that under section 9(1A) of the Act, except that there is no security of tenure at the end of the lease, and additional compensation may be payable if the sale of the freehold results in the diminution of value of or any other loss or damage in relation to any interest of the landlord in any other property.
5. If the landlord (on the assumption, where this is not admitted, that the claimant has the right claimed) intends to apply to the court for an order for possession of the premises for redevelopment under section 17 or use as a residence under section 18 of the Act, the notice must say so (Schedule 3, paragraph 7(3) to the Act). (Where a claim is to have a freehold, only certain public authorities or bodies can resist it on the ground of an intention to redevelop the property.)
6. If the landlord intends to object (under subsection (4) or (5) of section 2 of the Act) to the exclusion from the claim of property let with the house and premises to the tenant but not at the relevant time subject to a tenancy vested in him (see amendment to section 2(4) made by section 138(4) of the Commonhold and Leasehold Reform Act 2002), or to the inclusion of part of the house and premises which projects into other property of the landlord's, notice of his objection must be given before or with this notice, unless the right to give it later is reserved by this notice (Schedule 3, paragraph 7(2) to the Act). In any case, notice of the objection must be given within two months of the service of the claimant's notice.
7. Where there is a chain of landlords, this notice must be given by the landlord who is designated as 'the reversioner' (see paragraphs 1 and 2 of Schedule 1 to the Act). For this purpose the reversioner is either the landlord whose tenancy carries an expectation of possession of the house and premises of 30 years or more after the expiration of all the inferior tenancies (or, if there is more than one such landlord, the one whose tenancy is nearest to that of the tenant) or, if there is no such landlord, the freeholder.

© Crown copyright. The copyright in the content of this form belongs to the Crown. It is the Form given in the Schedule to the Leasehold Reform (Notices) (Amendment) (No.2) (England) Regulations 2002.

APPENDIX B

Flowcharts and checklists

B1

Collective enfranchisement timetable flowchart

Establish qualifying criteria

- self-contained building or part
- non-residential parts not more than 25%
- 2 or more flats held by qualifying tenants
- flats of qualifying tenants not less than 2/3rds of total flats
- participating tenants not less than 50% of total flats

Nominee Purchaser (NP) — [RTE Company]
  |
  [notice of invitation to participate]
  |
  +14 days

initial notice
|
2 months or later date specified in initial notice

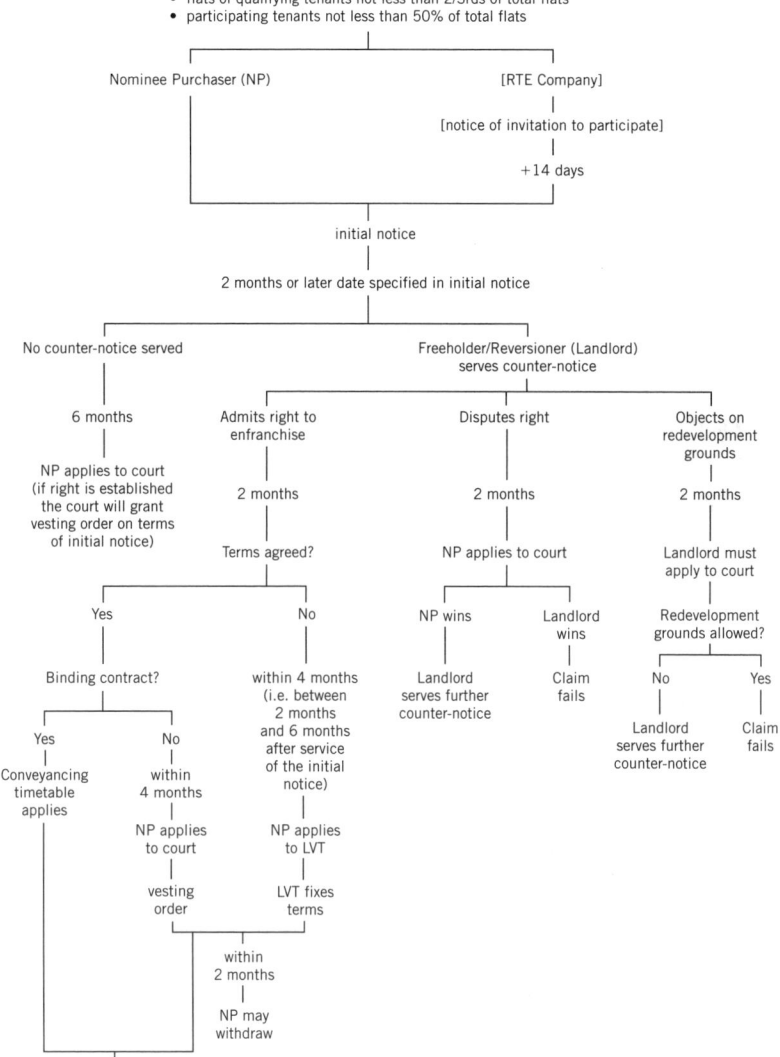

No counter-notice served | **Freeholder/Reversioner (Landlord) serves counter-notice**

No counter-notice served:
- 6 months
- NP applies to court (if right is established the court will grant vesting order on terms of initial notice)

Freeholder/Reversioner branches:
- Admits right to enfranchise → 2 months → Terms agreed?
  - Yes → Binding contract?
    - Yes → Conveyancing timetable applies
    - No → within 4 months → NP applies to court → vesting order
  - No → within 4 months (i.e. between 2 months and 6 months after service of the initial notice) → NP applies to LVT → LVT fixes terms → within 2 months → NP may withdraw
- Disputes right → 2 months → NP applies to court
  - NP wins → Landlord serves further counter-notice
  - Landlord wins → Claim fails
- Objects on redevelopment grounds → 2 months → Landlord must apply to court → Redevelopment grounds allowed?
  - No → Landlord serves further counter-notice
  - Yes → Claim fails

Completion

B2

Checklist of preliminary matters on collective enfranchisement claim

1. **Preliminary**
   1.1 Support in principle from sufficient tenants likely/established ☐
   1.2 Office copy entries for all flats/units in the building and of any superior interests obtained and checked ☐
   1.3 Where titles are unregistered, such initial analysis of titles as is practicable undertaken ☐
   1.4 Specimen flat lease obtained and checked ☐
   1.5 Indicative/rough estimate of value obtained ☐
   1.6 Table/spreadsheet of tenants and their leases and ground rents, etc. prepared ☐

2. **Qualifying criteria**
   2.1 Does the building qualify? ☐
       2.1.1 is it structurally detached or separated vertically, etc.? ☐
       2.1.2 no overhang or similar with any adjoining premises ☐
       2.1.3 plans obtained and inspected ☐
       2.1.4 site inspection undertaken where applicable ☐
       2.1.5 non-residential parts not more than 25% ☐
       2.1.6 no unusual features of the building ☐
       2.1.7 if 4 flats or less and not a purpose-built block, no resident landlord ☐
       2.1.8 if building part of an estate, issues arising considered ☐
   2.2 Qualifying tenants/tenancies ☐
       2.2.1 number of flats held on long leases ascertained ☐
       2.2.2 do such flats comprise at lease two-thirds of the flats in the building? ☐
       2.2.3 do the participating tenants hold at least 50% of the total number of flats in the building? ☐
       2.2.4 any tenant owning three or more flats in the building excluded ☐

CHECKLIST OF PRELIMINARY MATTERS – COLLECTIVE ENFRANCHISEMENT

2.2.5	are the relevant leases 'standard' long leases? if there are any special features, investigate further	☐
2.2.6	note made if any flats of participating tenants for which marriage value will be payable i.e. where there will be 80 years or less remaining at the time of service of the initial notice?	☐

3.	**The landlord**	
3.1	Has the freeholder and any relevant landlord been identified and their address for service ascertained?	☐
3.2	Information notice served where necessary	☐
3.3	Response to information notice received or copies of relevant documents requested and obtained	☐
3.4	No landlord falling into a special category such as an ecclesiastical landlord or the Crown	☐
3.5	Relevant landlord ascertained, where more than one	☐
3.6	Landlord's title(s) checked where possible	☐
3.7	Issue of intermediate leasehold interests to be acquired or potential leasebacks considered where applicable	☐
3.8	Index map search made of proposed premises to be acquired	☐

4.	**Matters between tenants**	
4.1	Participation agreement drafted, agreed and signed by all participators	☐
4.2	Tenants' contributions collected and/or provided for	☐
4.3	System of communication established	☐

5.	**Nominee purchaser/RTE Company**	
5.1	Where applicable, nominee purchaser/RTE Company formed	☐
5.2	Suitable Articles of Association/constitution prepared and agreed	☐
5.3	Initial corporate formalities dealt with, such as the appointment of officers, membership/shareholdings etc.	☐
5.4	[Notice of invitation to participate – RTE Company – served]	☐

6.	**Valuation**	
6.1	Valuer instructed	☐
6.2	Valuation obtained	☐
6.3	Issues arising from valuation listed and addressed	☐
6.4	Apportionment of values between landlords' interests where more than one	☐

APPENDIX B2

7. Other premises and rights

7.1 Additional premises to be acquired considered ☐

7.2 Additional rights to be required or covenants to be imposed considered ☐

8. Initial notice

8.1 Up-to-date precedent obtained and used ☐

8.2 Contents checked against statutory criteria ☐

8.3 Draft sent to and approved by tenants' representative ☐

8.4 Draft sent to and approved by valuer ☐

8.5 Engrossment prepared with date for landlord's response left blank ☐

8.6 Signed by all participating tenants, including both where there is a joint tenancy of a flat ☐

8.7 Date agreed for landlord's response being at least two months after the intended date of service of the notice, leaving a margin for error ☐

8.8 [Time for response to notice of invitation to participate – RTE company – expired, at least 14 days for service.] ☐

9. Service of initial notice

9.1 Landlord(s)' identity(ies) and address(es) rechecked ☐

9.2 Notice served by hand or some other method as well as by post where practicable ☐

9.3 Service on solicitor where such has agreed to accept service ☐

9.4 Service effected on all relevant landlords ☐

9.5 Receipt obtained where service by hand ☐

10. Steps following service of initial notice

10.1 Register at HM Land Registry or Land Charges Registry as appropriate ☐

10.2 Date diarised for time for service of landlord's counter-notice ☐

10.3 Review likely future timetable and anticipate subsequent steps ☐

B3

Right to manage timetable flowchart

Establish qualifying criteria

- self-contained building or part
- 2 or more flats held by qualifying tenants
- flats of qualifying tenants not less than 2/3rds of total flats
- internal floor area of non-residential parts does not exceed 25% of total internal floor area of the premises
- participating tenants not less than 50% of total flats

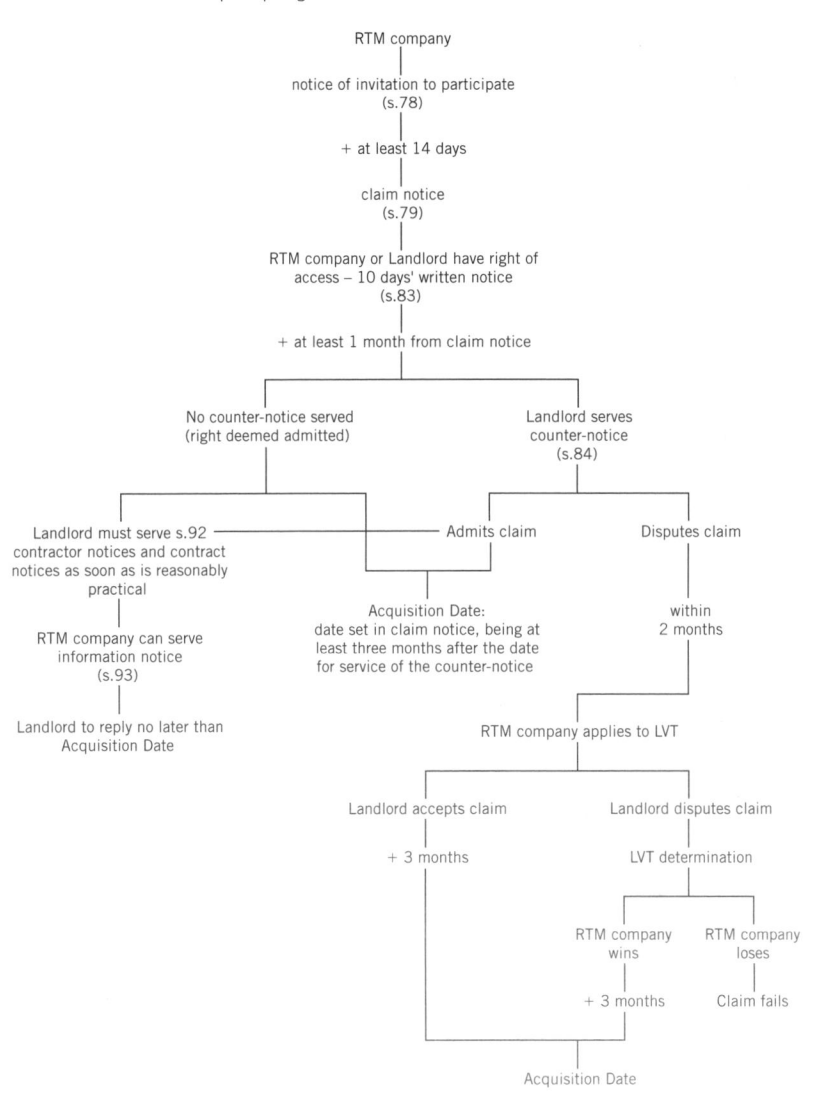

RTM company
|
notice of invitation to participate
(s.78)
|
+ at least 14 days
|
claim notice
(s.79)
|
RTM company or Landlord have right of
access – 10 days' written notice
(s.83)
|
+ at least 1 month from claim notice
|
┌─────────────────────────────┴─────────────────────────────┐
No counter-notice served   Landlord serves
(right deemed admitted)   counter-notice
                                                          (s.84)
                                                            |
                                              ┌─────────────┴─────────────┐
Landlord must serve s.92 ─────────── Admits claim   Disputes claim
contractor notices and contract
notices as soon as is reasonably
practical
| | |
RTM company can serve   Acquisition Date: within
information notice   date set in claim notice, being at   2 months
(s.93)   least three months after the date
                                for service of the counter-notice
| |
Landlord to reply no later than   RTM company applies to LVT
Acquisition Date |
                                                          ┌───────────────────┴───────────────────┐
                                                    Landlord accepts claim   Landlord disputes claim
                                                              | |
                                                        + 3 months   LVT determination
                                                                                                   |
                                                                                    ┌──────────────┴──────────────┐
                                                                               RTM company   RTM company
                                                                                  wins   loses
                                                                                    | |
                                                                               + 3 months   Claim fails
                                                              └──────────────────────┤
                                                                              Acquisition Date

B4

Checklist of preliminary matters on right to manage claim

1. **Preliminary**
1.1 Support in principle from sufficient tenants likely/established ☐
1.2 Office copy entries for all flats/units in the building and of any superior interests obtained and checked ☐
1.3 Where titles are unregistered, such initial analysis of titles as is practicable undertaken ☐
1.4 Specimen flat lease obtained and checked ☐
1.5 Table/spreadsheet of tenants and their leases and ground rents, etc. prepared ☐

2. **Qualifying criteria**
2.1 Does the building qualify? ☐
    2.1.1 is it structurally detached or separated vertically, etc.? ☐
    2.1.2 no overhang or similar with any adjoining premises ☐
    2.1.3 plans obtained and inspected ☐
    2.1.4 site inspection undertaken where applicable ☐
    2.1.5 non-residential parts not more than 25% ☐
    2.1.6 no unusual features of the building ☐
    2.1.7 if building part of an estate, issues arising considered ☐
2.2 Qualifying tenants/tenancies ☐
    2.2.1 number of flats held on long leases ascertained ☐
    2.2.2 do such flats comprise at lease two-thirds of the flats in the building? ☐
    2.2.3 do the participating tenants hold at least 50% of the total number of flats in the building? ☐

CHECKLIST OF PRELIMINARY MATTERS – RIGHT TO MANAGE

3. The landlord

3.1	Has the freeholder or any other relevant landlord and third party to any relevant lease been identified and their address for service ascertained?	☐
3.2	If any manager appointed under Landlord and Tenant Act 1987, their details obtained	☐
3.3	Served a preliminary information notice under section 82 where applicable	☐
3.4	Response to information notice received or copies of relevant documents requested and obtained	☐
3.5	Landlord's title(s) checked where possible	☐

4. Matters between tenants

4.1	Letter of intent or participation agreement drafted, agreed and signed by all participators	☐
4.2	Tenants' contributions collected and/or provided for	☐
4.3	System of communication established	☐

5. RTM company

5.1	RTM company formed	☐
5.2	Initial corporate formalities dealt with, such as the appointment of officers, membership/shareholdings, etc.	☐
5.3	Notice of invitation to participate prepared using prescribed form and contents checked	☐
5.4	Notice of invitation to participate served on all qualifying tenants not members of the company	☐

6. Management

6.1	Proposed managing agents selected in principle	☐
6.2	Assessment of potential management issues	☐
6.3	Timetable for acquisition of the right considered including tie in to possible key dates, such as insurance renewal or financial year end for service charges	☐
6.4	Funding of RTM company for payment of service after acquisition date considered	☐
6.5	Issues relating to repairs/building defects considered	☐
6.6	Prospective officers of RTM company aware of responsibilities of themselves and of company	☐
6.7	Management functions to be acquired noted	☐
6.8	Information regarding current management and contracts for services obtained insofar as practicable	☐

APPENDIX B4

7. Other premises and rights

7.1 The extent of any appurtenant property over which the right to manage is to be claimed ascertained ☐

8. Claim notice

8.1 Up-to-date precedent of prescribed form obtained and used ☐
8.2 Contents checked against statutory criteria ☐
8.3 Draft sent to and approved by tenants' representative ☐
8.4 Date agreed for landlord's counter-notice being at least one month after the intended date of service of the claim notice ☐
8.5 Date agreed for acquisition of right being at least three months after the date for the landlord's counter-notice ☐

9. Service of claim notice

9.1 Name and address of landlord(s) and manager parties checked ☐
9.2 Notice served by hand or some other method as well as by post where practicable ☐
9.3 Service on solicitor where such has agreed to accept service ☐
9.4 Service effected on all relevant landlords/manager parties ☐
9.5 Receipt obtained where service by hand ☐

10. Steps following service of claim notice

10.1 Date diarised for counter-notice and acquisition ☐
10.2 Consider exercising right of access where necessary ☐
10.3 Service of section 93 information notice (note may need to reserve after right admitted, deemed admitted or determined in the RTM company's favour) ☐

B5

Right to extension of lease of a flat timetable flowchart

Establish qualifying criteria

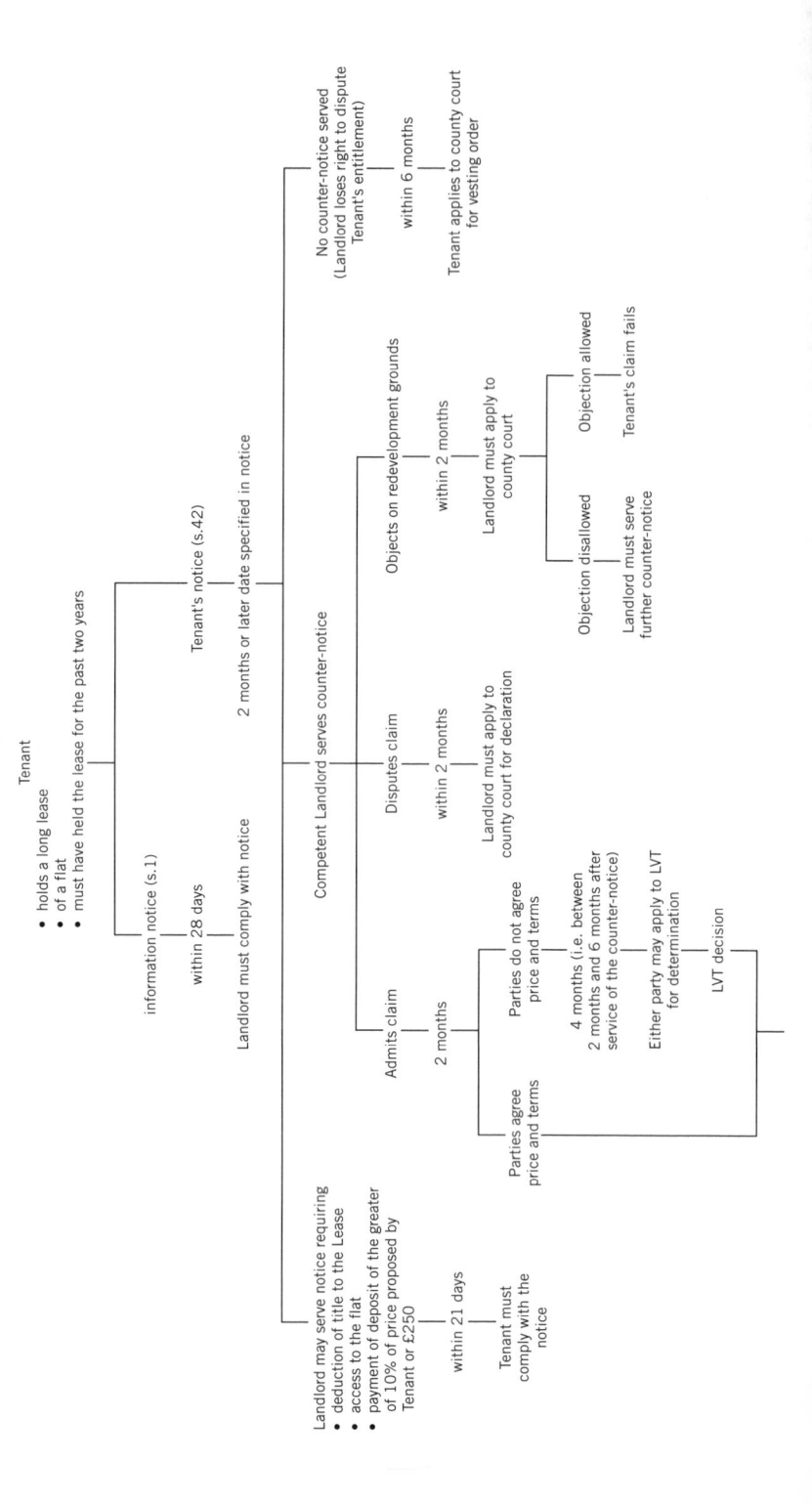

Tenant
- holds a long lease
- of a flat
- must have held the lease for the past two years

↓ information notice (s.1)

within 28 days

Landlord must comply with notice

↓ Tenant's notice (s.42)

2 months or later date specified in notice

Landlord may serve notice requiring
- deduction of title to the Lease
- access to the flat
- payment of deposit of the greater of 10% of price proposed by Tenant or £250

within 21 days

Tenant must comply with the notice

Competent Landlord serves counter-notice

Branches:

- **Admits claim** → 2 months
  - Parties agree price and terms
  - Parties do not agree price and terms → 4 months (i.e. between 2 months and 6 months after service of the counter-notice) → Either party may apply to LVT for determination → LVT decision

- **Disputes claim** → within 2 months → Landlord must apply to county court for declaration

- **Objects on redevelopment grounds** → within 2 months → Landlord must apply to county court
  - Objection allowed → Tenant's claim fails
  - Objection disallowed → Landlord must serve further counter-notice

- **No counter-notice served** (Landlord loses right to dispute Tenant's entitlement) → within 6 months → Tenant applies to county court for vesting order

276

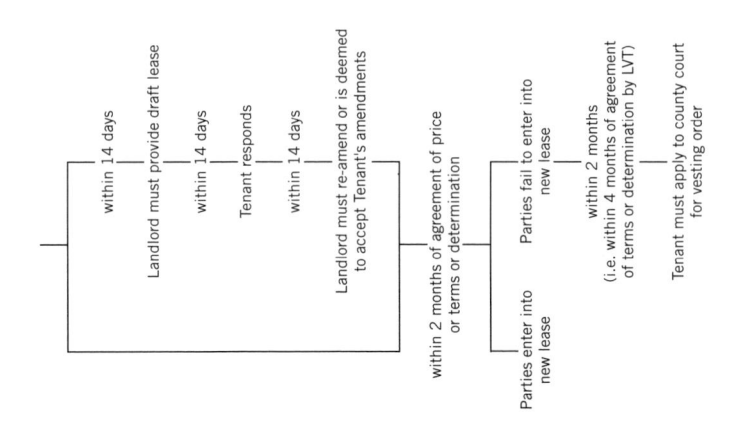

- within 14 days: Landlord must provide draft lease
- within 14 days: Tenant responds
- within 14 days: Landlord must re-amend or is deemed to accept Tenant's amendments
- within 2 months of agreement of price or terms or determination:
  - Parties enter into new lease
  - Parties fail to enter into new lease
    - within 2 months (i.e. within 4 months of agreement of terms or determination by LVT): Tenant must apply to county court for vesting order

B6

Checklist of preliminary matters on service of tenant's notice to extend the lease of a flat

1. **Qualifying criteria**
   1.1 Is the property in fact, a flat? see 3 below ☐
   1.2 Is the tenant's interest held under a long lease? ☐
   1.3 Has the tenant held the lease for more than two years from the date registered as proprietor? ☐

2. **Tenant's lease**
   2.1 If applicable, office copy entries of the tenant's title obtained ☐
   2.2 Copy of tenant's lease obtained and key information noted ☐
   2.3 Position investigated where tenant's lease is not a 'standard' long lease ☐
   2.4 Existence of any supplemental lease, deeds of variation, licences or similar checked for and copies obtained ☐
   2.5 Remaining term calculated and checked for critical date with regard to the impact of marriage value (where lease has, or is likely to have, 80 years or less unexpired as at the date of the tenant's notice) ☐
   2.6 Details of whether any other party to the lease other than the landlord and the tenant noted ☐
   2.7 Lease checked for defects which may need to be remedied in the new lease ☐

3. **Flat and premises**
   3.1 Checked to confirm that it is a flat ☐
   3.2 Plans obtained and checked ☐
   3.3 Confirmed no significant overlap with any other premises ☐
   3.4 Check to ascertain any other premises also demised for a tenant on a long lease, such as a garden, garage, for which a claim should also be made ☐
   3.5 Site inspection undertaken where necessary ☐

CHECKLIST OF PRELIMINARY MATTERS – TENANT'S NOTICE TO EXTEND LEASE

4. Valuation

4.1 Valuer instructed ☐
4.2 Valuation obtained ☐
4.3 Valuation discussed with tenant ☐
4.4 Apportionment of price between landlords where more than one ☐
4.5 Funding of likely premium and costs considered ☐

5. Landlords

5.1 Name and address of any landlord and other party to the lease ascertained and noted ☐
5.2 Section 41 notice requiring information served where necessary ☐
5.3 Reply to section 41 notice obtained ☐
5.4 Office copy entries of superior titles and copies of superior leases obtained and checked ☐
5.5 Identity of competent landlord ascertained where there is more than one ☐
5.6 Landlord in special category position checked and investigated ☐

6. General

6.1 Whether any collective enfranchisement procedure in force in respect of the building or anticipated ☐

7. Tenant's Notice

7.1 Up-to-date precedent used ☐
7.2 Contents compared against statutory criteria ☐
7.3. Value inserted and divided between landlords and such that can be reasonably supported by evidence ☐
7.4 Notice sent to tenant for signature with date for landlord's counter-notice left blank ☐
7.5 Notice signed personally by the tenant or all of them if more than one ☐

8. Service of Notice

8.1 Insert date for landlord to serve counter-notice, being a date at least two months after the date of service ☐
8.2 Notice served on competent landlord with copy served on any other landlord ☐
8.3 Service of copy of the notice on any other party to the tenant's lease ☐
8.4 If notice served by hand, receipt obtained ☐

APPENDIX B6

9. Steps following service of Tenant's Notice

9.1   Notice registered against the competent landlord's title at the Land Registry or as a Land Charge ☐

9.2   Date diarised for service of the landlord's counter-notice ☐

9.3   Is tenant in the position to pay deposit and deduce title if requested to do so by the landlord following service of the tenant's notice? ☐

B7

Right to acquire the freehold of a house timetable flowchart

Establish qualifying criteria

- Lease of a whole house
- must be a long lease
- Tenant must have held the lease for past two years

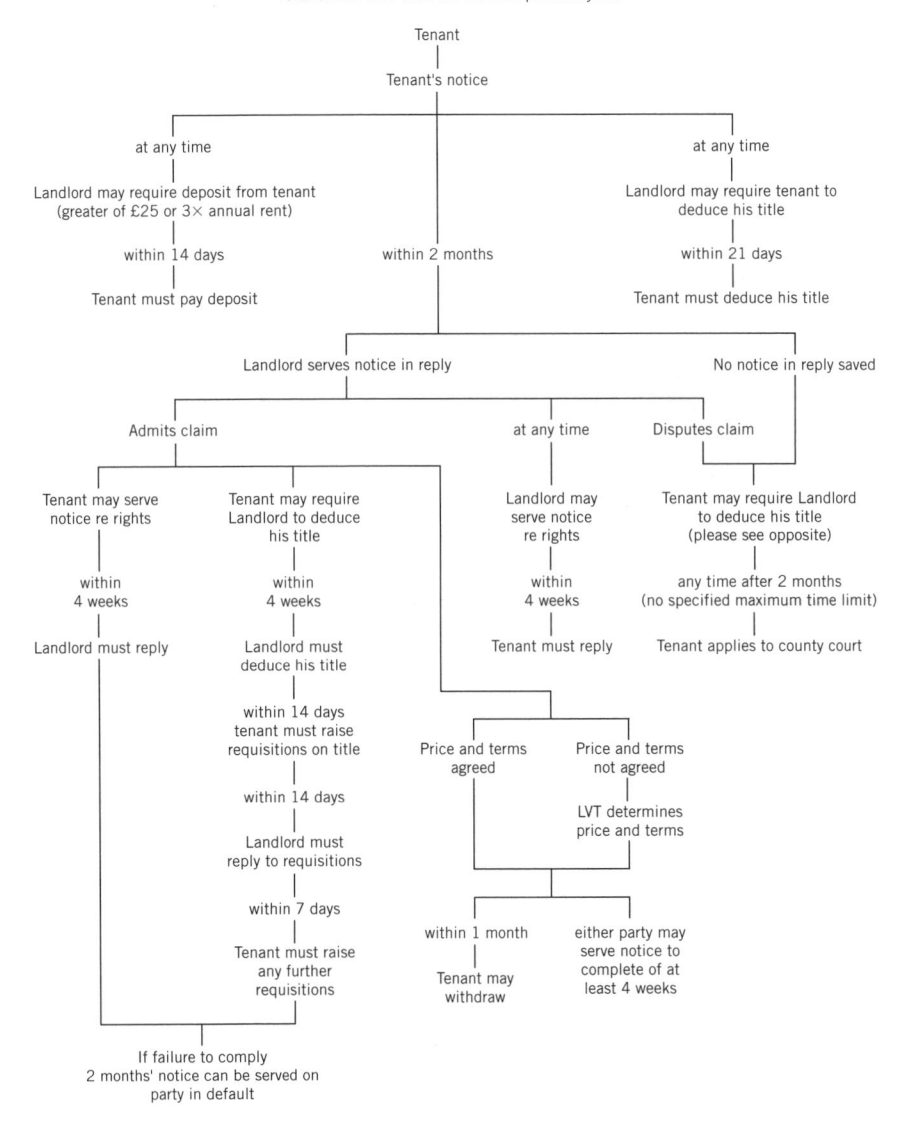

Tenant
|
Tenant's notice

at any time
Landlord may require deposit from tenant
(greater of £25 or 3× annual rent)
|
within 14 days
|
Tenant must pay deposit

within 2 months
Landlord serves notice in reply

at any time
Landlord may require tenant to deduce his title
|
within 21 days
|
Tenant must deduce his title

No notice in reply saved

Admits claim

Tenant may serve notice re rights
|
within 4 weeks
|
Landlord must reply

Tenant may require Landlord to deduce his title
|
within 4 weeks
|
Landlord must deduce his title
|
within 14 days tenant must raise requisitions on title
|
within 14 days
|
Landlord must reply to requisitions
|
within 7 days
|
Tenant must raise any further requisitions

If failure to comply 2 months' notice can be served on party in default

at any time
Landlord may serve notice re rights
|
within 4 weeks
|
Tenant must reply

Price and terms agreed

Price and terms not agreed
|
LVT determines price and terms

within 1 month
|
Tenant may withdraw

either party may serve notice to complete of at least 4 weeks

Disputes claim
Tenant may require Landlord to deduce his title
(please see opposite)
|
any time after 2 months
(no specified maximum time limit)
|
Tenant applies to county court

281

B8

Checklist of preliminary matters on service of tenant's notice to acquire the freehold of a house

1. **Qualifying criteria**
   - 1.1 Is the tenant's interest held under a long lease (i.e. original term granted more than 21 years)? see 2 below? ☐
   - 1.2 Is the property in fact, a house? see 3 below ☐
   - 1.3 Has the tenant held the lease for more than two years from the date registered as proprietor? ☐

2. **Tenant's lease**
   - 2.1 If applicable, office copy entries of the tenant's title obtained ☐
   - 2.2 Copy of tenant's lease obtained and key details noted ☐
   - 2.3 Position investigated where tenant's lease is not a 'standard' long lease ☐
   - 2.4 Existence of any supplemental lease, deeds of variation, licences or similar checked for and copies obtained ☐
   - 2.5 Remaining term calculated and checked for critical date with regard to the impact of marriage value (where lease has, or is likely to have, 80 years or less unexpired as at the date of the tenant's notice) ☐
   - 2.6 Tenant meets residency test (NB only relevant in very limited circumstances) ☐

3. **House and premises**
   - 3.1 Checked to confirm that it is a house, e.g. is it or could it be lived in as a permanent residence, is it a permanent structure? ☐
   - 3.2 Plans obtained and checked ☐
   - 3.3 Confirmed no significant overlap with any other premises ☐
   - 3.4 Check to ascertain any other premises also demised to the tenant on a long lease, such as a garden, garage, for which a claim should also be made ☐
   - 3.5 Site inspection undertaken where necessary ☐
   - 3.6 No special circumstances such as business tenancy, designated rural area or resident landlord ☐

CHECKLIST OF PRELIMINARY MATTERS – TENANT'S NOTICE TO ACQUIRE FREEHOLD

3.7	Any other rights or covenants required checked for and noted	☐
3.8	Analysis undertaken of whether house meets the low rent and rateable value, etc. criteria, where this may be relevant	☐

4.	**Valuation**	
4.1	Valuer instructed	☐
4.2	Basis of valuation discussed and agreed with valuer	☐
4.3	Valuation obtained	☐
4.4	Valuation discussed with tenant	☐
4.5	Apportionment of price between landlords where more than one	☐
4.6	Funding of likely price and costs considered	☐

5.	**Landlords**	
5.1	Name(s) and address(es) of the freeholder and intermediate superior landlord to the lease ascertained and noted	☐
5.2	Office copy entries of superior titles and copies of superior leases obtained and checked	☐
5.3	If landlord in special category position checked and investigated	☐

6.	**Tenant's notice**	
6.1	Up-to-date precedent of prescribed form used	☐
6.2	Contents compared against statutory criteria	☐
6.3	Notice sent to tenant for approval	☐
6.4	Notice signed either personally by the tenant (by both or all if more than one) or by their solicitor or other agent	☐

7.	**Service of Notice**	
7.1	Notice served on the freeholder and any intermediate landlord	☐
7.2	If notice served by hand, receipt obtained	☐

8.	**Steps following service of tenant's notice**	
8.1	Register the notice against the freeholder's title at the Land Registry or as a Land Charge	☐
8.2	Diarise date for service of the landlord's notice in reply	☐
8.3	Is tenant in the position to pay deposit and deduce title if requested to do so by the landlord following service of the tenant's notice? (deposit is £25 or 3 times the annual rent, whichever is the greater)	☐

APPENDIX C

Useful addresses

The Association of Residential Managing Agents (ARMA)
178 Battersea Park Road
London
SW11 4ND
Tel: 020 7978 2607
Fax: 020 7498 6153
Email: info@arma.org.uk
Website: **www.arma.org.uk**

Communities and Local Government
Eland House
Bressenden Place
London
SW1E 5DU
Tel: 020 7944 4400
Fax: 020 7944 9645
Email: contactus@communities.gsi.gov.uk
Website: **www.communities.gov.uk**

Estates Gazette Interactive
Tel: 0845 0778811
Fax: 020 7911 1770
Email: customer.services@egi.co.uk
Website: **www.egi.co.uk**

Land Registry
Head Office
32 Lincoln's Inn Fields
London
WC2A 3PH
DX: 1098 London/Chancery Lane
Tel: 020 7917 8888
Fax: 020 7955 0110
Website: **www.landregistry.gov.uk**

The Lands Tribunal
Procession House
55 Ludgate Hill
London
EC4M 7JW
Tel: 020 7029 9780
Fax: 020 7029 9781
Email: Lands@dca.gsi.gov.uk
Website: **www.landstribunal.gov.uk**

The Law Society
113 Chancery Lane
London
WC2A 1PL
DX: 56 London / Chancery Lane
Tel: 020 7242 1222
Fax: 020 7831 0344
Email: info.services@lawsociety.org.uk
Website: **www.lawsociety.org.uk**

The Leasehold Advisory Service
31 Worship Street
London
EC2A 2DX
Tel: 0845 345 1993
Fax: 020 7374 5373
Email: info@lease-advice.org
Website: **www.lease-advice.org**

The Residential Property Tribunal Service
Website: www.rpts.gov.uk

APPENDIX C

London: London Rent Assessment Panel
Residential Property Tribunal Service
10 Alfred Place
London
WC1E 7LR
Tel: 020 7446 7700
Fax: 020 7637 1250
Email: london.rap@odpm.gsi.gov.uk

Manchester: Northern Rent Assessment Panel
Residential Property Tribunal Service
First Floor
25 York Street
Manchester
M1 4JB
Tel: 0845 100 2614
Fax: 0161 237 3656 or 0161 237 9491
Email: northern.rap@odpm.gsi.gov.uk

Birmingham: Midlands Rent Assessment Panel
Residential Property Tribunal Service
2nd Floor
East Wing
Ladywood House
45–46 Stephenson Street
Birmingham
B2 4DH
Tel: 0845 100 2615 or 0121 643 8336
Fax: 0121 643 7605
Email: midland.rap@odpm.gsi.gov.uk

Cambridge: Eastern Rent Assessment Panel
Great Eastern House
Tenison Road
Cambridge
CB1 2TR
Tel: 0845 100 2616 or 01223 505112
Fax: 01223 505116
Email: eastern.rap@odpm.gsi.gov.uk

Chichester: Southern Rent Assessment Panel
1st Floor
1 Market Avenue
Chichester
PO19 1JU
Tel: 0845 100 2617 or 01243 779394
Fax: 01243 779389
Email: southern.rap@odpm.gsi.gov.uk

Corporate Unit
Residential Property Tribunal Service
10 Alfred Place
London
WC1E 7LR
Tel: 020 7446 7751 or 020 7446 7752
Fax: 020 7580 5684
Email: rptscorporateunit@odpm.gsi.gov.uk

The Royal Institution of Chartered Surveyors
RICS Contact Centre
Surveyor Court
Westwood Way
Coventry
CV4 8JE
Tel: 0870 333 1600
Fax: 020 7334 3811
Email: contactrics@rics.org
Website: **www.rics.org**

Index

Administration charges
   Commonhold and Leasehold
      Reform Act 2002 provisions 177
   failure to pay 183

Collective enfranchisement *see also*
   Collective enfranchisement
   conveyancing; Collective
   enfranchisement, notices and
   counter-notices
   absent landlord 32–3
   collective enfranchisement
      structures 164–6
   costs 27, 51, 195–6
   court, application to 52
   excluded premises 30
   key features 25–6
   key matters 28
   key practice points 30, 40, 42, 46, 49
   key terminology 25
   landlord's response 41–3, 44–6
   leasebacks 50–1
   leasehold interests, intermediate 30
   Leasehold Valuation Tribunal
      (LVT), application to 53, 221–2
   leases of participating tenants,
      extending 54–5
   legislation applicable 24
   nominee purchaser
      death of a participator 35
      generally 34–5, 164–5
      key considerations 166
   other issues 54
   overview 24
   participation agreement 19, 190–4
   precedents
      articles of association, company 198–206
      basic information spreadsheet 197
   collective enfranchisement
      timetable flowchart 267
   costs, breakdown of 195–7
   Leasehold Valuation Tribunal,
      application to 221–2
   letter of intent 188–9
   participation agreement 190–4
   preliminary matters checklist 268–70
   preliminary investigations 28–34, 268–70
   purchase outside the statutory regime 26–7
   qualifying criteria 28
   qualifying premises 29, 30
   qualifying tenants 31
   RTE (right to enfranchise) companies
      key points 36
      notice of invitation to participate 36
   timetable and procedure after
      service of initial notice
      conveyancing timetable and
      conveyance 47–8, 267
      landlord's response 41–3, 44–6
      overview 40–1
   valuation example, Fig 10.1 161
   valuation and price 33–4, 42–3, 157
   valuer and 153
   who is the landlord? 31–2
   withdrawal from the process 53–4

Collective enfranchisement conveyancing
   completion
      costs 51
      discharge of mortgages 51
      SDLT returns 51

INDEX

Collective enfranchisement conveyancing (*cont.*)
    vendor's lien and service charges 52
    conveyance contents
        air, right of 48
        key practice points 49
        management schemes 49
        other encumbrances and rentcharges 49
        rights to be included 48
    conveyancing timetable and conveyance
        contract 46, 47–8
        conveyance 46, 47–9
        title, deducing 47
    leasebacks
        mandatory and optional 50
        terms of 50–1
    leases of participating tenants, extending 54–5

Collective enfranchisement, notices and counter-notices
    counter-notice
        contents and service 43–4
        key practice points 46
        landlord admits claim 45–6
        landlord disputes right 45
        landlord disputes validity/form of initial notice 44
        landlord's intention to redevelop 45
        none served by landlord 46
    information notice 33
    notice, initial
        effect of service 40
        generally 37–39, 207–13
        key practice points 40, 42
        landlord disputes validity and form 44
        service 39
        timetable and procedure after service 41–8
    notice of invitation to participate 36, 188–9
    precedents
        counter-notice 214–20
        initial notice 207–13

Commonhold and Leasehold Reform Act 2002, general rights *see also* Collective enfranchisement; Freehold of a house, tenant's right to acquire; Lease of a flat, right to extend; Lease of a house, right to a new; Service charges
    administration charges 177
    manager, appointment of a 181
    overview 172
    summary 172–3

Companies and corporate formalities
    articles of association, precedent 198–206
    collective enfranchisement structures 164–6
    company limited by guarantee 165–6
    company limited by shares 166
    corporation tax and VAT 169
    directors' duties 167–8
    nominee purchaser 164–5, 166
    overview 164
    priority of 164
    RTE (right to enfranchise) company 167
    RTM (right to manage) company 167
    voting rights 168

Consultation
    long-term agreements on services, landlord's obligation to tenant 180
    long-term agreements, works under, landlord's obligation to tenant 181
    major works, landlord's obligation to tenant 179–80

Costs
    breakdown of costs, precedents 195–6, 224–5
    collective enfranchisement 27, 51
    contributions and process management 18, 22
    estate charges under estate management schemes 179
    freehold of a house, tenant's right to acquire 134–5
    lease of a flat, extending 100, 113
    Leasehold Valuation Tribunal and 148, 179
    right to manage claim notice 77
    withdrawal from collective enfranchisement 53–4

Estate charges under estate management schemes 179

Forfeiture and possession
    breach of a covenant or condition in the lease 183
    failure to pay service charge/administration charges or small amounts for a short time 183

Freehold of a house, tenant's right to acquire see also Freehold of a house, tenant's right to acquire, notices; Freehold of a house, tenant's right to acquire, procedure
    contracting out
        design of houses 137–8
        overview 137
    costs, amount of and types of 134–5
    forum 137
    intermediate landlords 135
    key features and terminology 117
    landlord, missing 138
    landlord, position where more than one 135
    legislation applicable 116–17
    merger 133–4
    outline of right 116
    precedents
        preliminary matters checklist 282–3
        timetable flowchart 281
    preliminary investigations by tenant
        general 121, 282–3
        landlord, information about 122
        rights of way and covenants 123
        title, checking the 121–22
        valuation and funding, obtaining 122
    premises included 123
    qualifying criteria
        house, what is a ? 119–20
        long tenancy 119
        low rent test 120
        other points to note 118
        primary criteria 118
        residency test 120
        special criteria 118
    special landlords 137
    tenant, death of 138–9
    valuation
        bases of, summary 133
        date of service of tenant's notice 132–3
        obtaining 122
        principles 157
        valuer and 154
        withdrawal, consequences and key practice points 134

Freehold of a house, tenant's right to acquire, notices
    landlord's response
        considerations 125–6
        key practice points 128
        landlord's notice in reply 127–8
        landlord's obligations 127
        landlord's own residence 126–7
    precedents
        claim, notice of 258–62
        reply to tenant's claim, notice 263–4
    tenant, death of
        after service of claim 138
        before service of claim notice 139
    tenant's notice
        effect of 125
        key points 123–4
        key practice points 125
        service of claim notice and method 124
        when can it be given? 124
    withdrawal, tenant's notice and consequences 134

Freehold of a house, tenant's right to acquire, procedure
    common facilities and maintenance 130
    completion
        failure to comply with contract terms or completion notice 131–32
        practical matters on completion 132
        summary 131
    conveyance/transfer, contents and preparation of 130
    covenants, overriding position on 131
    key practice points 129, 131
    landlord's title 129
    merger 133–4
    mortgages and debentures 136
    overview 128–9
    rentcharges 136

INDEX

Freehold of a house, tenant's right to acquire, procedure (*cont.*)
  restrictive covenants 129, 130–1
  right of way 129
  rights reserved 130
  tenant's mortgage 136

Ground rent, demands 178–9

History
  collective enfranchisement right, impending changes 5
  initial stages and rationale 3–4
  Leasehold Reform, Housing and Urban Development Act 1993 4–5
  post-1967 Act concerns 4
  pre-1967 Act legislation 4
  right to manage 5–6

Insurance
  information from landlord, obtaining 178
  tenant's own insurer 178

Landlords *see also* **Tenants** and under separate rights
  assignment of freehold, notice to be given to tenant 175
  consultations with tenants 179–81
  first refusal on disposal of building consisting of flats, right of 8, 174–5
  ground rent demands 178–9
  information, obtaining from 173, 178
  insurance information from landlord 178

Lease of a flat, right to extend *see also* Lease of a flat, right to extend notices; Lease of a flat, right to extend conveyancing procedure
  absent landlord 114
  assignment of right 112
  collective enfranchisement 112
  competent landlord, the 98–100
  costs 100, 113
  evaluating the premium 100
  key issues 98
  key practice points 101
  key terminology 96
  landlord, special category of 115
  landlord, the 98–100
  legislation applicable 95
  overview 95
  precedents
    preliminary checklist for tenant's notice 278–80
    timetable flowchart 276–7
  preliminary investigations 98–101
  price 113–14
  qualifying criteria
    flat, what is a ? 97–8
    long lease 97
    ownership, length of 97
    summary 97
  redevelopment compensation 113
  terms of the lease 100
  urgency 100
  valuation and 157–8
  valuation example Fig.10.2 162
  valuer and 154
  withdrawal and effect 112–13

Lease of a flat, right to extend conveyancing procedure
  completion 109
  key practice points 109
  new lease
    content of 110–11
    exclusion of certain terms 111
    Leasehold Valuation Tribunal (LVT), variation powers 110
    mortgages 111
    other landlords 111
    terms of 109–11
  overview 108

Lease of a flat, right to extend notices
  absent landlord 114
  access, right of 104
  assignment of right 112
  collective enfranchisement notice 112
  costs 113
  counter-notice
    admitting the right 107
    contents of 105, 252–5
    disputing validity of tenant's notice 106
    key points 104
    landlord's considerations 105
    no counter-notice served 107–8
    not admitting the right 106
    redevelopment 107
    timetable following service 108

valuation 107
deposit 104
key practice points 104
precedents
  counter-notice 252–5
  notice of claim 248–51
procedure following service of tenant's notice
  contents of 101–102
  generally 103–4
  key points 101
  key practice points 103
  service and effect 102–3
title 104
withdrawal and effect 112–13

Lease of a house, right to a new
key features 140–11
legislation applicable 140
overview 140
precedents
  claim, notice of 258–62
  reply to tenant's claim, notice 263–4

Leases, variation of
leases (houses) 182
principle 181
single lease (flat) 181–2
two or more leases (flats) 182

Leasebacks 50–1

Leasehold Valuation Tribunal (LVT)
application to 53, 221–2
appeals to 148
collective enfranchisement, application to for terms 53
costs 148, 179
decisions of 148
dismissal for abuse of process 146
hearings and intermediate hearings 147
key points of the procedure and overview 145–6
lease of flat, extension and terms of new lease 110–11
postponement 147–8
pre-trial review, statements of case and inspections 146–7
service charges, unfair or unsatisfactory, reference to 82, 179
valuers and 154–5
variation of leases 181–2

Management contracts
appointment 181
contract and contractor notices 78
function 77
service of notices 79

Management schemes, collective enfranchisement and conveyance 49

Managing agent, appointment, considerations on 60–1

Managing the collective process
assessing potential interest 16
assessment of the options 17
costs and contributions 18, 22
general 15–16
information, communication and provision of 17–18, 22
looking forward 22–3
nominee/RTE/RTM company 20
participation agreement 19
participation agreement precedent 190–6
preliminary information, obtaining 16
solicitors, professional issues for 20–3
tenants, binding into the process 18–19
valuation 16–17

Money laundering 21

Participation agreement
precedents 190–6, 228–32
tenants, binding the 19

Right to manage *see also* Right to manage, notices and counter-notices; RTM (right to manage) company
absent landlords 68–9
acquisition date, meaning and timing 67–8
general comments 58–9
key features 57–8
key matters on preliminary investigations 59–61
key practice points 63, 64, 71, 73, 76, 83
key terminology 57
landlord, issues for the 85–6
legislation applicable 56–7
management contracts 77–9
managing agent 60–1

291

INDEX

Right to manage (*cont.*)
  overview 56
  participation 61, 228–32
  precedent
    breakdown of costs 226–7
    invitation to participate 244–6
    letter of intent 224–5
    participation agreement 228–32
    preliminary matters checklist 272–5
    right to manage timetable flowchart 271
  preliminary investigations 59–61
  qualifying criteria
    appurtenant property 63
    exempt premises 63–4
    information, formal request for 65 5
    information from and about the landlord 64–6
    information and management contracts 66
    key practice points 63, 64
    participators, requisite number 62–3
    post-claim notice 66
    pre-claim notice 65
    qualifying premises 63
    qualifying tenants 62
    summary 61–2
Right to manage, notices and counter-notices
  claim notice
    contents of 70–1, 239–41
    costs of 77
    form and requirements 69
    key practice points 71
    service of 69
  claim notice, position following service
    access, right of 71–2
    timetable 71
    information from and about the landlord
    post-claim notice 66
    pre-claim notice 65, 234–8
    information notice, nature and key practice points 72–3
    invitation to participate 67, 244–6
  landlord's position following claim notice service
    considerations 74, 75–6

  counter-notice 74
  counter-notice, contents 74–5, 242–3
  key practice points 76
  management contracts
    contract notice contents 78
    contractor notice, contents 78
    contractor notice, service 79
  precedent
    claim notice 239–41
    counter-notice, contents 242–3
    information notice 233–7
  RTM company's position if the right is disputed 76–7
  withdrawal of claim notice 79
Rights generally
  collective rights
    collective enfranchisement 7
    first refusal 8, 174–5
    manage and miscellaneous rights, right to 8
  comparison, pros and cons
    collective enfranchisement 9–10, 26
    houses, rights in respect of 12
    right to manage 10–11
    tenant's right to extend lease of flat 11
  individual rights
    enfranchisement and right to a new lease of a house 9
    miscellaneous rights 9
    new lease of a flat 8
  overview 7, 172
RTE (right to enfranchise) companies
  meaning 25
  nominee purchaser and collective enfranchisement 36–7, 167
RTM (right to manage) company
  audit/accounts 85
  company issues 84–5
  company's position if the right is disputed 76–7
  directors 89–90, 167–8
  existing management structure and functions, taking over 58–9
  formation of 66–7
  management after acquisition date
    considerations and issues 79–80
    general management 80
    key practice points 83

292

INDEX

service charges, sources and contributions 80–1, 85–6
service charges, unfair or unsatisfactory and Leasehold Valuation Tribunal 82
management contracts, termination of prior 77
management functions and lease covenants 82–3
meaning 57
meetings 87
membership of 61, 86–7
memorandum of association 90
miscellaneous issues 84–5, 92
requirements for 66
right to manage, cessation of 92
statutes, modification of 84
structure, permissible 167
voting 87–9
voting provisions, example 88
withdrawal of claim notice 79

Service charges
considerations 175
demands for 176
failure to pay service charge 183
further information, right to 177
general provisions, Landlord and Tenant Act 1987 176
RTM company management after acquisition date, and 80–1, 86–7
statement of account, right for a 176–7
unfair or unsatisfactory, reference to Leasehold Valuation Tribunal 82

Solicitors
conflicts 21
cost information 22
information and costs management 22
money laundering 21
professional issues for 20–3
who is my client? 20–1

Taxation
capital gains tax (CGT), landlord's perspective 170–1
capital gains tax (CGT), tenant's perspective 169–70
corporation tax and VAT 169
stamp duty land tax (SDLT) 171

Tenants *see also* **Landlords** and under separate rights
assignment of freehold, notice of 175
binding into the process 18–19
extending leases of participating tenants 54–5
manager, appointment of a 181
participation agreement 19
participation, right to manage 61, 62–3
qualifying tenants, collective enfranchisement 31
qualifying tenants, right to manage 62
right of first refusal on landlord disposing of building consisting of flats 8, 174–5

Valuation
additional compensation 34
collective enfranchisement
  landlord's response, 41–3
  price, and 33–4
  valuation example, Fig 10.1 161
deferment rate 159
flat lease extension, example Fig.10.2 162
hope value 34, 160
houses, tenant's right to acquire freehold 158
key terminology 149–50
managing the collective process and 16–17
marriage value 34
principles of
  collective enfranchisement 153
  flats, lease extensions 154, 157–8
recent developments in valuation 157, 158–9
tenant's offer 158–9

Valuer
collective enfranchisement 153
collective enfranchisement, structuring and financial considerations 155
fees of 152–53
flats, lease extensions 154
generally 153
houses, tenant's right to acquire freehold 154
instruct, how to 151–52

293

Valuer (*cont.*)
   introduction 149
   key practice points 153–4
   Leasehold Valuation Tribunals and 154–5
   negotiations by 155–6
   report of, understanding 154–5
   selection of 150–1